1

© 2014   Inspiration Press – Brussels (Belgium); Prof. dr. Pieter
          Klaas Jagersma/Revised and Expanded Third Edition

ISBN 90-810776-1-9

NUR 163

Preface

The book you're about to read has taken many years to develop. It is concerned with global strategy. The goal of this book is to break down the walls between international business and strategic management – and to expose the foundations of performance – in the important area of growth.

The book is founded upon established research traditions. However, a substantial amount of material is not available elsewhere. The book is divided into six parts. It contains eighteen chapters of text and an extensive epilogue. Each section is designed to stand alone by containing the necessary material to understand the theme, for instance, "global strategy and growth", "global strategy and organization" or "global strategy and competition".

I have attempted to make this book practical. This calls for a compromise between mathematical precision on the one hand and realism on the other.

There are a number of people and institutes I would like to acknowledge for their contributions and support while I completed the book.

First, I owe a special thanks to many chief executives, chairmen and presidents. Their contributions to the practice of international business and strategic management have had a major impact on my thinking on international growth strategies. In addition, I benefited greatly from their comments, time, inspiration and encouragement during the process of writing this book.

I was lucky enough to have brilliant teachers to introduce me into the field of international business and strategy theory. Hans Krijnen (Groningen University) inspired me to explore the cross-border implications of strategy theory. Sytse Douma (Tilburg University) taught me to make things simple, and my former McKinsey colleagues taught me the power of asking the right questions.

I have been fortunate to teach great students and executives at a diverse array of universities and business schools. This book is an outgrowth of strategy and international business courses I developed and have taught at Nyenrode University, Vrije Universiteit Amsterdam, and many other universities and business schools.

It is a pleasure to acknowledge the help received at various stages of this project from Désirée van Gorp. I would also like to thank all the people whose entries made the case studies possible. Many executives and managers agreed to be interviewed by the author. Their wisdom found its way into this book.

Furthermore, with gratitude I acknowledge the many global companies and academic institutions that made this book possible, especially: ABN AMRO, Nyenrode Business University, Royal Dutch Shell, Motorola, Nokia, Goldman Sachs, Bayer, Novartis, Unilever, Nestlé, McKinsey & Co., Bain & Co., Boston Consulting Group, Rabobank, Philips, HP, Fortis, Virgin, Accord, Danone, Telefónica, Fiat, Sony, Toyota, Ford, Club Med, American Airlines, BP, Microsoft, Southwest Airlines, Apple, LVMH, Time Warner, 3M, Bang & Olufsen,

Siemens, IBM, Porsche, Morgan Stanley, Yahoo, Ricoh, and BMW.

At home, my greatest debt is to Yvette Eimers, Smirnoff (our labrador retriever) and my parents who are great supporters of everything I do. The book is dedicated to my parents Ruud and Lia.

Prof. dr. Pieter Klaas Jagersma

Winter 2006 (first edition)

Winter 2007 (second edition)

Spring 2009 (revised and expanded third edition)

Summer 2014 (revised and expanded third edition)

Contents

Part III. Global Strategy and Competition

Part IV. Global Strategy and Reputational Capital

Part V. Global Strategy and China

Part VI. Cases in Global Strategy

Foreword

Rapid improvements in information, communication and transportation technologies lead to better informed and more demanding customers everywhere in the world and to increasingly open and interlinked markets where global players compete.

The importance of nationality for organizations in such a world is a matter of dispute. Some argue that nationality has effectively become irrelevant for global organizations, as they have to operate locally in different markets around the world. Others, on the other hand, maintain the view that a corporation's home base (in terms of education, industry structure, customer sophistication, and fierceness of competition) determines much of its competitive potential world wide.

Nowadays, the challenge for many organizations is not whether to expand globally, but how to. For such companies, the rationale for expansion appears to have become overwhelming. From an offensive viewpoint, geographic expansion offers one of the few opportunities for growth when the home market is mature or domestic competition is already concentrated. From a defensive viewpoint, the arguments for expansion can be even more compelling – and more urgent.

Whatever you may think about the current globalization-hype, it is difficult to turn a blind eye to the fact that Europe, the Americas, and Asia is restructuring; in many industries, customers, suppliers and competitors are getting bigger and becoming increasingly global, and purely national competitors are looking increasingly vulnerable.

Unfortunately, while the need for international expansion may appear ever more pressing, the risk of destroying value through inappropriate initiatives is also getting more and more real. You do not need to be a great visionary to forecast that raiders will be shifting their attentions from today's multibusiness organizations towards those multicountry organizations that have failed to extract real value from geographic expansion and diversification.

What, then, is the answer? In many cases, simply not expanding at all may be the value-maximizing strategy – either finding a sustainable national niche or disposing of selected businesses to those companies better able to justify a global role.

However, where geographic expansion makes sense, my experience – and that of today's more successful global players – suggests that there are different keys to success, which I describe more fully in this book.

The purpose of this book is to reflect on the major global challenges facing the leadership of organizations in the coming years.

This book will be unpretentious in its objective. If we can step away from it with an incrementally sharper understanding of key challenges or a better sense of priorities, it will have fulfilled its mission.

Prof. dr. Pieter Klaas Jagersma   Summer 2014

Part I. Global Strategy and Growth

1

Aspiration and Leadership

'I skate to where the puck is going to be'.

- Ice-hockey legend Wayne Gretsky

How does one turn the herd roughly south, changing the actions of thousands of people dispersed across many organizational units and geographies? With difficulty for sure. Nevertheless, a corporate aspiration may be an important first step.

A corporate aspiration is a compelling statement of what the company aspires to become that reflects a view of the future. Sometimes it exists informally in the heads of a few, often it is a formal statement which can be quoted and repeated. It provides a rationale for action.

I know from my work in companies that the term corporate aspiration itself does not help, with its connotations of images rising from the mist. Although corporate aspirations are not a part of our everyday vocabulary, it is not as esoteric as it sounds. Most of us know that the first step on the road to success for companies is to decide where they are going and how they are going to get there.

Management needs an aspiration as to how the company will work in the future. It needs a guide for corporate priorities. A corporate aspiration drives the choice of objectives, required corporate and individual skills and capabilities, and corporate values. Therefore, corporate aspirations must be coherent, powerful, and realistic about the internal and external conditions the company is likely to encounter.

Box 1 Corporate aspirations

"To make a contribution to the world by making tools for the mind that advance human kind".

- Apple (USA)

"Unilever aims to be the foremost company meeting the daily needs across the world in foods, cleaning and personal care".

- Unilever (Netherlands/UK)

"We want to honorably serve the community by providing products and services of superior quality at a fair price to our customers".

- Motorola (USA)

"Our corporate aspiration is to advance the art of engineering".

- Ferrari (Italy)

"We want to provide value to our customers – to make their lives better via lower prices and greater selection; all else is secondary".

- Wal-Mart (USA)

A corporate aspiration is key to the continuity and organizational morale of the company. It helps create economic and cultural value necessary for continuity and focuses the energy of the employees in the organization. Any company – local or global - must be driven by an aspiration that energizes and motivates the company from top to bottom. Yet very few of us know how a corporate aspiration can help to bring about focus and direction, or how to develop or execute one. This chapter attempts to fill some of those gaps.

What is a corporate aspiration?

Sometimes called 'strategic intent', 'guiding philosophy', 'core ideology', or a 'statement of corporate beliefs', a corporate aspiration reveals the long-term goals of an organization in terms of what it wants to be and who it wants to serve. It is not an advertising slogan (for example, Coca-Cola's 'It's the real thing') or an abstract or broad statement (like 'global leadership', 'excellence' or 'innovation') as a stand-alone idea.

Additionally, a corporate aspiration is not the equivalent of corporate 'mission' or 'strategy' (see box 2). A corporate 'mission' captures an organization's reason for existence, and, therefore, describes a reality. A corporate strategy, on the other hand, seeks sustainable competitive advantage over the competition by finding alternatives to produce a better relationship between cost and value in serving customers. Since customer segments and competitors change constantly, so too do winning strategies. In fact, the formulation of an effective corporate strategy is a recurring top management challenge that entails careful analysis, close interaction with the customer, and an enormous amount of learning through experimentation, and trial and error.

In contrast, the purpose of any corporate aspiration is to create an environment in which the company can carry out

17

its mission and formulate and execute winning corporate and competitive strategies. Therefore, they must reflect the realities of the societal and business environment so that they facilitate the shaping and reshaping of the company's mission and strategy and the building of the key skills necessary to execute the strategy well.

Mission and strategy are the metaphorical equivalents to a company that food and water are to the body. They are not the point of life, but without them, there is no life. To achieve a corporate aspiration, there must be a mission and a strategy to provide the operational logic for what the company hopes to accomplish.

Box 2 Differences between mission, aspiration and strategy

Question	Answer	Meaning
Who are we?	Mission	Statement explaining why a company exists
Where are we heading?	Aspiration	Crystallization of what the leaders want the company to become
How do we get there?	Strategy	Plan for how to serve customers and how to beat present and potential competitors

Powerful corporate aspirations are not mere wishful thinking as is the case with so many 'corporate slogans' or 'corporate themes'. It is a hard-nosed practical concept based on deep understanding of the dynamics of industries, markets and competition, and the potential of the corporation to influence and exploit those dynamics. It may express a range of goals, from the strictly quantified, for example, 3M's "To become the industry's leading innovator with over 50 percent of our profits from products that we did not have five years ago" to the highly qualitative, for example, Porsche's "To earn the respect and loyalty of our customers" or Ferrari's "To advance the art of engineering".

Because of the thousands of people who are often affected by the corporate aspiration, the leaders should select every word in the theme with care, compare it with other possibilities, and try to test alternative themes for impact before choosing the final aspiration. Getting the right wording will make a great deal of difference. What one set of words implies at headquarters may not be the same at lower levels or in the field. Pretesting is especially critical in organizations where the aspiration must cross country and cultural boundaries. Since words can take on different meanings in different situations, the leaders should explore any negative connotations of the corporate aspiration and remove or counterbalance them.

How to develop and execute a corporate aspiration?

Do corporate aspirations make a company more competitive and successful? On average, companies with explicit corporate aspirations create more long-term economic value than comparable companies that lack it [1]. Nevertheless, very few of us know what a corporate aspiration is, how it can help to bring about results, or how to develop one.

Fly in Formation

Hamel and Prahalad found in the mid-1990s that less than three percent of top management's time is devoted to building a corporate aspiration [2]. The problem with a lot of executives is that they do not know how to formulate a corporate aspiration. They have spent years in education, learning to be pragmatic; but developing a corporate aspiration is about realizing dreams. This requires both a new way of thinking and of acting. As George Bernard Shaw once said, "You see things; and you say, 'Why'?' But I dream of things that never were; and I say, 'Why not?'"

According to my research population, the process of creating a corporate aspiration is almost more important than the end result. To outsiders, corporate aspirations often sound like 'motherhood and apple pie'. But as one CEO said: "Unless the corporate aspiration is backed up with specific targets and strategies, the words become meaningless."

Box 3 My research on corporate aspirations

Over the past few years, I have been systematically researching the question of what makes successful corporate aspirations tick. During a ten-month period, I interviewed 51 (former) chief executives, presidents, managing directors and chairmen of (21) US, (24) European and (6) Japanese global companies. The executives represented a wide diversity of nationalities and industries.

Furthermore, I used a variety of printed and electronic sources, including annual reports, the Financial Times, the Wall Street Journal and Frankfurter Allgemeine, and several Web sites containing information on corporate aspirations. Additionally, I conducted electronic searches for any announcements of (new) corporate aspirations of chief executives, presidents, managing directors, and chairmen. Finally, I consulted eight senior partners of three strategy consultancies to add any corporate aspirations that had not been identified.

Some companies see the process of composing a corporate aspiration as a means of bringing the senior executives together to sort out their differences. The lengthy process surrounding the drawing up of the new Philips aspiration, a few years ago, suggests that the process is sometimes part of a major restructuring of the enterprise, initiated by a new CEO and his management team.

The CEO and senior executives need to set a corporate aspiration that is deemed formidable, yet achievable, but not impossible (not a pipe dream). By imbuing broader meaning into the effort, this kind of purpose appeals to management's desire to excel, to be part of an exciting organization. This means translating the corporate aspiration into an inspiring set of values to guide behavior, required capabilities that might be needed to fullfil the corporate aspiration, which is to form the basis of action programs, and clear and meaningful measures and targets to satisfy and motivate the needs of stakeholders. An effective corporate aspiration provides the directional intensity needed to coalesce people much like a magnet aligning iron filings.

Answering four questions helps a company set its corporate aspiration:

• How might the future of the industry unfold?

Understanding and reviewing the future of an industry will form the basis for setting the company's aspiration. Even after the best industry assessments, however, there will often remain a few important uncertainties about the future that could be described as a limited number of credible scenarios. In these cases, a corporate aspiration would need to reflect these scenarios – either by building in flexibility to win as different events unfold, or by reducing the uncertainty by leading the industry in a favorable position.

- What is the biggest challenge for the company three or five+ years from now?

Setting the corporate aspiration engages the emotional involvement of leaders more acutely than logic or specified external pressure. The corporate aspiration has to capture the hearts and minds of the company. Without such an aspiration, embedded in the biggest company challenge, confusion and frustration are likely to reign. Corporate aspiration-setting is a very effective "pull" rather than "push" leadership style.

- Is the corporate aspiration achievable?

It is very important that corporate aspirations be underpinned and measured by using a scorecard. They need to be measured against realities to avoid hallucinations. Given the long-term nature of corporate aspirations, there is little value to being overly scientific with the analysis. Nevertheless, they have to be actionable and measurable. A CEO and his management team has to test the reasonableness of the corporate aspiration by assessing gaps between current and required performance. Gaps that are either readily attainable or impossible to close indicate the corporate aspiration needs modification. If today's performance on the scorecard is likely to fall well short of the corporate aspiration, it may be insufficiently challenging. If the gap is large but reasonable, management could use the size of the gap to inspire and motivate the company along a number of performance dimensions. Assessing the reasonableness of the corporate aspiration is iterative with respect to developing the strategy and tactics.

- How will you roll back the future to the present?

Rolling back the future automatically creates the road map (strategy) that bridges the gap between the company's current performance and the corporate aspiration. The specificity and form of the road map will vary, depending upon the degree of uncertainty to be faced. For instance, in industries where uncertainty is relatively low (for example, transport, hardware, and engineering), detailed and specific road maps with clear performance targets provide senior executives and front-line employees with the most direction. The CEO and senior executives can help employees internalize the corporate aspiration by translating it into a few inspiring themes that highlight major performance challenges. These themes should provide the rationale for subsequent initiatives. Companies in industries facing a high degree of uncertainty (for example, biotechnology, medical devices, and entertainment) will also have road maps. However, strategic initiatives may lack the detailed performance targets usually built into near-term plans.

Each company should constantly review its near-term road map and long-term corporate aspirations to ensure that they will remain in line with emerging knowledge of the future. This means answering a lot of questions. Important questions to answer are: "Are we on track toward interim targets", "What (new) barriers exist to achieving our corporate aspiration", "How are we performing with respect to required capabilities", and "How has our understanding of the future changed"?

Building understanding

Delivery is always more important than statements. The key question, therefore, is how can you build understanding throughout your company? Building organizational understanding means following two steps:

- *Creating broad awareness and excitement for the aspiration.* This is first and foremost about broadcasting the (new) corporate aspiration. A corporate aspiration will not do anything for the organization until all the employees know about it. Yet, conveying the overriding aspiration to the whole organization is just the beginning. A further step is needed.

- *Creating individual passion.* Most people want to make a real contribution to the company they are associated with. They want to feel like they have an impact on what gets done, and they want to have a set of values that underlies what the organization is trying to accomplish. Therefore, each company has to personalize the corporate aspiration to move beyond merely broadcasting the aspiration in a one-size-fits-all approach. A company has to translate the aspiration into terms that have personal meaning for down-the-line employees. Inspiration for most employees is not found in balance sheets, but in a search for meaning. Employees want to be part of something significant and to achieve things that are consistent with a sense of self. They must know what the corporate aspiration means for them, personally, so that they can aim directly for the resulting goals and targets in their day-to-day work. Ideally, the corporate aspiration should make employees want to align their own aspirations, and, therefore, behavior, with the company's (new) goals. For employees, the most powerful incentive to achieve the goals of corporate aspirations is to feel that those goals are crucially important to them, as individuals.

Executing a corporate aspiration is often about change management. A corporate aspiration always leads to the important question: how will individual behaviors have to change? Answering that question will mean spelling out the changes required from all those groups that affect the company's fortunes – customers, suppliers and shareholders, as well as employees and managers. Clear corporate aspirations support change.

A successful corporate aspiration rollout builds involvement, because each manager and employee feels a personal tie to it, understands his role in making the aspiration happen, and is motivated to overcome obstacles on the way to realizing the corporate aspiration (see box 4). Individual commitment is crucial in setting the right priorities to achieve the corporate aspiration and for executing it more effectively and more quickly than the rivals do.

Box 4 Advice from the executive suite

"A corporate aspiration helps to develop creative 'out of the box' thinking rather than 'business as usual'. Therefore, it lengthens management's time horizon."

- S. Jobs, CEO Apple

"A corporate aspiration provides a framework to set corporate-wide performance objectives."

- B. Arnault, CEO LVMH

"Corporate aspirations describe an inspiring *new* reality. They align an organization around a shared sense of direction and can energize people to achieve the aspiration."

- D. De Sole, former CEO Gucci

"Noncommitted executives can bury a corporate aspiration before it is born."

- B. Verwaayen, CEO British Telecom

"A company should develop a new corporate aspiration if many people in the organization need to be aligned toward a new goal."

- J. Ollila, CEO Nokia

"The ultimate corporate aspiration test is whether the dream is actually related to reality."

- Dr. H. von Pierer, former CEO Siemens

"Spotting a 'visionary company' is easy; The tricky bit is becoming one."

- P. Brabeck, CEO Nestlé

"A corporate aspiration is a very effective picture of the future."

- N. Idei, former president Sony

Can all this be encompassed in a single statement? One sentence or paragraph could hardly describe the variety of behaviors and performance targets required to achieve the goals. An effective corporate aspiration will comprise many layers of detail in the minds of executives and managers, not all of which will be evident from the start. This brings us to the role of leadership.

Aspiration and leadership

Martin Luther King, Jr. once observed that "people cannot become devoted to Christianity until they find Christ, to democracy until they find Lincoln and Jefferson and Roosevelt, to Communism until they find Marx and Lenin" [3]. Employees become committed through a leader who personify ideas about the future. Many attempts to develop and execute corporate aspirations have been naive. A wide gap has emerged between rhetoric and reality, and between ambitions and achievement. The exciting challenge for a leader is to integrate corporate aspirations and operations into a dynamic whole.

Each corporate leader has four fundamental tasks: to develop a corporate aspiration, to set specific goals and targets, to create and roll out effective strategies, and to energize and mobilize the organization toward those goals, targets and strategies through actions, commitment and performance measurement. Additionally, great leaders have the ability to tell and retell a convincing story that carries shared meanings. A story that affects the thoughts, feelings and actions of individual employees. If leaders are to be effective, they must embody the story in their own lives. Discrepancies between the values in the corporate aspiration and top management's behavior will have a disproportionately damaging effect on the usefulness of the aspiration.

Behind every successful corporate aspiration lies an ambitious leadership team with a corporate philosophy of what it will take to make the company an outstanding performer. It takes more than a leader, however, to establish a compelling corporate aspiration. Other important ingredients are:

- *A sense of urgency.* A corporate aspiration without a sense of urgency is almost unheard of. This sense of urgency could be triggered by a crisis or catastrophic event. It could also arise from the gradual buildup of negative forces, such as the Chinese penetration of US and/or European consumer markets. In rarer cases, a zealous leader could create a feeling of urgency without the aid of outside catalysts.

- *A cohesive, committed team.* Few corporate aspirations remain the sole property of the single originator or leader. Others must share, as well as shape, a leader's corporate aspiration and beliefs. A leader needs not only the support and contributions of the people at the top, but also an army of "defenders of the faith" throughout the organization. His most important task, however, is to quickly assemble a team at the top that subscribes to the urgency and basic elements of the corporate aspiration. Unless he does this, nothing will happen. Human nature rules against it.

- *A participatory process.* Building conviction and consensus among the group at the top is the leader's second task. Inevitably it entails discussions, interchanges, and debates during which key managers have the opportunity to challenge, shape, and internalize the corporate aspiration as it is evolving. Of value at this stage are drafts that can be circulated, shared, and finalized in multiple sessions. The team at the top must test, question, probe, and modify until it has a real feeling of ownership – not simply understanding and acceptance. Otherwise, it could neither support the leader when he needs it or help him take the heat that invariably accompanies the roll-out of corporate aspirations.

- *Integrating themes.* Corporate aspirations need integrating themes to reinforce the importance, priority and critical elements of certain related goals. The best themes are memorable; in other words, simple, clear, and catchy. They are also few in number. They produce a sense of pride and excitement throughout the organization, particularly in the firing line - where the rubber meets the road.

- *Constant reinforcement.* If the team at the top feels real ownership of the corporate aspiration and commitment to the themes, it will reinforce the message by basing key decisions on the themes and by taking on new patterns of behavior that remind the organization of what the effort is about. Managers at lower levels have an uncanny ability to spot mixed signals about the top's determination to realize goals. If there is ambiguity in the CEO message or 'way of doing things', people will opt out.

One of the most important contributions of an effective corporate aspiration is that it sets the stage for the fundamental values – the basic beliefs and convictions which govern behavior - that drive excellent companies. 'Values-based leadership' holds that, if managers and employees share certain values, the bond between them will be stronger than if they simply follow the same commands. The corporate aspiration indicates the relative importance of value versus cost, the levels of quality and service to be provided, and the kinds of human resources the organization wants in its fold.

From the corporate aspiration we can determine, for instance, whether the company prefers decentralized innovation or controlled cost effectiveness; whether it is conservative and cautious or aggressive and risk prone; whether it seeks transactional types of employees or the more normal long-term relationships. This is a complex management conundrum. In the words of Roger Enrico, former CEO of Pepsico and chairman of DreamWorks, "The soft stuff is always harder than the hard stuff."

With a clear aspiration and values, communicated through management, the employees are in a position to determine operating priorities and make decisions that maximize the organization's performance. The importance of devolving initiative and responsibility was never more clearly expressed than by Alfred Sloan, the man who built General Motors. He once said: "I just want my man in Denver to stay awake, and be thinking about the future of the company, and the only way I can do that is to push some decisions in his direction." You can't say it more economically than that.

Box 5 Can your company pass the aspiration test?

Through the rigorous application of the following best practices, your company can pass the corporate aspiration test:

- Do you and your leadership team believe in, and consistently reinforce, the same high corporate aspiration? Is it specific and measurable?

- Can your division/group and business unit heads and their direct reports articulate the corporate aspiration and their businesses' three-five year objectives and plan to achieve them?

- Does your corporate aspiration and strategic thrust (e.g. innovation, industry leadership) govern investment decisions in your divisions/groups and/or business units?

- Do you have a process for identifying discontinuities (e.g. technology breakthroughs, rising new geographies, customer and political changes) that could represent new opportunities? Do your management processes and organizational culture support such a bifocal perspective?

- Is your performance target-setting process truly aspiration-based: are targets stretching, and the consequences – both success and failure – significant for your division/group and business unit heads?

- Do your measurements focus on your corporate aspiration, and your incentive and performance evaluation systems reward risk taking (to realize your corporate aspiration)?

Achieving clarity and transparency in the corporate aspiration process is not an easy task. However, every corporate aspiration should be clear about the broad competitive arenas (e.g. industries and geographies), the capability areas in which the company intends to excel, the philosophy of its financial and people resources, and the primary themes and messages that top management will use to inspire, motivate, and build institutional pride.

Where do we go from here?

What lessons can we draw from this study? First of all, without exception, corporate aspirations are necessary. A shared corporate aspiration can help unite a large, scattered workforce. One major benefit of an effective companywide aspiration is that it sets the stage for the values and norms that drive most excellent companies. Clear corporate aspirations form a powerful tool for improving corporate performance.

Secondly, there is no single right way to develop and execute corporate aspirations. They are not all things to all people. Different executives and organizations produce corporate aspirations in all sorts of different ways, and tailored to their specific needs. What works at Exxon, Toyota and Danone is clearly different from what works in AOL Time Warner, British Telecom, Telefónica, Ernst&Young or Goldman Sachs. And what works well for General Electric, Nike or Sony is clearly not mirrored in Air France-KLM, Nokia or Gucci. The development, execution, and rejuvenation of corporate aspirations is a process driven by cultural forces and business dynamics.

Thirdly, corporate aspirations require effective execution, and, therefore, leadership. The challenge is to move from the rhetoric of aspiration to the reality of action. The success of this transition rests on how well leaders understand their employees and the right road maps to build a high-performance organization. The only way executives achieve high performance is through the work of others. Ultimately, aspiration and leadership make a successful company tick.

Fourthly, the formulation of an effective corporate aspiration is a recurring senior executive challenge that entails careful timing and analysis, close interaction with employees and other stakeholders, and a certain amount of experimentation. Corporate aspirations are based on beliefs, experience and willingness to speculate, but they must also reflect the realities of the societal and business environment.

Last, but not least, companies with serious problems should focus on solving their problems before embarking on a time-consuming corporate aspiration-setting exercise. But once the house is in order, aspiration-setting is the greatest available lever for increasing shareholder and stakeholder value.

References

[1] J. Collins and J. Porras, "Organizational Vision and Visionary Organizations", Research paper 1159, Stanford (Graduate School of Business), 1991.

[2] G. Hamel and C.K. Prahalad, "Competing for the Future", Harvard Business School Press, Boston/MA, 1994.

[3] Martin Luther King , Jr. as quoted in L. Bennet, "What Manner of Man", Johnson Publishers, Chicago, 1964: page 127.

2

Cross-border Alliances

Advice from the Executive Suite

Cross-border alliances are poised to become a building block of the global network economy. A look at the top executives around the world illustrates the increasing importance of a global and collaborative mindset. No one player can master everything. Therefore, more and more cross-border alliances take place. In recent years, there has been a dramatic proliferation of these arrangements. Everyone seems to trumpet their value, although businesses have long blurred the boundaries between competition and cooperation.

The reasons for these ventures are not always easy to understand, but cross-border alliances are an increasingly popular reaction to competitive forces in the business environment. They have gained momentum as the best way to access the capabilities of other companies, as well as the best ways of dealing with fragmented and deregulated markets. Deregulation is changing the ground rules for competition, growth opportunities are taking place outside traditional customer networks, and the competitive environment demands relentless attention to cost reduction and profitable growth. Companies are unable to meet challenges and address opportunities sufficiently through internal actions alone. A vice president of Nokia who participated in the survey (described below) said, "We don't view cross-border alliances as one-off situations but as an essential way of doing business."

Because of the increasing need for cross-border alliances, executives in the USA, Europe and Asia have ranked cross-border alliances as a top agenda item for the years to come.
But a healthy dose of scepticism underlies the trend. While CEOs publicly extol the virtues of global partnering, they privately express confusion as to their efficacy. Is it easier to run a 100% owned company? Of course it is.

Many companies have avoided cross-border alliances because of the inherent difficulties in successfully negotiating, managing and exploiting them to achieve a company's strategic objective. History has shown that companies have a hard time sustaining intimate, longer-term relations. Pride and ownership make companies want to be the best at everything, to do everything themselves. Company pride gets in the way. Many executives still adhere to the traditional competitive model of the corporation where cooperation is regarded with skepticism.

So how does a company make its way through the cross-border alliance jungle? This chapter addresses several issues facing companies considering or managing cross-border alliances. Given the inherent cultural, economic, and political difficulties associated with cross-border alliances, designing and managing any cross-border alliance is an extremely challenging task. Overcoming these issues in cross-border alliances has proven to be even more difficult and, given the increasing importance of foreign markets and foreign competitors, more critical to a company's success.

This chapter summarizes the reasons for the increasing number of alliances taking place and identifies a number of issues facing the CEO and his management in deciding whether to establish cross-border alliances and how to manage them. My research study indicates that some simple guidelines can improve the success rate of a cross-border alliance.

What's in a name?

Cross-border alliances can be legally defined and therefore readily counted. Their number has surged since the mid-1990s, a trend particularly evident among U.S., European and Asian companies. According to Booz-Allen & Hamilton, more than 20.000 cross-border alliances were formed between 1996 and 2003.

Almost all companies surveyed (box 1) agreed that cross-border alliances would grow in importance to their business. Most cross-border alliances are concentrated in relatively few industries - those typified by high entry costs, globalization, scale economies, and rapidly changing technologies - and span all elements of the value chain with particular emphasis on joint development activities (e.g., R&D and Operations).

Given the range and scope of cross-border activity and an equivalent range and scope of themes in cross-border alliances, it is not surprising to see that the result is a complex patchwork of cross-border alliances, with emphasis on short- and long-term issues. As this occurs, the industry structure and the rational behavior of major players within the industry structure is also undergoing major change.

Cross-border alliances are international agreements on collaboration between two or more independent companies who exploit a tangible or intangible asset. They consist primarily of joint ventures and cooperative business arrangements involving shared risk, cost, or reward without full ownership and with a significant degree of exclusivity. Supplier contracts are the loosest form of cross-border alliance. Management or technology contracts are often a "stepping stone" to further investment, and joint ventures are a more significant commitment of both tangible and intangible resources. My study focused on cross-border joint ventures.

Cross-border alliances are only one of three options executives can use to achieve corporate goals and objectives in the face of changing market conditions. They are formed when they yield benefits that cannot be achieved in-house or through outright acquisition or merger. They have been used by managements to:

- Secure economies of scale in the R&D and manufacturing functions to offset the higher cost and risk of bringing new products to the market without losing the identity or independence of the company in the market place.
- Reduce the cost and time required to establish major positions in new geographic markets compared with the cost of direct investment or acquisition.
- Eliminate difficulties in successfully consummating mergers of equals that are complementary and where two managements can agree on a common vision and plan, particularly given the poor experience of cross-border mergers in the 1980s and 1990s.
- Participate in some of the more rapidly growing markets where involvement of a local partner is either required (e.g. joint ventures in parts of Asia and South-America) or desirable (e.g. joint ventures in Italy, Spain, and Greece).

Once in place, however, cross-border alliances are frequently difficult to manage and have their own costs. Few of them have been used as vehicles to pursue multiple opportunities and even fewer could be considered a complete success on the scale needed to make a fundamental impact on the development of the company. In particular, links with a partner can create inflexibility, coordination difficulties and risk of competitive conflict.

The complex management challenges are higher in collaborative ventures that involve division of activities in the value chain and issues of division of markets and decision responsibilities. Managing cooperative ventures is a process to be learned by trial and error. It requires mutual adaptation to each other's business cultures (especially among direct competitors) and need to live with reduced autonomy. Cross-border joint ventures are especially difficult to manage and organize. They represent the highest level of interaction, shared commitment, and administrative complexity among the forms of cooperative agreements.

Box 1 About the research

I conducted 106 face-to-face interviews and 86 telephone interviews in 2003 in Europe, North-America, and Asia-Pacific among chief executives and top managers from 89 global companies. The project covered large cross-border alliances.

The study includes the views of senior executives of public companies (Unilever, Siemens, Akzo Nobel, Toyota, United Airlines, Royal Dutch Shell, GM, Ford, Motorola, Toshiba, Sony, Porsche, Daimler Chrysler, Nokia, Allianz, Telefónica, Fortis, Fiat, Nestlé, AXA, Carrefour, Ahold, Philips, Ericsson, ABB, and Novartis) as well as state-owned enterprises (especially in the energy sector), subsidiaries (of big global firms) and private (family) companies.

% of interviewees

By region

Europe	48
North-America	27
Asia-Pacific	25

By industry

Heavy, light and chemical industry	24
ICT (incl. telecom)	15
Financial services	19
Business services	11
Consumer goods	16
Other	15

By interviewees' titles

CEO	18
Owner	4
President	9
Chairman	8
CFO	3
COO	6
Vice President	12
Board director	18
Non-executive director	3
Senior vice-president	5
Executive vice president	6
Director of Strategic Planning	1
Other	7

Of those interviewed, 75 percent believed cross-border alliances were the best form of corporate combination for access to new customers and broader product ranges without the disruption of cross-border mergers. Most said that any future combinations would be with another partner from within the same industry. Almost 80 percent of interviewees said they believed future opportunities for corporate combinations lay in crossing geographical boundaries.

Rather than pursuing such combinations as a reactive strategy to defend positions, companies are acting for offensive reasons: 55 percent said they were improving their positions through cross-border alliances; 28 percent cited changes in the competitive landscape and 11 percent mentioned regulatory forces.

Forms of cross-border alliances

The form of a cross-border alliance often follows directly from the objective. For combining complementary resources, cross-border joint ventures are most often used, especially for new market entries and new business start-ups. For acquiring technology, either a joint venture or direct parent interaction can work, often in combination with a technology licensing agreement.

For managing industry rivalry, parent-to-parent cooperation is typically best for developing technical or industry standards. For improving vertical linkages, non-equity arrangements such as long-term contracts are usually best because of the conflicts inherent between suppliers and customers. There are exceptions, but the need for an equity relationship should be challenged in any vertical relationship.

If cross-border alliances are viewed as temporary, the venture form is probably the least desirable form of a cross-border alliance: it is least flexible and requires a substantial effort in ongoing management. Contractual forms of alliances with built-in notion of temporaries are often preferable.

Box 2 Separate ventures or parent-to-parent collaboration?

One of the most important decisions is whether to establish a separate equity venture or to establish a direct parent-to-parent alliance. Cross-border ventures are appropriate when:
- it is possible to establish a stand-alone business with dedicated resources provided by all parents;
- a high degree of integration of specific parent resources is required to achieve goals;
- it is desirable to create loyalty to a new business distinct from the parents because their interests might other wise prevent the success of a collaboration. Toshiba and Motorola, for example, created a

semiconductor manufacturing alliance, even though the two parents compete in downstream product areas.

Direct parent-to-parent collaboration (often including licensing or long-term contractual agreements) is appropriate when:
• assets or resources are best kept in separate parent organizations;
• parent interests are competitive so that close parent control is required, and
• success can not be measured in terms of performance measures that apply to stand-alone businesses (for instance, the main purpose is to learn).

Issues in cross-border alliances

As companies move away from the concept that the majority of key activities can be managed through operating units that are 100 per cent owned, managing the enterprise inevitably becomes more difficult for the chief executive and his management team.

Most cross-border alliance failures stem from strategic flaws. While many companies announce "strategic alliances", many lack "alliance strategies". An effective cross-border alliance strategy is the result of asking three important questions.

I Do we need to collaborate to compete?

According to the survey, cross-border alliances are appropriate for four broad purposes (many cross-border alliances involve multiple objectives):

1. *To combine partner resources to develop new businesses or reduce investment*. Typical examples include new business start-ups with parents contributing specific complementary capabilities that constitute the basis for a new business. For instance, ten leading drug companies, including Smith Kline

Beecham, created a $ 45 million joint research consortium to study variations in human DNA.

Airbus was a joint venture between French, German, British and Spanish manufacturers that eventually became a single company. Each national partner has specialized in one bit of aircraft manufacturing. The French became experts in aircraft electronics and cockpit design, the British became world leaders in wing manufacturing, the Germans concentrated on making fuselages and the Spaniards focused on aircraft tails.

2. *To eliminate risks*. During the past few years, Renault, General Motors and DaimlerChrysler have bought stakes in Nissan, Fuji Heavy Industries (which makes Subaru brand cars), and Mitsubishi Motors, respectively. The idea is that a stake in a Japanese carmaker, with a network of factories and dealerships in Asia, is a less risky way to expand into the world's fastest-growing automotive market than a full merger.

Pilkington, the UK glass manufacturer, has joint ventures with Saint-Gobain of France, one of its fiercest rivals, in Brazil. The two companies take turns to build glass-making plants. Each side manages its own plants but they share the profits. Building a glass plant is hugely expensive. Through their cross-border joint ventures, they reduce the risk of having too much capacity for the local market.

3. *To learn*. Learning may entail improving skills through working with a partner or gaining access to countries. Turner Broadcasting, which is part of Time Warner, has completed a deal with Philips, a Dutch electronics company, where Philips will get the right to name a new sports arena that TB is building in Atlanta. But TB's main motive is to find out more about European consumers and about the digital communications hardware that is Philips's stock-in-trade.

British Rover improved its manufacturing through the Honda alliance. GM learned about quality control, work teams, flexible assembly lines from Suzuki and from Nummi (i.e. the GM/Toyota global alliance), then transferred these capabilities to Saturn. Mazda has helped Ford improve its emissions testing - critically important as global regulations tighten. Ford has also gained access to Japanese manufacturing practices, including kaizen (constant improvement).

Having watched several of its peers make expensive mistakes trying to buy stores or go it alone, Britain's Tesco wanted to penetrate South Korean markets without making the same mistakes. It formed an alliance with Samsung and began many joint ventures in the 1990s with foreign firms because they couldn't do a cross-border acquisition.

4. *To change the name of the competitive game*. To manage industry rivalry, Star Alliance, which includes Lufthansa and United Airlines, began as a series of loose arrangements to share codes and direct passengers to partners' flights; now it is beginning to look more like a quasi-merger, with shared executive lounges and pooled maintenance facilities.

II How do we select a partner?

Each cross-border alliance requires different approaches to screening partners. The survey participants suggested "make-or-break" questions to ask about each partner. If any of the answers are "no", a cross-border alliance with this candidate should be avoided:

- Can the partner perform as required to make the venture a success?
- Can you agree with the partner on a clear objective for the alliance?

- Have you minimized (or can you manage) the risk of competitive overlaps and friction with the partner? Does your partner have any alliances with your competitors? How will you cope with that situation?
- Is the balance of contribution fair and in line with expectations, e.g. does the partner appear to be willing to contribute the resources and skills necessary to make the alliance a success?
- Does the partner have a positive track record for previous alliances?
- Does the partner agree with your vision of how the cross-border alliance might evolve?
- Will this cross-border alliance fit with your alliance network of the future?
- Are the business and "cultural" chemistry compatible?
- Have you compared this partner with other candidates in terms of potential value creation?

The name of the "company screening game" is applying knock-out factors. Lessons learnt in applying knockout factors include:

- keep the number of criteria manageable (i.e. five to seven criteria);
- link prioritization criteria to a company's alliance goals;
- identify prioritization criteria that will allow discrimination among the potential candidates;
- apply prioritization criteria in order of increasing difficulty of measurement.

The partner screening process is an iterative and time-consuming process. Nevertheless, potential foreign partners should always be screened along three dimensions: their ability to meet a company's strategic objectives, their compatibility with the company and the likelihood of completing the deal.

III What are the key factors for capturing value?

Having determined the best partner, a company's next challenge is to structure the cross-border alliance in a way that is most likely to lead to success. Winners in cross-border alliances follow common patterns in how they structure alliances. The structuring - especially the form, scope, ownership and financial arrangements, governance, and exit provisions - should be driven by the specific objectives. According to the majority of the interviewees, it is essential to:

1. *Develop a business plan jointly with prospective partners to generate enthusiasm before negotiating thornier issues of management control, ownership, and financial contributions.*

Rather than being a separate exercise, the alliance structure should be an end product of developing a detailed business plan. Make sure there is common ground to begin with and build synergies on paper between the companies.

Top-level commitment is critical to overcoming tough negotiation hurdles as the deal reaches closure. Given that cross-border alliance negotiations can easily last for 5 to 12 months, with the possibility that partners fail to reach agreement, backup strategies (go-it-alone; other partners) should be pursued in parallel with alliance negotiations.

2. *Build an alliance organization with strong conflict-management capabilities.*

Building in conflict resolution capabilities is critical for managing early problems and enabling the cross-border alliance to evolve over time. In 2002, Ahold unravelled the cross-border alliance it had established with Capabro, a Spanish colleague. "It became apparent that the cross-ownership and cultural differences were depriving both companies of the flexibility to take fast management action in the consumer business in Spain," said Cees van der Hoeven, CEO and President of Ahold.

Aim for 50/50 ownership whenever possible to ensure that both partners are fully committed. Of the 252 cross-border alliances in the study, 70 percent succeeded in realizing strategic and financial alliance objectives when ownership was equally divided, compared with only 35 percent of those with an uneven shareholding split. However, even where ownership is equally divided, one partner should be clearly responsible for ultimate management control. There were very few instances of a successful cross-border alliance where management control was shared evenly between the owners.

Control should be channeled through a strong chief executive with considerable operating autonomy. Cross-border alliances should also have strong boards, able to insulate them from conflicts between their parents. Direct involvement by chief executives of the partner companies is of the utmost importance. They should be prepared to devote considerable time to ensuring that cooperation develops smoothly. That underlines one of this study's central findings - that cross-border alliances depend on the degree of commitment by the partners to make them work.

3. *A cross-border alliance strategy should always include an explicit view on whether the goal is to buy or sell position in the alliance over the long term - or whether to create a truly independent business that will evolve separately for the parents.*

Companies should decide at the outset whether they want to end up as the buyer or the seller of a partnership and shape their approach to structuring and managing it accordingly. Of the cross-border alliances studied, more than 80 percent were purchased by one partner while the rest were either sold to a third party or dissolved.

The termination of an alliance is not a sign of failure - even if its life span has been short. A cross-border alliance is often a transitory structure. According to Cees van Lede, Akzo Nobel's CEO, "you always have to anticipate the end game; you have to plan ahead". If you are the likely seller, pre-negotiate exit terms in advance because your bargaining power will decrease over time. The desired position as buyer or seller must drive the alliance strategy.

It is difficult for the cross-border alliance to cover every eventuality. But the companies do need to agree in advance how they will end the relationship and divide the assets. They have to accept that they may one day be competitors rather than collaborators. Debate about the exit clause or prenuptial agreement is a valuable way to clarify corporate strategy for the business involved but typically it receives minimal attention from the negotiators. Exit provisions should be defined based on the desired position as buyer or seller. The exit clause should include a valuation formula or methodology and a clear definition of events that can trigger termination or acquisition.

When it is unclear which partner will be the buyer or seller (e.g. both want to buy), and when the future value is highly uncertain, a "shotgun auction", where either partner proposes a price at which the other partner can either buy or sell, may be appropriate. A similar approach is a "revolving auction" where either partner can offer to buy the other company's shares at a specific price. The other company can accept the offer or make a counter offer to purchase the partner's shares at a higher price.

4. *Understand that many of the qualities required of alliance managers are quite different from those expected in their parent company.*

Alliance managers have to be impartial, not fiercely committed to one company or brand. They must be able to tolerate different ways of doing things. The role of alliance managers requires great sensitivity. They have to be clear about the different objectives and the variances in culture.

The managerial and people challenges thrown up by cross-border alliances are immense. At the heart of cross-border alliances is a willingness to dissolve boundaries, both between organizations and within people's minds. Knowing how to develop a cadre of employees, both (alliance) managers and specialists, capable of working in various complex yet temporary alignments will become a key source of competitive advantage.

Box 3 Designing successful cross-border alliances

Five key principles for successful cross-border alliance design, and hence the challenges faced by any company entering a cross-border alliance, are as follows:

- *Strategic objective*. The form of the alliance, the chosen partner, the agreed ownership structure and the scope of alliance activity must be designed to meet the strategic objectives of each partner.

- *Mutual dependence*. The alliance must become a critical part of the overall strategy for each parent, such that the partners have the utmost incentive to provide the commitment and resources required to make the alliance successful.

- *Alliance independence*. The alliance must be of substantial size and be given sufficient scope to allow it to reach the critical mass necessary to develop "a life of its own" and the ability to sustain itself without excessive reliance on the parents.

- *Shared vision and rewards.* Mechanisms that allow and encourage partners to develop a common vision for the alliance and share in the rewards and benefits of working together, regardless of the success of a specific venture, should be in place.

- *Barriers to exit.* Structural or operational barriers to exit that make it difficult or painful for any of the partners to walk away and establish an independent business also need to be in place.

Managing a cross-border alliance

To manage a cross-border alliance effectively requires an accomodation between apparently conflicting administrative requirements for unified, unambiguous direction and control, on the one hand, and for effective participation by all the partners, on the other hand. There is no simple structure or management approach that will accomodate all these needs. Each cross-border alliance will need a mix of formal and informal organizational and other managerial devices.

Depending on the type of cross-border alliance, the management challenge can be quite different. In the case of a to-be-formed global joint venture with a stand-alone organization, the classic issues of organization structure and "cultural fit" are the most critical. In the case of a cross-border alliance with little or no organizational integration between the partners, the critical issues often center around how to gain momentum and meet performance targets in the absence of a dedicated organization.

Regardless of the type of partnership, managing a cross-border alliance successfully means being able to resolve conflicts between the partners. Therefore, anticipating potential conflicts beforehand and making conflict resolution policies part of the final agreement is critical. Since an alliance has more owners, all major issues relative to parents must be resolved before the deal is signed. By contrast, in post-merger or post-acquisition management, the owner has the power to decide these items after the merger or acquisition.

Cross-border alliances often fail and rarely continue in force longer than seven years. Most are dissolved or acquired within seven years. Not all of these are failures: many cross-border alliances have sunset provisions or become attractive takeover candidates for one of the partners. Many satisfactory alliances are disbanded once they have outlived their purpose. However, many do fail, as judged by the interviewees (see box 4 for a "top 10" of pitfalls).

A historical view of cross-border alliance success patterns shows that those formed between strong partners are the most likely to succeed, whereas those in which one or both of the partners is weak are much more likely to fail. Cross-border alliances are extremely unlikely to improve the situation of a weak company.

Box 4 Top ten pitfalls, ranked by interviewees

1. No real consensus; failing to agree explicitly on objectives and vision.
2. An unrealistic outlook on market trends and synergy value embedded in an unrealistic or incomplete business plan.
3. Overlay complex alliance management and organization structure.
4. Unclear division of responsibilities between parents (i.e. lack of accountability).
5. Poor communication between partners embedded in cultural incompatibility.
6. Inflexibility of the alliance agreement, e.g. no capability to evolve.
7. Failing to develop the right amount of trust among partners (Trust in cross-border alliances means different things to different people).
8. Overestimating the expected synergies significantly and underestimating required investments.
9. Insufficient resources dedicated to alliance management.
10. Emphasis on legal safeguards rather than cooperation.

Measuring success

Defining what success means for both partners and for the cross-border alliance, and ensuring 100 percent clarity on and mutual understanding of the objectives upfront, constitute an important hurdle on the way towards a successful cross-border alliance. Falling short here will most likely result in unmet expectations and dismay for at least one of the partners.

Survey participants suggest that, in contrast to cross-border acquisitions, where much of the integration planning is often done after the deal, in cross-border alliances it is imperative to assess the synergies and create detailed plans for working together before a deal is signed, since neither partner will have full control thereafter. The parties must develop a joint perspective on market outlook and industry trends and establish an agreed-upon baseline against which different alliance options will be measured.

Clear performance targets have to be established for sales volumes, cost efficiency, intercompany prices, and other areas. Any significant deviation from targets could cause conflict between the partners because it might adversely affect either partner's income beyond his own control. However, the risk of conflict between partners is even larger without clear performance agreements up front.

A managerial compromise

The rapid growth of cross-border partnerships, from distribution agreements and collaborative research to equity partnerships, has been one of the most striking features of international business in the past decade. The top 1000 global firms now draw nearly 12 percent of their revenues from cross-border alliances, a fourfold increase since 1994, according to The Boston Consulting Group.

Box 5 Lessons from successful cross-border alliances

1. Appreciate that business and national cultures are different: international success increasingly comes in proportion to a company's willingness to accept differences.
2. Be prepared to recognize and react to factors beyond the direct control of your partner and always understand the advantage of the cross-border alliance to the partner.
3. Maintain strong executive sponsorship continuously.
4. Negotiate business logic before control issues: first identify the "pie" (e.g. synergies and opportunities), then allocate the "slices" (e.g. profit and ownership issues).
5. Commitment, courage and capability throughout the participating company's organizations are key to a successful cross-border alliance.
6. Communication oils the wheel of cross-border alliances and nothing is worse than to have two partners in the same bed with different dreams.
7. It pays to do your homework: dedicate resources and significant (senior) management time and carefully define meeting frequency at the outset.
8. Build in "go/no go" checkpoints to ensure that both sides are satisfied with ongoing developments and insist on frequent/full disclosure of progress toward key objectives.
9. Build in some quick wins and constantly review your alliance's viability.
10. High expectations are a common source of problems. Corporations may overestimate the expected contributions of their partners. Each partner may also overestimate its own contribution.

There is no doubt that cross-border alliances are not managerially the ideal solution. However, recognizing the increasing consolidation and globalization of major industries through the world, some form of cross-border alliance may become critical for many companies. But despite high aspirations and enthusiasm for the concept of cross-border alliances among stakeholders in business, there is little systematic understanding of how to structure, manage and organize them. Corporations that can successfully do so will gain a competitive edge.

51

References

Bamford, J., D. Ernst, and D.G. Fubini, "Launching a World-Class Joint Venture", Harvard Business Review, p. 91-100, February 2004.

Bleeke, J. and D. Ernst, "Collaborating to Compete", John Wiley, New York, 1993.

Contractor, F.J. and P. Lorange, "Cooperative Strategies in International Business", Lexington Books/D.C. Heath and Co., Lexington, 1988.

Gomes-Casseras, B. "The Alliance Revolution", Harvard University Press, Cambridge/Mass., 1996.

www.bah.com

www.bcg.com

Yoshino, M. and U.S. Rangan, "Strategic Alliances: An Entrepreneurial Approach to Globalization", Harvard Business School Press, Mass., 1995.

3

Cross-border Acquisitions of European Multinationals

More and more companies expand the scope of their activities beyond national frontiers. This globalization of corporate activities takes place through alliances, mergers and/or acquisitions or start-up of new activities. This chapter presents a study into the cross-border acquisitions of European companies. It is structured as follows. The next paragraph describes the purpose of the study. Subsequently, the findings of the study are presented. Finally, it puts into perspective some widespread beliefs that frequently turn out to be misconceptions. This chapter ends with lessons learnt for boards and general managers.

Eye-catching growth vehicles

Of all methods of internationalization that a company could follow, acquisition is the most spectacular and usually the most drastic one. At macroeconomic level, this phenomenon is studied by analyzing the fluctuation of acquisition activities and the effects thereof on, for instance, market forces. This chapter, however, concentrates on the business considerations that play a part in the acquisition of a company and leaves the macroeconomic effects aside. It offers a qualitative analysis of the phenomenon of international acquisitions; it charts the characteristics of a large number of observed and studied cases.

It is important to make a distinction between acquisitions and mergers. Through the years, many different interpretations of acquisitions and mergers have been used. To a considerable extent, this is caused by the incomparability of the results of many studies into the acquisition and merger behavior of companies. In this chapter, the following distinction is made on the basis of common terminology: acquisitions are the result of the combination of two companies of different qualities, not necessarily by mutual agreement. Acquisitions show a disproportion in the levels of control.

Mergers, on the other hand, are the result of the amalgamation of two equal companies. The amalgamation is realized with the consent of both parties. In this case the levels of control are equivalent. Finally, cross-border acquisitions are concerned when the companies in question are from different countries. My extensive database included cross-border acquisitions made by European companies during the period 1976-2000.

The analysis in this chapter has been structured around the following twelve research questions.

1. Why are foreign companies acquired? Different motives can be identified:

- *Expansion*: acquisitions make it possible to quickly anticipate a strong market growth. This way, a company is able to seize a significant part of this growth.

- *Market entry*: acquisitions make it possible to enter a market without extremely high initial expenses. It avoids the costs of market penetration and market development. In addition, acquisitions are a way of circumventing (intended) protective measures.

- *Scale*: cross-border acquisitions enable companies to achieve a critical mass in a short time. A certain minimum size is required for a company in order to keep up with its competitors.

- *Geographic*: by spreading the activities geographically, a company becomes less vulnerable.

- *Finance*: through acquisitions, local cash cows can be acquired. It is possible, for instance, to formulate a new ambitious corporate strategy with the support of financial means of the acquired local company. The internationalization in zone B can be financed, for example, with the internationalization already realized (through acquisitions) in zone A.

- *Economies of skills*: as a result of acquisitions, companies are able to benefit from the mutual exchange of experiences, skills and capabilities within geographically spread segments.

2. In what region/country is the company established that is the acquisition target i.e. what is the "geographical direction" of cross-border acquisition activities? A distinction can be made between Europe, the USA, Japan and the category "other countries".

3. Is the acquisition paid in cash or in another way?

4. What about the consolidation method? Are acquired activities integrated in the existing business, or does the acquired company continue to exist in its original form, i.e.

without any organizational cross-connections between acquired and acquiring company?

5. Acquiring companies, were they small (less than 250 employees), medium-sized (250-1000 employees) or large (more than 1000 employees)?

6. Do acquiring companies want full control or do they agree to a partial control over the activities of acquired companies?

7. Is the acquired foreign company run by the same executives after the acquisition took place?

8. Do the acquiring European company and the acquired foreign company know each other well, or is the acquisition also the first time they make their acquaintance?

9. Acquired foreign companies, are they financially healthy or are they ailing or even insolvent or bankrupt companies?

10. Acquiring companies, are they mostly large European companies (that is to say, the largest companies of their industry), or do the medium-sized (250-1000 employees) or small companies (less than 250 employees) account for the majority of international acquisitions?

11. Are the activities of acquired and acquiring companies connected in some way, or are the two companies concerned operating in different stages of the value chain or in different industries? In other words: what is the "strategic direction" of cross-border acquisitions - related/horizontal or unrelated /diversified?

12. What European companies account for the majority of cross-border acquisitions: industrial or service companies?

Method of investigation

This study aims for valid and reliable results by using a research method based on case studies, using the following complementary data sources:

- Official communications to the financial press (press releases), especially *The Financial Times*, *The Wall Street Journal* (US and European edition), Reuters and Bloomberg.
- Volumes (if possible from 1976 onwards) of well-known (financial) daily newspapers, like for instance *The Financial Times*, *The Wall Street Journal* (Europe), *Frankfurter Allgemeine*, *Het Financieele Dagblad* (the Dutch equivalent of The Financial Times) and *Financieel-Economische Tijd* (the Belgian equivalent of The Financial Times).
- Annual reports of the top 500 European enterprises of *The Financial Times* (edition 2000) and annual reports of the top 100, 500 and/or 1000 companies of different European countries (published by different management magazines and newspapers), at different points in time (if possible, from 1976 onwards).
- Databases of investment banks Goldman Sachs, Morgan Stanley, Merrill Lynch, CSFB, and UBS Warburg.

I have traced and extensively studied 2.933 well documented cross-border acquisitions made by European companies in a 25-year period (1976-2000). A separate and extensive file was opened of each cross-border acquisition. The international acquisitions were effectuated by a cross-section of European businesses. All data were entered in an electronic database. The aforementioned questions were used as starting point and guideline for the empirical study. A review of the results of this study is made in the next paragraph.

Of the 2.933 cross-border acquisitions of European companies, the relative geographical spread of the acquiring parties is as follows:

Great Britain	31,2 %
France	12,9 %
Benelux (the Netherlands, Belgium, Luxembourg)	20,9 %
Germany	7,1 %
Scandinavia (Norway, Sweden, Denmark, Finland)	12,7%
Central Europe (Switzerland, Austria)	6,1 %
Southern Europe (Portugal, Spain, Italy, Greece)	6,9 %
Eastern Europe (Poland, Bulgaria, Slovakia, Czech Republic, Hungary, [former] Yugoslavia, Rumania)	2,2 %

Conclusion: British and Benelux companies account for the majority of cross-border acquisitions in my database. British, Dutch and Belgian companies are very active on the international market for corporate control. Scandinavian companies also use this form of international expansion quite often. The large number of Swiss cross-border acquisitions is remarkable, as is the relatively small number of German cross-border acquisitions.

The small number of Eastern European cross-border acquisitions is closely related to the lack of experience in respect of this form of international growth. In addition, it has to be pointed out that it is difficult to trace international acquisitions made by Eastern European companies because they are often not well documented. The same applies to the cross-border acquisitions made by Southern European companies, although remarkable improvements have taken place in recent years.

Results

The results of this study will be addressed point by point, in accordance with the research questions that were formulated earlier in this chapter. In connection with the size of the research study, I consciously choose to present the results in this specific way. In the future I will realize a comparative analysis of cross-border acquisition behavior of companies from different European countries. The tables represent a relative score (that is to say, the scores of the 2.933 cross-border acquisitions in respect of the possible answers to the questions), expressed as a percentage.

Major types of rationales

There are many explanations for cross-border acquisitions. The motive of shaping and giving meaning to a more intensive exchange of experiences, skills, and capabilities between various parts of corporations, (i.e. achieving economies of skills) had the highest score: 32 percent.

Remarkably, this motive has become increasingly important through the years, which applies to companies from all European regions. Economies of skills are the result of bundling and disseminating experiences and competencies from different corporations (i.e. the acquirer and acquired company) in order to be able to respond more effectively (in terms of value added) and efficiently (in terms of lower costs) to the local and global market. This is also called the realization of horizontal synergy (see chapter 6).

According to my database, the more internationalizing companies develop foreign activities located in more than one country, the higher is the importance of economies of skills. This applies to all companies from all European regions.

The desire to achieve economies of skills indicates that the management of many European companies give priority to the strategic and operational dimensions of an acquisition instead of to the financial and tax-related dimensions. Cross-border acquisitions are made because companies want to strengthen their strategic position and to improve their business operations through the achievement of economies of skills. The decision to make a cross-border acquisition is first and foremost a strategic one, and to a much lesser extent a financial one.

Box 1 Why are foreign firms acquired?

Economies of skills	32%
Expansion	27%
Economies of scale	25%
Market entry	12%
Geographic risk spreading	3%
Financial	1%

ABN AMRO is an example of a multinational bank that has given a lot of attention to the potential of skills, capabilities and experience of the foreign acquisition candidate and to whether or not this potential could be used to the benefit of other ABN AMRO businesses located elsewhere. British publisher Reed Elsevier was able to expand its activities in professional information in Europe successfully through cross-border acquisitions in the eighties and nineties, partly because of the knowledge, skills and experience of professional information companies acquired in the seventies in the United States.

The motives of expansion and economies of scale played an important part (scores of respectively 27 and 25 percent). International acquisitions made it possible to rapidly expand scale and thus achieve objectives as profitability and market leadership in the short term. For that matter, many cross-border acquisitions of European telecommunications companies during the second half of the nineties show that these growth and scale objectives were by no means always achieved.

Another motive frequently found was the one of gaining a foothold in an important growth market (12 percent). For this reason, cross-border acquisitions were continuously made in developing markets or fast growing product markets. Striking examples of this are the recent acquisitions by European companies in the Far East (to an increasing degree also in China) and those that took place in the eighties in the services sector in the United States. During a certain period (second half of the eighties till first half of the nineties), the Argentine market was also an attractive hunting ground for Spanish and other European companies that wanted to expand their interests in Argentina.

Apart from geographical markets, acquisitions can result in gaining a foothold on fast growing global product markets. This way, Daimler-Benz acquired important interests in the international aviation industry. For this same reason, Swiss financial service providers (especially retail and wholesale banks) took over many specialized investment banking activities in the United States and Great Britain in the eighties and nineties. This concerned both large, eye-catching acquisitions as well as a few dozen medium-sized and small acquisitions of high-quality research firms and small and medium-sized local investment companies.

Due to reasons in particular related to risk spreading, cross-border acquisitions were seldom made in other currency areas (3 percent). In the chemical industry, European companies like Bayer, Basf and Akzo Nobel frequently acquired medium-sized and large companies in the United States and the United Kingdom. Similarly, in the services sector, European companies frequently acquired publishers and insurance companies in the United States for this reason. European retail organizations as Ahold and Carrefour made frequent acquisitions in the Far East on the basis of this argument.

Remarkably, the financial motive was hardly ever found (1 percent). The takeover of the Dutch company Worldonline by the Italian Tiscali in 2000 can be described as a cross-border acquisition primarily based on financial motives. Due to the deep financial pockets of Worldonline, Tiscali was able to considerably strengthen its position in the rest of Europe. In a way, Worldonline served as a financial springboard for the rest of Europe.

Geographical direction

The majority of acquiring companies want to expand their activities in Europe, North America and Japan. Large companies in particular feel that their position, as global players, has to match the economic potential of the three most important regions.

The vast majority of the acquisitions were made in Europe (49 percent) and the USA (41 percent). Japan makes a relatively low score (2 percent), just like the category "other countries" (8 percent). In the global market for corporate control, the trend is clearly set by the home market (Europe) and the United States.

A permanent preference for Europe and the United States can be observed. Japan and the category "other countries" have not gained in popularity in the last few years as destination for international acquisitions of European companies.

Box 2 What is the geographical direction?

Europe	49%
United States of America	41%
Japan	2%
Other countries	8%

The high score of the United States (one country) calls for some explanation. Many European companies are active in the American market for corporate control, especially companies from Great Britain, the Netherlands, Sweden and Switzerland. British and Dutch companies in particular have close ties with the United States from way back. In the second half of the seventies, the American acquisitions of, for instance, Dutch companies, accounted for more than one third of the total value of all acquisitions (therefore not only international acquisitions!).

Both British and Dutch companies acquired more companies in the United States in terms of value than in Europe in the first half of the nineties. Swiss and Swedish companies - both from the industrial and services sectors - are striking runners-up. They also concentrate to a great extent on the United States. Although numerically speaking more acquisitions are made in Europe, the biggest international acquisitions of Swedish and (especially) Swiss companies are usually made in the United States.

By way of illustration: The turnover of the US operations of the Dutch retailer Ahold and insurer Aegon was considerably higher in 2000 than the turnover of both companies in other parts of the world, including Europe, their home market. The same can be said for Swiss pharmaceuticals and private banks.

Some companies have been active on the US market for decades. The concentration of many European companies on the US market can be explained on the basis of:

- *size* - which creates a large level of support for all kinds of activities (there is enough room for each company to compete and to grow);
- *diversity* - as a result of which many market niches can be accessed - also by smaller European companies, and
- *"psychological distance"* - which is relatively small in view of the historical ties between the United States and Great Britain and the Netherlands in particular.

In addition, the US has few restrictions for many European companies (there is a positive attitude towards the business sector in general), it is a highly dynamic market (for many companies, the US market is the most flexible and innovating market in the world and therefore the home of many new products and services) and it enables an anti-cyclic policy.

Furthermore, also the majority of the (for instance Asian) competitors of the globalizing European business sector have found their way to the United States. In order to compete effectively on a global level, it is almost essential to be present in the US. Companies that are not present on the US market are at risk of losing global competitiveness.

Method of payment

The majority of transactions (46 percent) were cash, financed from the cash flow. The takeover price was seldom financed with loans (11 percent). Cash deals also dominated the exchange of shares (43 percent). Paying a cross-border acquisition in shares results in a dilution of the profits per share, which, in general, is not accepted by existing shareholders. This explains why many European companies prefer to pay acquisitions in cash.

Box 3 Is the acquisition paid in cash or in another way?	
Cash	46%
Loans	11%
Exchange of shares	43%

It is striking, however, that Southern and Eastern European companies show a dominant preference for cash transactions. Relatively speaking, companies from Great Britain, the Benelux, Scandinavia and Central Europe frequently use loan capital. These companies also score relatively high on share transactions.

Consolidation method

An important question for the acquiring company is whether the acquired party is integrated into the existing portfolio or continues to be an independent activity. The majority of acquired companies was integrated in one way or another in order to profit from advantages like cost and revenue economies. In addition, from a control point of view, it was easier to manage the new combination.

The vast majority of cross-border acquisitions were followed by one or more reorganizations. According to my database this was related to, among others, the:

- financial condition of the acquired company (not always as profitable and well-functioning from an operational point of view);
- necessary adjustments in order to rearrange both companies (integration) or to align business operations (coordination), and

- harmonization of strategic and operational policies (among others, the alignment or incorporation of information systems and business processes that most of the time were different and for that reason did not communicate well with each other).

Box 4 What is the consolidation method?	
Integrated	81%
Independent	19%

Size of the acquisition

Acquired companies frequently were medium-sized (34 percent) or large (45 percent). In all probability, the group of large acquired companies dominates the database because of the visibility of this kind of cross-border acquisitions. Against this background, the number of medium-sized acquisition candidates is remarkable. European companies have a preference for medium-sized or large cross-border acquisitions.

Small companies are regarded as less attractive (21 percent). This is understandable if we relate the size of cross-border acquisitions to the motives dealt with above. The preference for medium-sized and large foreign companies explains, for instance, the high score of strategic motives of "increase in scale", "expansion", "market entry" and "economies of skills". Size is an important precondition if a company wants to materialize many of the aforementioned motives (i.e. latent advantages) for acquisition.

Many small cross-border acquisitions involved local companies that were not performing well from a financial point of view. In general, these companies were acquired because they had an interesting/unique product that made them stand out in the line of business in which they operated and competed (among others with larger companies, often the acquiring parties). This way, a local (though weak) competitor (which in itself had an interesting product that fitted in with the product portfolios of the acquiring company), was taken off the market.

Box 5 Size of the acquisition - small, medium-sized or large?

Small (< 250 employees)	21%
Medium-sized (250-1000 employees)	34%
Large (> 1000 employees)	45%

The fact that a relatively high number of small companies was acquired is also due to the political sensibility related to acquisitions of larger companies. A smaller company does not attract attention and when acquired, it causes less political turmoil. This appears to play a role especially in the financial services and media sectors as well as in defence-related industries.

Partial or total control

Acquiring European companies showed a distinct preference for total acquisition (79 percent). Acquired companies were forced to follow acquiring companies' corporate and competitive strategies. Important reasons to make total instead of partial cross-border acquisitions were:

- to gain a better grip on the business operations of the acquired company;
- to expand globally or locally at a higher pace, and

- to have the possibility not to disclose the results; for instance, in the United States, many majority participating interests are under the obligation of disclosing their results, whereas 100 percent participating interests are often released from this obligation.

Senior executives strongly prefer full acquisitions. The full ownership of a new acquisition means having control over all dimensions (both strategic and operational).

Box 6 Do acquiring companies want full or partial control?

Full control	79%
Partial control	21%

Some European companies deliberately use a "multi-tiered" acquisition strategy, i.e. gaining total control over a company by acquiring it in different phases. Especially in the financial services sector and the information sector (particularly media and multimedia companies), often a participation of 51 to 60 percent in the foreign company is acquired (in my terminology a partial acquisition). In time, the participating interests are expanded. This way, majority interests are often increased to 100 percent (a full acquisition), especially when the region in which operations take place is of great or increasing importance to the internationalizing company.

Various European service providers like publisher VNU (the Netherlands), retailer Delhaize (Belgium), Swiss banks and insurance companies have used this strategy - particularly in the United States.

Continuation of management

After acquisition, the acquired company is practically always continued under the same management (and often also under the same name). Acquiring European companies - from all regions - are hesitant to adjust (read: replace) management of the acquired company directly after the acquisition. They prefer to maintain the existing management. This way, an acquiring company is able to take advantage of the experience and commercial relations of sitting management.

Compared to an acquiring company, an acquired company is often much better acquainted with a local market and its customers, in particular because of this management. Acquiring parties also seek to profit from strong ties between existing management of an acquired company and local and national political leaders.

Box 7 Is the acquired foreign company run by the same executives after the acquisition took place?

Same management	87%
New management	13%

In fact, acquiring companies only break with existing management of an acquired company if it has been responsible for a really bad - in particular financial - performance.

Acquaintance

In many cases, acquiring and acquired companies had been in contact with each other in one way or another some considerable time before the acquisition (this applies to 88 percent of the acquisitions).

The fact that companies involved are acquainted reduces their insecurity in respect of each other's capacities and consequently, the possibility of failure. In itself, this result is understandable. In general, companies take over others that are in the same line of their own business, i.e. colleagues whom they know well (see also research question 11).

Box 8 Do the acquiring and acquired companies know each other well?

They know each other well	88%
They don't know each other well	12%

The results for this question show that many European companies, before actually acquiring another business, apparently orient themselves quite well on the potential international market for corporate control. This applies to companies both from Northern and Central Europe as well as from Southern and Eastern Europe.

Financial health

European companies mainly acquire financially sound foreign businesses. The share of acquired bankrupt companies in the total number of cross-border acquisitions was small.

European companies want to expand their geographical scope with solid acquisition partners. The fear of being burdened with a financial shipwreck is high. This also is - at least partly - the reason that cross-border acquisitions normally are well prepared. A vast majority of acquiring parties make intensive use of the services of top lawyers, strategy consultants, investment bankers and tax consultants.

Box 9 Acquired companies - financially healthy or not?

Financially healthy	84%
Financially not healthy	16%

In general, companies are willing (and have the capacity) to pay substantial amounts for acquisition candidates. A high acquisition price is perceived to indicate that the foreign company (in all likelihood) is not a "risk factor". Many managers of acquiring parties feel that the other side of "buying a pig in a poke" is pitch-black. A disastrously executed international acquisition frequently results in the end of the career of a top manager. I have constantly found this psychological factor in my study. "Best" is perceived as "expensive" in the end. This psychological factor is found in all European regions. For that same reason, European companies often dislike large-scale restructuring processes of foreign acquisition candidates. In this context, the evident preference for financially sound companies is only natural.

Size of the acquiring company

The majority of cross-border acquisitions were made by the largest companies from the respective industries. This pattern applies to all European regions.

Box 10 Size of the acquiring company - small, medium or large?	
Small	2%
Medium	36%
Large	62%

The research results show that the largest companies make the largest acquisitions. This result is in line with the results of the previous research question. In general, companies like BP, Vodafone, Philips, LVMH, VW, Daimler-Benz, UBS, Unilever, Royal Dutch Shell, Deutsche Bank and Akzo Nobel are responsible for the largest acquisitions. Large European companies rarely acquire small foreign companies. In isolated cases, medium-sized companies are acquired. The "bigger is better" strategy is dominant.

In general, medium-sized companies take over small foreign companies. European medium-sized companies rarely take over medium-sized foreign companies. Small European companies only venture onto the field of international acquisitions in isolated cases. For the majority of the small companies, a cross-border acquisition is a bridge too far.

Relatedness

It appeared from my study that to a high degree the majority of cross-border acquisitions is related to the core activities of the acquiring company (94 percent). Related cross-border acquisitions are less venturesome and make it easier to achieve economies of scale and experience.

European companies rarely make cross-border acquisitions in non-related industries. For the same reason non-related diversification hardly ever occurred. A successful non-related cross-border acquisition was that of the American cosmetic giant Cheesebrough-Pond's by Unilever in 1987 for an amount of $3.1 billion. In my database, this was one of the rare successful non-related cross-border diversifications.

Box 11 Are the activities of acquired and acquiring companies related or unrelated?

Related	94%
Unrelated	6%

The majority of cross-border acquisitions had a horizontal character. If we look at the top 25 cross-border acquisitions made by European companies initiated for instance in 1998, it is remarkable that more than 20 had a horizontal character. Well-known examples from that top 25 are acquisitions of Amoco by BP, Chrysler by Daimler-Benz, Giant Food by Ahold, Banco Real by ABN AMRO, Courtaulds by Akzo Nobel and of Fina by Total - all horizontal cross-border acquisitions.

Looking at the largest cross-border acquisitions of European companies in the year 1999, a similar image emerges. The following eight examples are included in the top ten of the largest international acquisitions in 1999:

- American Airtouch Communications by Vodafone for as much as $69.3 billion;
- Swedish Astra by the British Zeneca for $37.7 billion;
- American Arco Atlantic Richfield by BP Amoco for $34 billion;
- French Rhone Poulenc by German steel group Hoechst for $22 billion;
- Argentine YPF by Spanish oil company Repsol for $15.45 billion;
- British One 2 One by Deutsche Telekom for $13.6 billion;

- American TransAmerica by Dutch insurer Aegon at a price of $9.7 billion, and
- Rothmans International by British BAT Industries for $8.51 billion.

Horizontal cross-border mega-acquisitions realized right at the end of my research period were acquisitions of the American Bestfoods by Unilever (for $25.07 billion), Orange by France Telecom (for $46 billion), and of Credit Commercial de France (CCF) by HSBC Holdings (for $11.2 billion). Non-related cross-border acquisitions by European companies are isolated cases in the practice of the European business sector.

Kind of company

Industrial companies account for the majority of cross-border acquisitions (78 percent). In this respect, there are significant differences between the different European regions. British - and to a lesser degree Dutch and French - companies are more active than other companies as acquiring party in the information-intensive services sector like banking, insurance, publishing, media and multimedia. Both Southern and Eastern European companies are mainly active as acquiring party in the industrial sector.

On the whole, European services companies account for a much smaller part of the total number of cross-border acquisitions than industrial companies do. In a way, this is understandable. The majority of globalizing companies is still involved in the production or trading of goods (I included trading companies - borderline cases - in the category of industrial companies). The majority of service companies, especially those in Southern and Eastern Europe, simply lack experience to expand their activities by making foreign acquisitions.

Box 12 Which European companies account for the majority of cross-border acquisitions?

Industrial companies	78%
Service companies	22%

It appears to be difficult to make cross-border acquisitions in services industries. National characteristics like government restrictions (for instance, in respect of sectors like banking and insurance) often are a barrier for foreign services companies to enter a foreign market. For that reason, acquisitions of information-intensive companies - especially media companies in the larger European and non-European countries - is often either impossible or accompanied with annoying, mostly superfluous, preconditions (so-called "informal barriers").

From the end of the seventies and the beginning of the eighties onwards, cross-border acquisitions made by publishers, insurers and banks have been increasing. The number of cross-border acquisitions of (multi)media companies also has increased rapidly in recent years. Nearly all large services companies made one or more cross-border acquisitions in the nineties. The number of medium-sized and small European services companies that use cross-border acquisitions are, however, few and far between.

Strategic issues

In a way, my extensive database obscures the view of reality. Further analysis shows that the majority of European companies internationalize mostly along the path of organic expansion. ABN AMRO, Gucci and Unilever are striking examples of this: these companies make many eye-catching cross-border acquisitions, but on further analysis of the company specific data, growth is achieved particularly through internal development.

Apart from strategic matters addressed in this study, more tactical matters can be distinguished. These tactical matters also determine whether or not cross-border acquisitions are made. For example, negotiating on an acquisition price influences both a negotiating climate and pricing. In this study, I have merely concentrated on some strategic dimensions and a number of related questions, not taking into account tactical and operational considerations. Two additional strategic issues regarding the content and results of this study will be discussed in this paragraph:

- the influence of the European Union (EU) on the cross-border acquisition behaviour of European companies, and
- the international character of cross-border acquisitions.

EU

The euphoria surrounding the euro and the EU has to be differentiated. For a long time, the euro/EU had an almost magic undertone. With the approximation of the real internal market, various predominantly non-European companies started to expand in Europe in general, and in particular to make acquisitions. These acquisitions were often motivated by fear of a second (after 1992) "Fortress Europe".

From the point of view of anticipating management, it was a widespread belief that for the same reason, European companies also had to expand to other countries. If they did not, they would come off worst in the rising multi-market competition battle for market leadership. The results of this study indicate otherwise, however.

The coming of the EU has rarely been decisive for international growth through acquisitions by European companies. No significant relation could be found in the study between the increasing integration of the European market on one hand, and the cross-border acquisition behaviour of European companies on the other hand.

Furthermore, the coming of an integrated Europe did not significantly influence the cross-border acquisition behaviour of (especially Eastern-) European companies that were not part of the EU. Without a doubt, the fact that they were already located in Europe will have something to do with this. Nevertheless, I was surprised about the absence of this connection so often assumed in the financial press.

European companies have strategic and operational motives to expand their activities through cross-border acquisitions. Political motives will play a significant role from time to time, but for the European companies that I studied, they were clearly of marginal importance.

Geographical concentration

I would also like to pass a comment on geographical diversity of cross-border operations. Acquisitions by European companies were often made in one region or country. Especially companies from Great Britain, the Benelux, Scandinavia and Southern Europe used this cross-border acquisition approach.

A few illustrative examples are the focus of:

- many large European publishers and various British and Dutch insurance companies on the United States;
- various large European retailers on North and South America;
- large and medium-sized Spanish multinationals (industrial and services companies) on the Spanish-speaking part of South and Central America, and

- many European banks on certain parts (especially the Mid West and North-East) of the United States.

Many other European companies also use this "geographical concentration strategy". This way, advantage can be taken of economies of scale and skills. The majority of internationalizing European companies are active in only one region/country. There are very few real global European companies.

Unique competencies and deep financial pockets

Almost all European companies that made many acquisitions had at least one unique, distinctive competence (that made them stand out abroad) and deep financial pockets. Most European companies internationalized their scope through acquisitions from a financially strong position. This applied to both small companies (that internationalized in lucrative market niches) and the better known medium-sized and well-known large companies. The presence of deep financial pockets is important, given the fact that the debt-equity ratios of various companies frequently were subjected to great pressure after a cross-border acquisition was made.

A few companies with unfavourable debt-equity ratios were forced, after a sizeable cross-border acquisition, to alienate certain components through divestments and break-ups. A case in point is divestments realized by various European telecommunications companies in the year 2000.

Value-maximizing reality requires a complex balancing act

Rapid improvements in information, communication and transportation technologies lead to better informed and more demanding customers everywhere in the world and to increasingly open and interlinked markets where global players compete. Nowadays, the challenge for many corporations is not whether to expand globally, but how to.

From an offensive viewpoint, geographic expansion offers one of the few opportunities for growth when the home market is mature or domestic competition is already concentrated. From a defensive viewpoint, the arguments for expansion can be even more compelling and more urgent.

It is difficult to turn a blind eye to the fact that Europe (but also the Americas and Asia) is restructuring; in many industries, customers, suppliers and competitors are getting bigger and becoming increasingly global, and purely national competitors are looking increasingly vulnerable. Unfortunately, while the need for international expansion may appear ever more pressing, the risk of destroying value through inappropriate initiatives is also getting more and more real.

One useful way of deciding between alternative cross-border expansion strategies is to assess how well each will meet - and not exceed - the company's objectives along three dimensions:

- *Control* - which functions need to be directly controlled in order to maximize value and which can be left to third parties?
- *Scale* - what scale is needed in each national market, and overall across the world? Clearly, this will be heavily influenced by which global and/or pan-European vision has been agreed.
- *Speed of expansion* - how fast the desired scale must be achieved, given the lifecycle of the product and the nature of local and global competition.

Clearly, if a cross-border expansion strategy under-delivers against the company's objectives, then the chances are it will destroy value, even if it looks attractive in the short term. Equally, exceeding these objectives can incur a cost - in terms of cash, human resources or risk - that will not be justified because it will not help to fulfil the overall company vision.

The different routes to global expansion deliver very different scores against the three criteria. Organic development - growing the business from scratch - will deliver complete control of all business functions but will usually be slow and will not, at least in mature markets, generally result in significant scale. Alliances, on the other hand, can generate scale rapidly, but will usually involve sacrificing complete control over some element of the business. Finally, acquisition will typically score high against all three criteria, but at a cost.

Unilever may be a good example of a company continuing to build leading positions separately in a number of national food markets, but also exploiting the benefits of global scale and skills - in product categories such as ice cream, frozen food and cosmetics. To maintain competitive advantage, it needs to control most functions - except distribution. And the maturity of most European and American food markets means that it has needed to build national scale rapidly. In Unilever's case, therefore, cross-border acquisition has been the preferred route.

When Electrolux began its expansion drive in the European white goods industry, it did not have the benefit of a unique value proposition. To gain competitive advantage, it needed to keep down costs by controlling and integrating most aspects of the business on a pan-European basis - including R&D, manufacturing, marketing and branding. It also needed sufficient scale to justify plants dedicated to specific products (all front loading washing machines to be produced in Italy, all microwaves in the UK). And it needed all of this fast - because the industry was already mature and competitors

80

were perfectly capable of following Electrolux's lead. In these circumstances, it is likely that neither organic development nor local alliances would have worked. Since 1990, Electrolux has made over 40 acquisitions in Europe alone.

Turning a cross-border acquisition into value-maximizing reality requires a complex balancing act - creating and pursuing opportunities with the utmost vigour whilst at the same time not getting carried away by the sort of management hubris that so often destroys value. This balancing act is not a task for the faint hearted. Few organizations can manage this balancing act by committee; either the CEO himself or his deputed "acquisition champion" must be given control of the process. Therefore, perhaps the single most important step that a CEO can take is to find and appoint an "acquisition champion" - someone who can lead the cross-border acquisition process through all of its inevitable pitfalls, both external and internal.

The two major challenges for the CEO and his acquisition champion are: winning over a potential acquisition candidate, and avoiding the temptation to overpay.

In continental Europe and Asia, hostile acquisitions are still a rarity. In may cases, local acquisition candidates will be controlled by banks or a small group of family shareholders, whose decision on whether or not to sell will be determined by many factors besides price.

Government too can often play a major role and may need to be persuaded against their instincts. Overcoming these challenges requires a lengthy "courtship". The champion needs to demonstrate perseverance, coupled with the ability to complete the negotiation rapidly once a deal has been struck in principle. Equally important, of course, is avoiding the temptation to overpay and end up destroying value.

If one wishes to avoid becoming the target of tomorrow's cross-border raiders, there is no alternative but to do one's homework now and be willing to walk away if the price is too high.

Lessons for practitioners

Many European companies that are aggressively pursuing cross-border acquisitions should not be. Companies that have significant opportunities to improve core business performance should do so. Companies that try to diversify away from problems in their core businesses through cross-border acquisitions are more likely to compound their problems than solve them.

Although having a strong core business is no guarantee of success with cross-border acquisitions, a strong core business is highly correlated with cross-border acquisition success. Better managed companies have a better chance of adding value.

My analyses of consistently successful European cross-border acquirers indicates that they have several approaches in common:

• They restructure candidates and use financial engineering to extract value and lower the effective acquisition price.
• They add both operating and strategic value to the acquired candidate and harness the candidate's superior capabilities to add value to their own business portfolio.
• They use a disciplined process to identify and value attractive candidates.
• They carefully manage candidates post-acquisition to ensure that value is extracted.

Nearly all cross-border acquirers use financial engineering within twelve months of the cross-border acquisition, to improve the economics of the acquired entity. Successful European acquirers employ a variety of restructuring and financial engineering approaches: selling businesses to companies that will pay handsomely for synergies, disposing of under-utilized corporate assets (e.g. real estate), changing capital structures, and stripping over-funded pension plans.

Virtually all successful European cross-border acquirers do more than restructure and financially engineer. They also add significant strategic and operating value. Successful acquirers use three approaches for adding value:

- *Skills transfer* (i.e., upgrading the general management and/or functional skills of the acquired company using people, systems, and philosophies from the acquirer). General management skill transfer can serve to create strategic and operational improvements. Functional skill transfer can take place in any and all of the major functional activities of the acquired entity, depending on the leverageable skill base of the acquiring firm and, of course, on which functional activities are key to competitive advantage.

- *Create and exploit functional economies of scale*, e.g. achieve critical mass in R&D (necessary to support major R&D investments), eliminate duplicative (development) efforts, consolidate manufacturing plants, and combine sales, distribution and service systems (i.e. consolidate and rationalize the assets and systems of the combined entities). The principal objective in this approach is to fundamentally improve the relative cost position of the combined firms.

- *Change industry structure*, e.g. solve structural overcapacity problems and change value-added supplier-customer relationships. This approach is particularly applicable to industries undergoing discontinuities due to deregulation, globalization, substantial technological change, or material changes in customer buying patterns. In these situations, opportunities arise to create new and sustainable competitive advantages by recognizing, early on, what the future competitive structure is likely to be. For instance, acquisitions to create global financial supermarkets (i.e. the international strategy of ING) were designed to change the basis of competition in multiple financial services businesses by locking up customer groups and offering one-stop shopping.

Furthermore, successful European acquirers asses their own strengths and weaknesses to determine how they will add value to acquired candidates, actively search for candidates instead of waiting for opportunities to be brought to them (the best (local/global) acquisition candidates are usually those that are not being shopped by investment bankers), and go to great pains to value a candidate accurately and do not overpay.

Successful European acquirers are able to add value after they acquire. Well thought-out post-acquisition integration is an essential part of their approach. The extent and type of post-acquisition integration needed depend on what needs to be done to extract value from the acquired company and thus offset premiums and create value for the shareholders of the acquiring company. A foreign acquisition that must be restructured/financially engineered to create value requires an integration program very different in extent and type from one that seeks to capitalize on functional economies of scale.

If restructuring/financial engineering is the primary means of adding value, management transfers and functional consolidation plans are not that important. In contrast, an acquisition predicated on functional synergies through skills transfer or economies of scale requires a great deal more organizational integration. In addition to integrating the two corporate centres, the acquirer must decide how synergistic businesses can be integrated to share functions. Should the acquired company be fully functionalized and integrated into the acquiring company's businesses or should only one function be broken out and shared?

Appropriate integration is key to capturing most functional and operational synergies. The actual integration process requires careful planning because of the large number of communications that need to be handled well. The extent of integration ultimately planned, has to be communicated to the top management team of the acquired company to ensure that their expectations are properly managed and key players can be locked in. Systems must be integrated in a series of steps carefully sequenced to minimize operational disruptions and departures of talented people.

Integration steps must be consistent with strategic, financial, and organizational needs. The focus must be on "beat the competition", not "beat those other guys". Successful cross-border post-acquisition management will be greatly facilitated by integrated thinking in which the challenges of the post-acquisition period are anticipated and incorporated into pre-acquisition planning.

Cross-border acquisition programs are not for every company. They are not a panacea to ensure corporate health. Well-managed European companies that have exhausted value creation opportunities in their core businesses should actively evaluate both cross-border acquisition programs and internal growth initiatives as vehicles for ongoing shareholder value creation. Companies with poorly performing core businesses should focus on fixing those businesses before pursuing cross-border acquisition opportunities. A corporation that has difficulty adding value to its core businesses is unlikely to add value to an acquired company.

Make haste with caution

The question of how to expand globally has moved to the forefront of many European CEOs' attention. The potential benefits are huge, but so too are the risks of inappropriate expansion. With the stakes so high, the best advice seems to be "make haste with caution". First, challenge and re-challenge the cross-border vision; if such a vision cannot be clearly articulated or if it lacks full corporate support, then do not expand globally. Second, make sure that an anorganic expansion strategy (i.e. growth through acquisition) is truly consistent with the objectives of the vision. Third, find an "acquisition champion" with the personal qualities and internal credibility to pursue international expansion vigorously and systematically.

There is no doubt that cross-border acquisitions are not the ideal solution. Numerous case studies underline the potential problems that can arise. However, recognizing the increasing enlargement of trade, economic and political unions (e.g. the expansion of the EU) through the world, this form of global expansion may be critical for many companies. Consequently, identifying and anticipating the problems well in advance must be of concern to the CEO and his general management team. Trade, economic and/or political integration will create continued momentum in the growth and importance of cross-border acquisitions.

4

International Divestments

An Empirical Perspective

Internationalizing the business scope is far from simple. Many multinational companies incur most of their losses abroad. A striking example of such a company is the Endemol entertainment business. Performance of the biggest entertainment business in the Netherlands in 1998 was unreservedly sound. The theater division, however, operated at a loss. This was the result solely of sub-standard performance of its "Holiday on Ice" shows in Latin America and its unsuccessful American musical "High Society". While Endemol was market leader in theater productions inside the Netherlands, outside the country the company bombed. Its copycat strategy of doing more of the same outside the Netherlands failed to bring success abroad. In its ambitious international theater adventure, Endemol overreached itself.

Another example is the industrial trading company Geveke. Its internationalization rate in the early nineties was much too rapid. In quick succession, foreign businesses were acquired. In the general sense, Geveke specialized in acquiring underperforming companies active in its own industry. While this strategy was highly successful in the Netherlands, Geveke was greedy when it started doing the same abroad. Its foreign acquisitions in Norway, Sweden, and Denmark culminated in divers financial debacles, bringing Geveke to the edge. Internationalization of the business scope proved to be, for Geveke, a bridge too far. Internationalization became synonymous for "operating at a loss".

Many other, large Dutch industrial and service companies preceded Endemol and Geveke [1]. What is striking in this context is that whereas the expansion strategies of multinational companies are the subject of an increasing volume of research, studies on international divestment strategies and the ensuing consequences are much scantier [2]. This is odd, given that recent years have seen the large-scale business portfolio restructuring of many Dutch multinationals. Where the sixties and seventies were the decades of continuous international diversification, since the early eighties a substantial wave of foreign divestments has occurred. In the past twenty or so years, partly as a result of this, many Dutch multinational companies have drastically changed their portfolios of activities.

To study this phenomenon, I conducted a detailed analysis and synthesis of 868 international divestments of Dutch multinational companies, focusing on the period of 1981 through 2000. The results offer some insight into the motives for, and ensuing consequences of, this activity.

This chapter is set out as follows. First, the reasons for deciding to effect international divestments are addressed in detail. I examine the generic forces impacting on the international divestment behavior of multinational companies generally and Dutch multinational companies specifically. Then, seven international divestment motives are reviewed. These motives provide a framework for the empirical research. The fourth section describes the design and approach of my extensive field study.

Next, I present the study results and, on the basis of a series of short case studies, some insights into international divestment motives. The chapter concludes with a short review of the consequences of the international divestments I have observed.

Background

Many multinational companies are currently finding themselves in a phase of drastically repositioning, rationalizing, streamlining, and restructuring their portfolios. Spreading risk by means of national and international diversification has resulted in a high incidence of underperforming multinational companies [3]. Large-scale divesting of foreign activities helps make them leaner, more effective, and thus more competitive.

In recent years, global realignment of multinational companies' business scope has become a major issue. International divestments are a prominent part, as are mergers, acquisitions, and alliances, of this global realignment process. Many local and global conglomerates are intensely preoccupied with this issue, it having much to do with the aggressive merger and acquisition (M&A) strategies these companies implemented in the 1960s and 1970s [4]. This resulted in very high growth rates of Dutch companies including Bruynzeel, RSV, OGEM, Akzo(-Nobel) and Unilever. The most prominent non-Dutch conglomerate was ITT [5].

Assertive M&A strategies would lead, the managers of these companies felt, to risk spreading and productive forms of operating and strategic synergy [6]. Both aspects would offer positive effects for profitability [7]. The conceptual tools developed in the 1970s by the Boston Consulting Group (BCG) justified investing in non-core activities [8]. Under the traditional BCG model, cash cows support new, as yet unprofitable, activities that require much cash (the "cross subsidizing" strategy) [9].

In the 1980s, many multinational companies incurred gigantic debts due to their costly M&A strategies. These companies were subsequently compelled to dispose of their peripheral activities. Many giants proved to have feet of clay. Substantial companies, former thoroughbreds of the Dutch economy, such as OGEM and RSV went under with others hardly managing to stay afloat. Many foreign activities were divested under the "sink or swim" motto. Often, the (one-sided) financial argument was dominant. Domestic activities were being trimmed as well.

Moreover, governmental bodies at all levels were increasingly getting a taste of this rationalizing and divesting business, sometimes called "liberalization," sometimes "privatization". Downsizing combined with divesting those activities that are no longer the focus of attention is a major management trend among senior civil servants in many governmental ministries today.

The attention afforded to national and international divestments, as effected by for-profit organizations, is less than the phenomenon warrants. In retrospect, the study, for instance, of international divestment waves, divestment motives or consequences has been rather marginal. The discipline called Strategic Management suffers a significant research gap. We have neither a clear insight into the exact scope and development of international divestments nor a sound understanding of their causes and consequences. The decision-making processes underlying divestments are also poorly understood. Many international divestments effected by non-listed companies are not monitored by the authorities or by research and consultancy firms. Lists of international divestments are, therefore, either not available or sufficiently incomplete and unreliable only to provide a partial understanding of these issues.

The low level of attention afforded to the international process of contraction is interesting. In certain respects it is understandable, because the majority of business leaders or company managers are focused primarily on growth. This is, after all, what they are held accountable for with bonuses, incentives and status at stake.

International growth is frequently associated with good and solid operations. Especially in the Anglo Saxon world, growth guarantees "success", "promotions", "power" and "good prospects". Every business hopes to be spending the major portion of its life cycle in the future. And for this, many feel, you need growth more than anything else. Also, the issue of international divestment strategies, often wrongly associated by managers with "failure," is a sensitive one.

Effecting international divestments smells of "hand on brake", "treading water", "plugging leaks," and so on. As Woody Allen once said, "Perception is all that counts." From this perspective, the issue is understandably not an easy one to study. The fact that a company is preparing for and effecting international divestments is usually not broadcast to all and sundry.

Schmidt focuses on the question of why so many companies postpone making divesting decisions [10]. The item "For reasons of a sensitive nature" scores high. Frequently, companies do not divest a foreign activity for this very reason, even though all parties involved know it should be done.

Other reasons for postponing international divestment decisions are, according to Schmidt:

- the aversion to admitting making a mistake;
- the possibility that startup losses are higher than anticipated - the wish to "give it some time";
- the fear that another party might make a go of this foreign activity, with the associated loss of face;
- the need for and lack of additional resources to divest an international activity and make it attractive to a potential buyer;
- the fear of hurting other international activities with which the one being divested might be intertwined.

In this chapter, international divestment refers to rationalization by multinational companies of their business scope by closing down (liquidating) or selling a foreign activity, withdrawing an international form of collaboration entirely or partly, or expropriating a foreign activity or international form of collaboration. In other words, "separating" an international activity owned by a (multinational) company. An international activity is understood to be a foreign location engaged in the development, production, marketing, sales/service or distribution of activities.

Administrative organizations and financial and legal holdings, too, can be object of international divestment strategies. Nevertheless, an international activity is always a "real" activity, not a "paper tiger" (for instance, a legal structure), and involves concrete activities (e.g. locations, offices, operating companies, business units, divisions, etc.). The many, often quite diverse, forms of international collaboration are included in this definition of international activities.

This chapter does not address international licensing and patent contracts (so-called non-concrete activities). Instead, it focuses solely on international divestments involving the (financial) transfer from seller to buyer of an international activity. Letters of Intent, written statements of intent (in the legal sense not a contractual obligation) and announcements of international divestments (which in the end are not realized) are not international divestments and are therefore excluded from this study.

Dominant causes for international divestments

Seven dominant reasons for international divestments may be distinguished [11]:

- Poor financial performance.
- Alternative local or global growth opportunities.
- "Follow the market leader" behavior.
- An unfavorable political climate.
- The absence of strategic policy synergy.
- A lack of competitive edge.
- Conflicting policy views.

Poor financial performance

Internationalizing the business scope not always hit the bull's eye. In theory, internationalizing the business scope appears very promising whereas, in practice, it proves difficult to implement. The examples in the introduction to this study (Endemol and Geveke) speak volumes. Every foreign subsidiary not performing to the profitability standard set by head office is, in essence, a candidate for divestment.

Financial reasons underlying the failure to achieve such a standard are quite diverse. When the under-performance of an international activity is due, for instance, to structural industry-wide issues for a specific period of time, then this can be reason to divest the activity in question [12]. This is a reason why many international activities are not followed through. Sometimes, the causes for failure to realize a specific financial target can be attributed to an individual (top) manager. (Top) managers at home are seldom held responsible for international failures. They are sometimes so keen on international expansion that they skip solid preparation. Boosted by the tyranny of the quarterly figures (and personal ego) they decide to cut preparation time short or cut it altogether [13].

Poor preparation is one of the principal causes for financial failure [14]. A big ego and a lot of enthusiasm can never compensate for the lack of solid preparation. This is a cold shower for many business leaders. It was why Anton Dreesmann almost bankrupted Vendex International, and how Eckhart Wintzen of BSO (now [Atos] Origin) found out - only just in time - that you must be really fit to make it in the Olympic-size pool even if you may have outgrown the toddler pool that is the Netherlands.

Building up sales of a foreign activity to a level of profitable operations sometimes requires expenditures that bear disproportionately on a company's financial resources. In other cases, startup costs result in disproportionate burdens whereby the multinational company will lack, precisely at the moment that they are most needed, the resources to finance (usually) high-cost revitalization projects. An international activity thus becomes a millstone for the (top) managers of this multinational company. The fall of renowned, and initially rapidly growing, ICT company Infotheek is largely attributable to a number of bad buys abroad that could simply not be made profitable.

Ceasing a foreign subsidiary's activities is easier if the company has other strategic or structural problems as well. When this is the case, then drastic and expensive restructuring is called for. This will 'soften' the blow of having to divest the foreign subsidiary. The majority of companies require a "do or die" climate to find the strength to divest the "bleeders". It was for precisely this reason that, in the first half of the 1990s, Philips was able to divest many such businesses. This was the company's "do or die" era.

Divesting international loss-making activities may generate substantial funds. Philips is a fine example of this; the company filled its treasury not so much through its sound operations but rather through well-advised implementation of many international divestments. Many other multinational companies are also compelled, for this very reason, to sell foreign activities to achieve more profitable overall operations.

More attractive growth opportunities

A multinational company may decide to effect foreign divestments because it can realize higher profitability elsewhere. For this reason, some multinational companies migrate (usually after a long time) to another industry or industry segment. Non-profitable industries are left behind and exchanged for structurally profitable industries [15]. To guarantee the company's continuity, management sometimes needs to say goodbye to the company's past, expressed in part through its divesting domestic and foreign activities.

Such strategic behavior may be observed, for instance, where production locations are built up and phased out in Eastern Europe and developing and third world countries: the country offering lowest production costs is, for some companies requiring (a lot of) low skilled labor, the most attractive location. Global sourcing has thus become a major strategy for many production focused companies [16]. The availability, or sudden emergence, of high growth geographic markets can be another reason for relocating international activities [17].

To illustrate, in the early 1990s, the Czech Republic and Poland were principal favorites with many West European companies, whereas in the second half of the 1990s more distant (and more cost effective) countries such as Bulgaria and Rumania were more attractive to production focused Western European companies [18]. And, today, the attention of Western European companies focuses mainly on the Ukraine and Russia, whereas in the early 1990s these same companies were keen to set up shop close to former East Germany (Poland) and Austria (the Czech Republic) [19].

Migration by many European multinational companies to Eastern Europe and low-cost parts of South-East Asia was a concern for many national governments in the 1990s [20]. After all, a major source of employment and revenue was vanishing. In addition, they observed with some suspicion production know-how leaking away to foreign parts or distant countries. Once companies have made the first step on the global sourcing path, they invariably turn their backs on the home country [21].

Follow the market leader

Many multinational companies operate in oligopolistic industries, where the business domain is often global. Strategies of market leaders in such industries are frequently followed by others (see, for instance, competitive strategies in the electronics, computer and telecommunications industries). Knickerbocker produced an interesting doctorate thesis on this subject in the 1970s [22].

The "follow the market leader" adage evidently need not apply to realizing direct foreign investments (i.e. international expansion) alone, but can also apply to direct foreign divestments (i.e. international contraction). Specifically, the market leader starts divesting certain foreign activities and, subsequently, others in the industry start divesting similar foreign activities. The "herd instinct" of companies is expressed specifically in the phenomenon of multi-market competition [23]. Competition is a game of move and countermove, with parties monitoring and analyzing each other's (dis)investment behavior [24].

Political climate

The stance adopted by the guest country or that adopted by other countries towards the guest country may also play a significant role.

A negative stance adopted by the guest country toward the activities of a multinational company, expressed by it imposing a multitude of restrictions on the foreign company's operations, may contribute to a climate whereby a multinational company could decide to discontinue its activities in this country.

Local governments are in a position to hinder operations of domestic and foreign companies through all kinds of policy instruments. A national government may, for example, adversely influence cost levels of a multinational company's foreign location through its wage levels, taxes, as well as regulations hindering profit repatriation, thus favoring local (home-based) companies in the guest country. For many foreign companies this throws up quite a barrier. In international business such formal and informal impediments are bumps in the road that may prove difficult to overcome, even keeping a company from attempting to internationalize [25].

Moreover, a host country's attitude toward a multinational company's activities may change abruptly. Especially in politically less stable countries, a new regime may become an inconvenient even insurmountable factor in conducting corporate activities. Management can anticipate such political developments by divesting at the right moment.

Strategic policy synergy

Strategic policy synergy may be absent. A multinational company may, having changed its strategic direction, get saddled with internationally deployed activities that initially were interesting and (might still be) profitable but, under the new strategic policy objectives, have ceased to be a strategic core activity. Consequently, some foreign activities are no longer within the company's business scope.

If this happens, then the foreign activity or business unit in question lacks positive policy synergy. The multinational company runs the risk of its overall worth becoming less than the sum of its domestic and foreign parts. It is often only a matter of time for a good partner (in case of an alliance) or buyer (in case of an acquisition) for the international activity to be found, because profitable activities generally attract the attention of others sooner or later.

Multinational companies, rationalizing their scope of international activities for this reason, implement the "back to the core business" adage [26]. Many foreign activities are divested for this reason, creating value for the company's shareholders. The value of domestic activities (a) and of foreign activities (b) to be divested, when under the same umbrella (O ab), is smaller than the value of a and b, whereby a and b are autonomous (O a + O b). Thus: O ab < O a + O b

This situation presents itself specifically when the benefits generated by the multinational group of companies fail to outweigh the benefits generated by stand-alone and autonomous entrepreneurship [27].

No competitive edge

International competition has grown increasingly fierce in recent years. The ever more complex international landscape, and the rate at which it changes, makes for a true minefield for many international companies.

Many international activities operated by multinational companies must sell their products at lowest possible cost and highest possible quality. Competing in the international market under the accurate price/quality ratio is a very finely tuned mechanism.

International activities that have lost their capacity to compete in a market that is getting fiercer due to increasingly tight cost/quality ratios must eventually be divested (the infamous 'millstones' around top managers' necks). Lacking competitive edge is, therefore, a legitimate reason for divesting or terminating certain international activities.

Conflicting policy views

This rationale for international divestments applies only to international forms of collaboration.

International forms of collaboration in this context are all types of alliances, i.e. from very loose international distribution contracts to cross-border joint ventures. Companies ally internationally because each party individually is not capable of realizing an intended objective by itself. All explanations for international collaboration can be derived from this one, simple, generic explanation.

A relationship with a local company is often formalized as a joint venture (i.e. international joint venture). But such ties between a multinational company and its partner need not be without friction. The ties of multinational companies to foreign firms are often severed quite abruptly for any number of reasons, but they can all be reduced essentially to one phrase: "conflicting policy views."

This stage is often preceded by a disappointing series of events involving specific issues such as product lines to be established, marketing and sales approach to be decided, management style to be adopted, chain and quality management to be implemented, and production methods to be put into place.

After a while, the partners' general views on day-to-day management issues may start diverging to such a degree that it is wiser for one of the parties to withdraw from the collaboration. In such a context, the venture is often sold in its entirety to the partner or a third party.

The structure of the study

In the context of this study, the various information sources were consulted in three phases.

In phase one, twenty annual editions of *Het Financieele Dagblad* (the Dutch equivalent of *The Financial Times*), for the period 1981-2000, were consulted. Also, annual reports of Holland's top 1000 companies listed in Quote Magazine (the Dutch equivalent of *Fortune*) in 2000 were reviewed as far as feasible for the period 1981-2000. A total of 868 international divestments were traced.

In phase two, the 868 international divestments traced were studied in more detail using internal company documents, whereby access was obtained to both hardcopy sources and electronic databases available. Utilization of several internal information sources enhanced the reliability of the data generated. In phase three, the study's concluding phase, telephone or face-to-face in-depth interviews were conducted with relevant experts.

Experts included senior managers, executives and non-executive board members employed by those companies that effected, in the period 1st January 1981 to 1st January 2001, one or several of the international divestments under review. A total of 229 interviewees had been actively involved in the international divestments process.

The purpose of this phase was mainly to compare findings, to fathom better the emotional and rational process of an international divestment decision, and to enhance the validity of the results.

Results

Box 1 shows that two motives for international divestment were dominant: absence of strategic policy synergy, followed by poor financial performance of the activity in question. All other motives proved secondary.

Box 1 Study results

Absence of policy synergy/strategically irrelevant	53%
Poor financial performance	22%
Lack of competitive edge	13%
More attractive alternatives	4%
Follow-the-market-leader	4%
Political developments	2%
Differing policy views	2%

Absence of policy synergy/strategically irrelevant activities

Fifty-three percent of international divestment decisions were motivated by the argument that the international activity had ceased to fit the company's strategic direction and could therefore no longer be included in its strategic core.

This was the reason for Akzo Nobel, the chemicals group, to effect several international divestments over the past 20 years, particularly in the first half of the 1980s. In this period, for instance, the substantial foreign subsidiaries Brand-Rex (1983), Enka-USA (1985) and Armira Company were divested because these companies no longer fitted the strategic product portfolio envisaged by Akzo Nobel. The financial resources thus procured were used by Akzo Nobel to finance new investments (in international acquisitions and alliances) in the United States of America.

Unilever, too, effected several international divestments in the period 1981-2000. The sale, in 1985, of the group's lumber interest, Brooke Bond, suited the policy being implemented by Unilever from the mid-1980s to sell activities and interests not essential to the group's strategic activities.

To be viewed in this light also was Unilever's sale in 1987 of its American subsidiary, Stauffer Chemical, to the British group, Imperial Chemical Industries (ICI). Stauffer went to ICI for 1.7 billion euro. Stauffer was profitable reporting a profit before tax in 1986 of about 50 million euro – having been bought in 1985 as part of Unilever's acquisition of Chesebrough-Pond's. Stauffer Seeds had been sold earlier by the Unilever management for about 45 million euro to the Swiss group Sandoz. In the period 1984 and 1985, Unilever divested no fewer than fourteen international activities. In the period beginning 1986, and during the 1990s, another 37 international ventures were sold.

Sometimes, a number of foreign activities are divested as a package. Such transactions tend to be sporadic, but highly newsworthy and quite sizable.

In 1997, Unilever sold for about seven billion euro four chemical companies to ICI, i.e. National Starch and Chemical Company, Crossfield, Quest International and Unichema International. This divestment gave Unilever a markup of about 4 billion euro. Chemical activities were divested because Unilever wanted to concentrate on three core activities: food, detergents and toiletries. The four international ventures attracted the attention of more than 50 potential buyers including the American group Dupont.

Former Unilever CEO Morris Tabaksblat, commenting in a 1996 *Financial Times* interview, was clear on where the financial means would be allocated:

> "We intend to use the proceeds for further developments to benefit shareholders. This will be achieved in the longer term by investing in growing our existing activities and, where opportune, expanding these through acquisitions."

In 1998, Unilever struck again, this time selling for about 500 million euro its plant improvement business, Plant Breeding International (PBI), to the American chemicals and bio-technical group, Monsanto. PBI enjoyed a strong market position, was profitable, but no longer fitted Unilever's vision of its future. Unilever's focus was on food and on domestic and personal care products.

Poor financial performance

Poor financial performance as a motive accounted for 22 percent of the foreign divestment decisions of the Dutch companies studied. The downside of internationalizing business scope manifests itself a great deal in under-performing foreign initiatives and activities. The case of Philips offers an example.

In 1999, Philips sold its TV-tube plant in the Russian city of Voronezj for one rouble. Philips had acquired the plant in 1995 for about 2 million euro, committing to invest about 45 million euro in the near future for modernization and expansion. The plant employed about 7,500, and was to be the springboard for the conquest of the Russian market.

But, these prospects failed to materialize. Philips did not manage to make the activities profitable. Due to the poor economic situation, demand for TV sets slumped, local authorities put up heavy resistance against rationalization operations started by Philips almost immediately, and local competition proved extremely fierce after government lowered import duties. When energy prices rose four-fold within a period of twelve months, Philips' management decided to divest the activity. In the period 1995-1999, this Philips unit suffered a loss of no less than 54 million euro. The plant was eventually sold to the provincial authorities.

Speciaalzaken Ahold, my next example, had been active in the Far East since 1996. At the time, Ahold management's target was to realize about one tenth of its overall sales in the Far East in the year 2006. The 1997 financial and economic crisis in Asia, however, spoiled things. Sales in 1998 were a mere 1,5 percent of total group sales and operations proved highly loss making. In 1999, Ahold sold its retail activities in China, Singapore and Indonesia. These regions caused substantial losses, although sales turnover for the three exceeded 150 million euro. Since it would take many years to turnaround these operations, Ahold re-focused on its profitable activities in Malaysia and Thailand.

In 1996, Smit Transformatoren closed the production plant it had purchased in the United States in 1993. The US location was suffering heavy losses that could no longer be financed by the parent company in the Netherlands. The production plant failed to produce at market prices. To close down the location required an extraordinary expenditure provision of about 13 million euro, and compelled Smit to report a 1996 loss of some 20 million euro.

Automation group Triple P divested all its German activities in 1997. Although these activities represented one-fifth of Triple P's sales, they incurred increasing losses. The German activities started to hang around the neck of the fragile automation group like the proverbial millstone. By the second half of the 1990s, Triple P had got into financial difficulties in the Netherlands and could no longer cope with the added burden of a German financial problem. It was "do or die" time. Since 1997, a new management team has been working to rationalize and restructure the company. By divesting weak units, it plans to make the company profitable again.

In 1993, International Nederlanden Groep (ING) sold its heavily loss-making British operating company Life Association of Scotland (LAF). LAF realized sales of about 100 million euro and employed about 500. Since 1988, this company suffered losses totalling many tens of millions of euro. The company was sold to the British company, Britannia Life. The sale of LAF was in line with ING's policy of rationalizing its insurance activities in the UK. LAF was divested after earlier divestments of Orion and NRG Victory – the reason again, poor financial results.

It is striking that, as ING was gradually withdrawing from the British market, competitor Aegon was participating actively in that same British market [28]. In 1993, for instance, Aegon paid 1,3 billion euro to acquire Scottish Equitable.

More attractive alternatives

The companies in my study only rarely effected foreign divestments because their policy makers identified "(more) attractive alternatives." In only 4 percent of my 868 cases did this motive play a decisive and directly attributable role.

Publishing company, Wolters-Kluwer, sold in the winter of 1994 its 100 percent stake in the Swedish Skrivab company to the Swedish investment company Nordic Capital. At the same time, Wolters Kluwer announced its acquisition of the publishing activities of the Akelius Group in Sweden. This publishing company with locations in Sweden and Norway was active in the fields of fiscal law, administration and civil law. Its annual sales were over 10 million euro. The divestment of Skrivab was no surprise. The margin on Akelius' activities was significantly higher than that on Skrivab's activities. Both international initiatives were lucrative and fitted Wolters Kluwer's management policy of internationalizing in professional publishing activities enjoying higher added value.

Philips sold, in 1993, its American activities of Super Club (video rental) to the American company Blockbuster, market leader in the field of video rentals. Philips received about 150 million dollar for the sale. These financial resources Philips intended to use to strengthen the more profitable Super Club activities in Europe. In Europe, moreover, Super Club was much stronger than it was in the United States. Philips approached Blockbuster because the American activities were too vulnerable, even though they were profitable and realized sales of about 400 million dollar.

Follow the market leader

The "follow the market leader" phenomenon may be a relevant issue for direct foreign investments, but in the context of international divestments only a few examples inspired by this motive could be traced. This motive was responsible for only 4 percent of my sample, a rather surprising result.

In 1999, Van Melle, producer of confectionery, concentrated its production in a few countries, after global market leaders had proceeded to do likewise. Van Melle closed its British Fruit-Tella plant, making 170 employees redundant. In the global and European markets for confectionery, the battle for market share was won with increasing regularity by the company operating at lowest production costs. This was the main reason for shutting down production in the UK, and concentrating on the company's two plants already operational in the Netherlands (Breskens and Weert).

For precisely the same reason (concentrating production to control costs following other bigger competitors), in 1999 ASM International closed its American plant and transferred production to the Netherlands. In doing so, ASM International followed in the strategic footsteps of its international competitors who where all suffering from the micro-chip industry crisis that compelled them to cut and control costs.

In terms of its comprehensiveness, this study result is food for thought: international divestments are followed by direct competitors only to a relatively low degree. A chain reaction is not discernable. Dutch multinational companies demonstrate low to zero "herd instinct" where international divesting is concerned. A possible explanation is that the multinational companies of my study population are active in quite diverse industry segments, ones that play by different rules and face different circumstances.

Other explanations could be that managements of the companies in my study spend relatively little time monitoring the competition's strategic movements and initiatives or, that these same managements do spend a lot of time monitoring the competition but follow their own policy course not allowing the competition to influence them too much. This result will be tested in a follow-up study.

Political developments

Political developments play a decisive role only in exceptional cases. Only 2 percent of international divestments were demonstrably caused by political factors.

In the Netherlands, the sale by SHV of its Makro stake in South Africa, at the end of the 1980s, is still a keen memory. As a consequence of terrorist activities by the Dutch terrorist group RaRa, SHV – one of the top 10 Dutch multinational companies – was pressured into withdrawing from South Africa.

Also, packaging materials giant Van Leer divested, in 1986, its activities in its building materials division in South Africa, selling to the South African company Kwikot Ltd. Political pressure (in terms of being a 'good corporate citizen') is often brought to bear by customers, and in this period Van Leer was clearly feeling some discomfort. Van Leer, a company with corporate philanthropy as a high priority was, arguably, far ahead of its time in listening genuinely to its customers' voice.

In 1999, telecommunications giant KPN withdrew entirely from the Ukraine. It had been active in the Ukraine since 1991, one of the most promising markets of the future, and had invested about 55 million euro in two local telecommunications companies. Its Ukraine activities were the company's first foray into Eastern Europe - in the 1990s KPN's second home market.

Unfortunately, the explanation for KPN's withdrawal leaves a sour taste. The telecommunications group came to find it could no longer manage local political instability, making it impossible for KPN, in its own words, to "achieve regular operations". In the second half of the 1990s, the Ukraine political leadership continuously changed its policy towards foreign companies. This meant that, as a rule, foreign companies were being faced with increasingly higher costs. Not only KPN but also other foreign companies were compelled to bring ever fatter wallets for the privilege of being in the Ukraine market.

In *Het Financieele Dagblad* of 13 October 1999, a KPN spokesman commented as follows:

> "Recent decisions by the Ukraine Government were ultimately decisive. The political leadership is very self-involved, viewing only the short term. Funds are required to solve the Government's financial problems. This makes it quite hard on foreign companies, however. A reliable partner is simply absent."

Remarkably, KPN investments in a number of other Eastern European countries generated sound profits. In the words of the same spokesman in the same daily newspaper:

> "Investments in Poland, Hungary, and the Czech Republic are sound. These countries form a cultural barrier against the rest of Eastern Europe. The problems at times occurring there are mainly at the local political level, not to be compared with the Ukraine situation".

Pressured by the European Commission in 1999, Akzo Nobel sold its coating producer PRC De Soto International for 512 million dollar to the American group PRG Industries. The sale was unavoidable. The European Commission had ordered Akzo Nobel, after its acquisition of Courtaulds (in 1998), to phase out its dominant position in the airplane coatings and sealants markets (PRC De Soto was a substantial subsidiary of Courtaulds). Akzo Nobel's position in those markets was dominant to such a degree that it was contrary to public interest. Akzo Nobel used the financial proceeds to improve its debt exposure.

The role of the various antitrust authorities in Brussels, Washington and The Hague in the international divestment process is most likely to increase in the coming years. My database showed a clear growth of their influence, specifically since 1995.

No competitive edge

The "lacking competitive edge" rationale was indicated in 13 percent of the cases I studied as the main reason for divesting international activities. Aegon provides an example.

One of the largest insurers in the United States, Aegon decided to withdraw entirely in 1994 from the Belgian insurance market, where it had been for 100 years. The scale of those activities proved too small for it to play a significant role in local competitive rivalry, and the growth rate of the Belgian market was too slow.

Although, in the early 1990s, Aegon tried to increase its scale sufficient to match the competition, it met with limited success. Even though Aegon is among the largest insurers in the Netherlands, it failed to succeed in a country "just around the corner." Aegon's strategy rested on acquiring a presence confined to the limited number of geographic markets that it could dominate.

In 1999, beer producer Grolsch closed its operations in China and Brazil. Their competitive position in both these markets left something to be desired: Grolsch's activities lacked visibility and were, therefore, vulnerable, incapable of achieving a top three position. In both markets other beer producers had been competing for years and Grolsch had struggled. Consequently, the company's management re-focused attention on its top three positions in mature beer markets such as Europe and the United States.

Sanitation equipment producer Sphinx closed its Belgian plant Novoboch in 1998. Sphinx's activities were not in the Belgian market's top tier and, as a result, it was unable to beat its direct competitors. This competition was overtaking Sphinx with a combination of lower cost of wages and better customer relations – deteriorating market conditions did the rest.

Differing policy views

The motive "differing views on policy to be implemented" applies to two percent of my population of divestment decisions taken by Dutch multinational companies.

Further analysis shows that this motive may conceal more than it reveals. It seems that the reasons for dissolving or separating international joint ventures are often labelled, euphemistically, as the result of "differing views on policy to be implemented." Telephone and face-to-face interviews proved unable to shed more light on this aspect; interviewees consistently confined themselves to the commonplace "differing views" explanation. Further probing seldom led to a different more satisfactory or solid argument for international divestments.

Philips' disposal of its share in an international joint venture with AT&T in the first half of the 1990s is a striking example of a divestment decision arising when, after a while, both companies proved unable to sit at the same board table.

In 1984, Philips clustered its European telecommunications activities in a cross-border joint venture with AT&T, the latter wanting seriously to commit itself to a European expansion strategy. In the United States, the company already had a leading position – now it was Europe's turn. The objective of the international joint venture APT (AT&T Philips Telecommunications) was to assume leadership in the European telecommunications market. Philips, however, found in the early 1990s it was too small for the major league and too big for the minor league. Philips felt itself in a highly awkward situation. As a result, top management decided to withdraw from the international joint venture. After all, it was impossible to lead the electronics race on all fronts. Philips gradually withdrew from the joint venture, to be substituted eventually by the Spanish group, Telefónica.

In 1998, Grolsch sold its Polish stake in Elbrewery and Hevelius to a local partner, with whom the company had started the joint venture. Grolsch had genuinely sought a major stake in the local breweries market, but eventually this proved unfeasible. Grolsch did not divest all its Polish activities, the company continuing to market its proprietary brand in the local Polish beer market. Today, Grolsch is the biggest international beer brand in Poland (bigger, for instance, than the internationally much more renowned import beer produced by fellow brewer, Heineken).

October 1998 saw the failure of Ahold's third Spanish joint venture Store 2000 with the Spanish company Caprabo, for reasons relating to "differing views on the joint venture's strategy for the future." The joint venture with Caprabo comprised 45 supermarkets with annual sales of about 140 million euro. Caprabo was active primarily on Mallorca and in Catalonia, and was a family business based in Barcelona. The joint venture, Store 2000, operated mainly in the region around the capital Madrid.

The conflict between both parties focused mainly on the projected rate of growth. Ahold's growth plans were much the more ambitious. In *NRC Handelsblad* (the Dutch equivalent of

The Wall Street Journal) of October 9, 1998 an Ahold spokesman commented as follows:

> "We identify sound growth opportunities in Spain and aim at high growth rates. Our partner, somewhat smaller in scope, envisages a different rate."

Ahold had been active via a high-profile joint venture in the Spanish market on an earlier occasion, during 1974-1985. After a while, the company's views differed from its partner's, Candadia, concerning a range of strategic issues. Candadia also operated mainly around Madrid.

It is striking that Ahold keeps failing in its attempts to operate successfully via joint ventures in the Spanish market, whereas in Portugal the company has been in a successful collaboration with Jeronimo Martins, one of the country's biggest supermarket chains, since 1990.

Basic element

In the media, the good results of multinational companies often seem to obscure the poor results of certain foreign activities. Internationalization is not an easy matter. The great number of foreign divestments - often of substantial size - points to this.

In some countries, divestments by foreign multinational companies lead to awkward situations. Many countries' economic growth is increasingly being determined by incoming foreign direct investments. In balance of payments terms, one can conclude that a substantial portion of such investments reverts after a while to the multinational companies' home offices. Countries failing to retain those operations therefore have their backs to the future.

International divestments may be quite salutary for multinational companies. Periods of growth must be alternated with periods of pruning, which can prove revitalizing. The resources procured from pruning can be used to develop in more lucrative directions - horizontal expansion, vertical integration, diversification, and so on.

In my study, 68 percent of the 868 international divestments were realized by listed companies. In 78 percent of the cases, company share prices rose once the divestment decision had been announced. That initial increase was 3,9 percent; the average share price, once the divestments had been finalized, rose by only 1,8 percent. The increase partly evaporates when the "actual work" is being done. Still, the conclusion is warranted that, as a rule, stock-markets positively value international divestments.

The study has shown that of the many Dutch multinational companies that reconsidered their business scope in the 1980s and 1990s, top management variously concluded that the benefits of diversification, or risk spreading, no longer outweighed the drawbacks of coordinating a complex, overly broad-based business scope. In the end, over the years, managers came to prefer a simpler business scope - depth (more of the same) over width (more of something else).

Burgeoning international and local competition has put more pressure on multinational companies to rationalize their business scope. A need for less diversification can clearly be discerned: multinational companies are still divesting non-core activities. The dominant rationale, an absence of strategic policy synergy, illustrates this. Compared to the early 1980s, various Dutch multinational companies have become leaner and hence more agile, thereby enhancing their global competitive edge.

Developments such as fiercer competition, introduction of the euro, continuous reflection on corporate portfolios and business models, and more demanding shareholders and customers are increasingly compelling Dutch multinational companies – and probably others as well - to critically review their international ventures. Foreign divestment is thus a basic element of every multinational's strategic business policy.

References

[1] P.K. Jagersma, "Internationalization of Dutch Service Companies", Tilburg University Press, Tilburg, 1993.

[2] One of the first publications is by the hand of R.L. Torneden, "Foreign Divestment by U.S. Corporations", Praeger, New York, 1975 and A. Bettauer, "Strategy for Divestment", Harvard Business Review, pp. 112-119, March-April 1967. See also: R.H. Hayes, "New Emphasis on Divestment Opportunities", Harvard Business Review, pp. 55-64, July-August 1972 and T.H. Hopkins, "Mergers, Acquisitions, and Divestments", Dow-Jones, Irwin, Homewood, 1984. Interesting is the Ph.D study of J.C. Sachdev, "A Framework for the Planning of Divestment Policies for Multinational Companies", University of Manchester, 1976.

[3] R.P. Rumelt, D.E. Schendel, and D.J. Teece, "Fundamental Issues in Strategy: A Research Agenda", Harvard Business School Press, Boston 1994.

[4] H.W. de Jong, "Dynamic Market Theory", Stenfert Kroese, Leiden, 1985.

[5] R.V. Araskog, "The ITT Wars", Holt, New York, 1989. See also: A. Campbell, D. Sadtler, and R. Koch, "Break-up!", Capstone, Oxford, 1997.

[6] See for instance: H.I. Ansoff, "Corporate Strategy", McGraw-Hill, New York, 1965.

[7] R.P. Rumelt, D.E. Schendel, and D.J. Teece, "Fundamental Issues in Strategy: A Research Agenda", Harvard Business School Press, Boston 1994.

[8] C.W. Stern and G. Stalk Jr., "Perspectives on Strategy", John Willey & Sons, New York, 1998.

[9] R.P. Rumelt, D.E. Schendel, and D.J. Teece, "Fundamental Issues in Strategy: A Research Agenda", Harvard Business School Press, Boston 1994.

[10] R.J. Schmidt, "Corporate Divesture: Pruning for Higher Profits", pp. 26-31, Business Horizons, May-June 1987.

[11] P.K. Jagersma, "International Management", Stenfert Kroese, Houten, 1996.

[12] See for instance: M.E. Porter, "Corporate Strategy", The Free Press, New York, 1980.

[13] K. Barham and D. Oates, "The International Manager", The Economist, London, 1991. See also: P.K. Jagersma, "International Economies of Scale, Scope, and Skills", Inaugural lecture, Nyenrode University, October 1997.

[14] P.K. Jagersma and D. van Gorp, "International HRM: The Dutch Experience", Journal of General Management, Vol. 28, No. 2, p. 16-28, Winter 2002.

[15] See for instance: R.P. Rumelt, "How Much does Industry Matter?", Strategic Management Journal, Vol. 12, pp. 167-185, 1991 and R.P. Rumelt, D.E. Schendel, and D.J. Teece "Fundamental Issues in Strategy: A Research Agenda", Harvard Business School Press, Boston 1994.

[16] F.R. Root, "Entry Strategies for International Markets", Jossey-Bass, San Francisco, 1994. See also: P. Ghemawat, "Distance Still Matters", Harvard Business Review, p. 137-147, September 2001.

[17] M.E. Porter, "The Competitive Advantage of Nations", The Free Press, New York, 1990.

[18] P. Dicken, "Global Shift", Chapman Publishing, London, 1998; B. Parker, "Globalization and Business Practice", Sage, London, 1998.

[19] P.K. Jagersma and H.E. Ebbers, "Global Management: Text and Cases", Pearson, London, to be published in 2007.

[20] Financial Times, "Mastering Global Business", FT Mastering Series, London, 2000.

[21] T. Friedman, "The Lexus and the Olive Tree", HarperCollins, New York, 1999.

[22] F.T. Knickerbocker, "Oligopolistic Reaction and the Multinational Enterprise", Harvard University Press, Boston, 1973.

[23] B.J. Nalebuff and A.M. Brandenburger, "Co-opetition", Harper Collins, New York, 1996.

[24] R. D'Aveni, "Hypercompetition", The Free Press, New York, 1994.

[25] P.N. Doremus, W.W. Keller, L.W. Pauly, and S. Reich, "The Myth of the Global Corporation", Princeton University Press, Princeton/New Jersey, 1998.

[26] G. Hamel and C.K. Prahalad, "Competing for the Future", The Free Press, New York, 1994.

[27] See also: A.Campbell, D. Sadtler, and R. Koch, "Break-up!", Capstone, Oxford, 1997.

[28] P.K. Jagersma, "Internationalization of Dutch Service Companies", Tilburg University Press, Tilburg, 1993.

Part II. Global Strategy and Organization

5

Spin-out Management

Theory and Practice

Sooner or later in their life cycle, companies are confronted with slowing or declining results. This is generally the outcome of having paid insufficient attention to a core element of entrepreneurship – namely, innovation as applied not only to products and services but also to business models. Information communication technology (ICT), especially Internet, has caused a revolution in the business world at all corporate levels (a company's vertical linkages with customers, suppliers, and employees) and through all sectors of the business community (the horizontal linkages among firms within or between industries) [1].

The competitive battle is not so much between small and big enterprises or new and old ones, but more between adaptable and slow business models. This century's prevailing competitive paradigm seems to be: Adapt or die. Adaptivity is the name of the competitive game, and the ability to do so can break a business. The majority of large companies are rather slow movers. Because of rapidly changing economic environments, this has become a barrier for responding to client and consumer needs, which seem to be best served by smaller or flat, decentralized firms. This is especially the case for companies in the telecommunications and biotechnology industries, but it also applies to firms representing other sectors being subjected to fast economic changes [2].

The capabilities of adapting to new developments is mirrored in a firm's business model (see box 1). Business models have a life cycle and should be adjusted at a certain point in time. External changes in the environment should lead to internal organizational adjustments. The incumbents, especially larger companies, clearly have difficulties in radically adjusting their competitive strategies and business models in order to meet the quick-changing environment, while start-ups and small firms are often able to adapt quickly and flexibly to the challenges and threats of market and technology developments.

Box 1 Business models: what's in a name?

What is a business model? Ask ten managers and you will have ten different answers. Here I will use the following definition:

> A business model is an organizational model oriented towards adding value to stakeholders by combining tangible and intangible assets in a unique way.

Assets - intangible and tangible - are buildings, production lines, R&D centers, knowledge, employee experience, brands, reputation, distribution channels, growth and competitive strategies, organizational cultures, and so on. Stakeholders are, among others, employees, customers, government institutions, employee organizations, banks, and suppliers.

Since the mid-1980s, big companies have embraced some of the characteristics of smaller firms such as flexibility, entrepreneurship, and innovation. This is referred to as internal entrepreneurship, or intrapreneurship [3]. Since the 1990s, it has also been called corporate venturing [4]. It is only in the past few years that a new variation of corporate venturing has become increasingly popular: spin-out management [5]. The implementation of spin-out management has led to new business models.

In this chapter I focus on the practical consequences and added value of these new business models, elaborating on their characteristics, advantages, disadvantages, and key success factors. Four business cases are used to illustrate the concept, their selection based on the best practices I had experienced in five years of strategy consulting activities.

After gaining knowledge about this new form of corporate venturing, managers can then decide whether and to what extent spin-out management is suitable to use as an instrument for innovating or introducing their own business models.

Three discontinuities

A study among the top 500 biggest companies in the world, executed by The Economist Intelligence Unit and Booz-Allen & Hamilton, reports that 90 percent of the top managers surveyed believe the Internet will have a major impact on the management and organizational structures of their companies [6].

Since the introduction of this new technology, the relevance of traditional entry barriers, such as switching costs and access to distribution channels, seems to have decreased or disappeared. The borders between sectors, products, and services are blurring, partly as a result of online distribution channels. This means the market place is wide open to new competitors – and the competition is an even more complex, boundaryless game than before [7].

New start-ups frequently use the Internet to communicate directly with their customers, keep distribution costs low, respond effectively, and develop innovative activities. Recent experience with this new type of "hollow organization" has shown that it takes about two years before such a company launches an innovative business idea, develops an interactive website, and dominates a new sector or niche [8]. The speed of innovation is breathtaking. Many traditional or established enterprises lack the organizational infrastructure to compete with these high-speed firms, largely because of their difficulty in adapting to the fast changing environment [9].

Innovation is usually associated with new products or services from the R&D department, but it can include activities in sales as well. Creative sales employees develop new, innovative concepts that enable a company to sell more products to new customers. Most innovations are applied to existing products; this is know as "stretched innovation" [10]. Important revolutionary breakthroughs, such as the development of new products or product categories, demand a lot of time and energy.

At the same time, strategy life cycles are becoming shorter and shorter. In the past, followers had sufficient time to apply their copy-cat strategy in imitating products and selling them profitably. Now, as a result of increasingly strong price competition, this follower strategy is often no longer profitable. The Internet enables firms to serve more customers in a shorter period of time. More and more, innovation in a broad sense is a key success factor.

Three developments in particular have been credited for the insecurity among firms and their need for new innovative business models.

From tangible products to intangible solutions

First, whole industries are shifting from tangible products to intangible solutions. The differences between these two categories of value propositions are extensive.

The variable costs of tangible products are relatively high and those of intangible solutions relatively low, with the exception of the initial development costs. Prices of intangible solutions are not based on the "cost price plus" methodology, but on the perceived added value to the end-users. Product development and differentiation are easier due to "smart" reproduction of information, as well as the possibilities of adjusting it.

In the past, standard products were offered with possibly extra functionalities; today, it is exactly the opposite - unique products are standardized.

New sources of value

Second, there has been a change in the most important source of (added) value. The value of a product to one user depends more and more on how many users there are because of the so-called network effects and positive feedback [11]. A network effect occurs when the value one user places on a good depends on how many other people are using it. Positive feedback refers to the phenomenon of more and more users finding adoption worthwhile as the installed base of users grows; it makes large networks grow even larger.

Both of these factors may influence the shape and form of business models, affecting how companies communicate with their customers, how they use their resources, which partners they choose to offer customer value, and so on.

The more users, the more added value for them, and the more useful the product becomes. Until recently, value was created mainly by an increase in production combined with profits of scale advantages. The law of decreasing returns is valid only up to a certain point, after which the average costs per product rise instead of fall.

Moreover, the law of increasing returns is an important characteristic of today's network economy [12]. The number of users is positively correlated with increasing returns. The fax is a good example of this development. The larger the number of people connected, the greater the added value can be generated from it. Scale advantages are linked to individual enterprises, whereas network effects are felt by every single member of the network.

The internet

Third, the internet is a major change factor. It facilitates the strategy of entering a market and is available to every enterprise. With internet technology, a firm can, say, focus on smaller market segments that in the near future have a global growth potential. Moreover, it facilitates the sharing of experiences and knowledge. Thanks to the internet, sharing information on a worldwide basis is cheap.

Most important, the internet is the catalyst of companies' search for new models enabling them to adapt to the fast-changing economic environment. Innovation in this respect no longer relates only to products, services, and creative sale techniques and concepts, but much more to the strategy, structure, and processes of providing added value to customers and other stakeholders. First and foremost, the businessmodel should be innovative. It should enable companies not only to adapt but also to initiate innovative developments either individually or with partners.

I agree with Harvard Business School Professor Michael Porter that the outcome of developments in the networked economy is not a radically new approach to businesses [13]. However, unlike Porter, I do not think that the critical success factor in this mercurial environment is building on the proven principles of effective strategy.

Moreover, gaining competitive advantage requires first of all a "lean and mean" organization that is able to change its strategy (drastically, if necessary), regardless of how successful the strategy has proven to be in the past. Therefore, emphasis should be on the development and implementation of a strategy as a continuous process itself [14]. An adequate business model is, in my view, a decisive factor in this process [15].

Bigness = badness (?!)

Large, traditional firms have struggled for some years with the aforementioned discontinuities as a result of the "Big is bad" syndrome – the lack of confidence on the part of management that a big company can actually be as innovative and adaptive as a smaller one [16]. A number of big companies have established new venture divisions for that reason, such as KPN Ventures, Apple Strategic Investment Group, Shell Technology Ventures, Philips External Venturing, Lucent Technologies New Ventures Group, and Xerox Technology Ventures.

The trend of downsizing and decentralizing large companies is by no means new. Already in the 1980s and even before, the proliferation of hybrid organizational forms was seen as an important movement, with the greater emphasis on innovation [17]. However, the issue did gain growing attention in the so-called "new-economy" era.

In this respect, the issue of organizational structure plays a key role. An inappropriate structure may destroy any form of innovation in a firm. An appropriate one offers many possibilities, especially for fast growth in an innovative way. Because of the spin-out business model, the possibility of directly and continuously reacting to changes in the market, competition, high-tech developments, and customer preferences is closer than ever. ICT, in combination with new business models, leads to endless possibilities in innovative capabilities.

Spin-out business model

Spin-out management can be the answer to many of the challenges I have mentioned (box 2). It manifests itself through the "spin-out business model", defined here as:

> a process by which a new or existing part of an enterprise is separated from the parent company with the aim of independently developing related or unrelated activities by profiting from the parent's assets.

Box 2 The study

My focus here is on successful spin-out management: its ins and outs, the reasons behind it, its advantages and disadvantages, its implementation, and the requirements for it. I review the qualitative results of a study I made and interpret my research material. The following four companies were analyzed in detail: Dell, Cap Gemini Ernst & Young (CGEY), Infopulse, and 4BB.

I first elaborate on the more generic results and subsequently on the specifics of the four different cases. The research study was based on secondary and primary research. Interviews with senior management (primary research) were combined with the study of public and company files (secondary research).

Despite the fact that all companies included in this research belong to the ICT-sector, there is quite some heterogeneity. The companies are large (Dell and CGEY) or medium-sized (Infopulse and 4BB), young (Infopulse and 4BB are less than ten years old) or older (Dell and CGEY), international (Dell, CGEY, and Infopulse) or local (4BB), well-known (CGEY and Dell) or relatively unknown (Infopulse and 4BB) in the market, diversified (CGEY) versus non-diversified (the other three).

Nevertheless, the study is based on an analysis of a relatively small number of companies, which operate within the same sector characterized by a high technological and marketing intensity. Therefore, although it has a high internal validity, the external validity may be limited, raising the question: What is the value of the results of this study for other industries?

Therefore, the study needs a follow up. The conclusion to be drawn is the fact that spin-out management has become an issue on the agenda of the Dutch business community. (Dell, with its strong base in the Netherlands, acted as an international benchmark for this study). Any follow-up research should be more internationally oriented and less local in nature.

The independent operating company is supported by the parent through a professional infrastructure (back office), existing network (customers, business partners), reputation (brand), and channels (distribution concepts). The parent coordinates a portfolio of (relatively) independent subsidiaries with their own budgets, strategies, assets, and balance sheets.

There are two different forms of spin-outs: start-ups and going concerns. Start-up spin-outs are new business initiatives launched by the parent. Going concern spin-outs are activities initiated by the parent company in the past that subsequently, based on a senior management decision, are positioned independently from other activities.

At first sight, spin-out management has much in common with external corporate venturing [18]. Like the latter, it is about managing activities outside the hierarchy of the existing company. In both cases, activities are managed at arm's length. However, the two models differ significantly.

External corporate venturing includes joint ventures and external capital participation, whereas spin-out management refers exclusively to existing or newly established units owned by a company – that is, the majority of shares are in the hands of the parent company and are part of its business scope. External ventures may be owned by alliance partners and, unlike spin-outs, their strategies can be altered by an external party. A parent company always owns a spin-out and, therefore, always has the final say in its management, whereas external ventures do not always offer this possibility due to the division of shares and the shared control of the company.

Spin-outs are also different from incubators such as CMGI and Internet Capital Group. Incubators are investment vehicles. The parent company is mainly interested in the financial performance of the individual ventures, which immediately operate as independent entities. In the case of spin-outs, however, the parent has a primarily strategic rather than financial interest.

Different researchers maintain that this is why spin-outs are an integral part of the parent's business activities, which is not the case with incubators [19]. Implementing spin-out management brings at least three strategic advantages [20]:

• quicker mode of growth;
• entrepreneurship, and
• flexibility.

Mode of growth

Spin-out management facilitates the opportunity to grow with subsidiaries that operate autonomously in the boundaries of a large company - growing by becoming smaller. This is usually the primary reason for external start-ups (developing completely new activities with no parent). Internal start-ups can grow more quickly than external ones, but they generally lack the infrastructure and financial instruments needed for fast take-off and growth.

Spin-outs do not suffer from this disadvantage. For the parent company, spin-out management is an effective instrument for growth that ties employees with an entrepreneurial spirit to the company and supports a corporate culture in which entrepreneurship is the key success factor for boosting competitiveness.

Entrepreneurship

Spin-outs are not tied to structure and cultural status quo like bureaucratic companies. If necessary, they can quickly make and implement decisions. This is precisely the reason why they are an interesting medium for competing within a dynamic sector dominated by technology.

The entrepreneurial spirit of a spin-out may even positively influence the corporate culture of the parent company. It may prevent the parent from becoming a slow moving organization, or "target", based on principles of equalization. A positive side effect is that a spin-out, not having a dominant hierarchical structure, operates close to fair, "never lying" market principles.

Flexibility

Implementing spin-out management enhances flexibility. It can compensate for the negative aspects of large companies such as structural inertia, a weak record of innovation, rigidity, or risk aversion. It improves the speed of making decisions and responding to market demands. It weds the cost efficiency of the more traditional, centralized, functional, or divisional organizational structures to the flexibility of the decentralized market-driven business-unit structures. It enhances both effectiveness and efficiency.

Challenging opportunity?

In addition to the advantages of spin-out management, there are some important disadvantages to consider. Such expansion is often expensive and goes hand in hand with risks and internal conflicts. According to Jagersma (1997), spin-outs initiated as internal start-ups will only profit from cost advantages in the long term.

Companies aiming for growth mainly through such spin-outs will usually have a costly learning curve. Going concern spin-outs will not be quite as expensive. Moreover, spin-out management - certainly in the initial stage of the life cycle - is a risky growth strategy. Start-ups in particular have a high failure rate, since going concerns have a broader and less vulnerable product/market scope.

The implementation of spin-out management has considerable consequences, not only for the spin-out but for the parent company in general. The spin-out should be viewed as an integral part of the organization. In practice, it is often viewed as a threat by employees rather than a challenging opportunity.

Both start-ups and going concerns suffer from this perception. Political processes, which are difficult to manage, play a role when applying spin-out management, particularly in large companies. Employees are often dissatisfied with the preference and attention senior management gives to spin-outs, possibly resulting in serious political conflicts and internal competition over resources.

In the worst case scenario, this could lead to a weakened position on the market – not just the spin-out, but the whole company.

Case Studies

How do companies in general cope with spin-out management? Four cases can help supply answers: Dell, Cap Gemini Ernst & Young (CGEY), Infopulse, and 4BB.

All companies operate in the ICT sector and serve in many ways as examples for other companies. All have successfully operated with a spin-out business model for some time; Dell and CGEY have changed their model over time into a spin-out, whereas Infopulse and 4BB started out that way.

Dell

Headquartered in Round Rock, Texas, Dell Computer Corporation is the world's leading direct computer systems company and a premier supplier of technology for the internet infrastructure. In the United States, it is a leading supplier of PCs to business customers, government agencies, educational institutions, and consumers.

Dell has been operating for a couple of years with a high profile on the Dutch market. Renowned primarily for its direct sales model, it is also known for its efficient use of the internet. The direct sales model and the internet's open architecture are integrated, a strategy that has served the company well. Fifty percent of Dell's turnover is via the internet. Technical services to clients are also being provided more and more by using the internet as a distribution channel.

Dell's direct business model is relatively cheap and equipped to adapt speedily to changes in the business environment. The absence of retailers and other resellers means a quick time-to-market for new products. By using this model, Dell differentiates itself from its competitors in a unique way, with positive effects on its margins and, therefore, on its financial performance. In an industry with continuous pressure on margins, the direct business model, if adequately implemented, serves as an important competitive advantage.

Dell Ventures, a wholly owned strategic investment branch, is responsible for spin-out activities. It's aim is to constantly innovate Dell Computers through newly developed ideas and technological activities. Without this spin-out strategy, Dell would have an unfocused, sporadic awareness of new developments in the industry.

Dell Ventures provides a competitive advantage through direct investments that give visibility to new relevant technologies. That access helps Dell anticipate future customer needs and improve products and services. Dell Ventures is a long-term investor, and the strategic objectives of Dell guide its strategy.

Scouting for new technological opportunities and receiving requests internally via the business units or directly via external parties, Dell Ventures acts as the radar for the Dell Group companies. Typically, people at Dell start spin-outs as research projects. Proposals first undergo a review to assess the fit into at least one of Dells' prevailing industry clusters:

Servers & Storage, Notebooks & Desktops, Networking, Software & Peripherals and Services.

Thereafter, a corporate business development team investigates the venture on its basic financial, legal, management, and business aspects and decides whether the investment opportunity is sound. The team then contacts the appropriate Dell business group to encourage early relationship building between the venture and Dell. Finally, due diligence work is executed and the investment is proposed to the Board of Management for approval.

Dell Ventures has established more than a dozen young firms, exploiting ideas that would have either gone to waste or slipped away to make fortunes for others.

Examples of Dell Ventures' Network Infrastructure spin-outs are:

- Avici Systems, which develops high-performance routers and switches;
- Cidera, which delivers content via satellite to the edge of the internet;
- Finisar, a company that develops fiber optic subsystems and performance test systems for high-speed serial data communications, and
- XACCT, a specialist in IP metering services for internet carriers and network providers.

Dells' major spin-outs in Services are:

- Mobilian, which designs chips that allow devices to interact simultaneously with multiple wireless communication radio standards;
- Zeevo, which makes low-power wireless technology that integrates radio, analog and digital circuitry on a single chip, and

- SirF Technology, a specialist in semiconductors and software for making location data (via GPS) available to consumer devices and commercial applications.

Important Server & Storage spin-outs of Dell are:

- Interactive Silicon, which makes chips for parallel computing compression and decompression;
- Nishan Systems, which specializes in hardware that enables storage area networks to operate as IP/Ethernet networks, and
- LiveVault, a specialist in real-time data protection and data distribution software.

Dell uses a positive Internal Rate of Return (IRR) from a spin-out as an important financial source for new ones. That means that mature spin-outs finance younger ones. As a result of this policy, a spin-out should already be making profit at an early stage of its existence.

In Dell's business model, spin-out management has not yet spread through Europe, which is remarkable because the European and US markets have so much in common. Dell seems to use a "cascade strategy". First it implements spin-out management on the home market and subsequently rolls out this innovative business model into the rest of the world. In short, Dell is using spin-outs to optimize its existing direct business model.

Cap Gemini Ernst & Young (CGEY)

CGEY is one of the biggest global service providers in the field of management consulting and IT services. Even before its acquisition of Ernst & Young, Cap Gemini was a leading consultancy company, with a turnover of 4,3 billion euro in 1999 and about 40.000 employees in Europe, the US and the Far East.

At that time the mission of the firm was: "Cap Gemini works with clients to enable them to run their business better by developing knowledge-based solutions". It had already entered into many alliances, with Microsoft, Oracle, SAP, and Cisco Systems as partners. This kind of cooperation allowed the partners to provide total solutions for their clients in the field of management consulting, system integration and outsourcing.

CGEY has been using spin-outs for some time; they have emerged as its growth engine, fueling much of the profit creation and technological innovation. According to its top management, spin-outs have kept CGEY alive in world competition, bridging existing core activities with the new ones, which may ultimately become part of the core business.

Despite the bigger-is-better notion propagated by some investment bankers and takeover attorneys, CGEY - a corporate Goliath - is trying to spawn the Davids of the business world, creating smaller, highly decentralized units and giving managers greater flexibility and freedom with less staff review. It wants the best of both: a big company with the heart and hunger of a small, innovative one. Therefore, spin-outs first-and-foremost are counted on to contribute to CGEY's growth strategy; their financial performance is not the key issue.

CGEY invests directly in spin-outs with new, innovative ideas. Investment levels vary between 0,5 - 5 million euro. The head office takes minority stakes in the ventures in the first financing round or later and does not take board seats. Special funds are established for dedicated purposes.

Potential deals are sent to the relevant business units, which may decide to sponsor the venture. In this role, the business units are responsible for the interaction and communication between CGEY and the venture. Thus, CGEY attemps to achieve an active relationship with its spin-outs.

Bortiboll Communications is a medium-sized Dutch spin-out of CGEY that makes application software for electronic markets. Due to Bortiboll's market position, CGEY is a leader in the Dutch market for e-commerce applications. Twinsoft is one of CGEY's biggest spin-outs. It provides high-quality professional services in the European market for various platform-independent systems and applications. Twinsoft's services include consulting and assistance to analyzing, designing, maintaining, supporting, and managing critical enterprise systems and applications.

As a rule, CGEY's existing core activities will never be performed by a spin-out. Both start-ups and going concerns will be used only for non-core activities, which of course have the potential to eventually become part of the core business. According to CGEY, this is an important requirement for using spin-out management as an innovative growth strategy.

CGEY tends to use spin-outs only for activities that do not fit its corporate image. In such cases, they represent a brand on the market, and an eventual failure will not have a negative effect on the parent. The "golden rule" is: there must be an intensive, give-and-take relationship between the parent company and the spin-out - CGEY directs resources to the spin-out, and the spin-out returns know-how to its parent.

Spin-out management also seems to be an effective way for CGEY to keep its employees satisfied and tie them to the company. Talented consultants with the intention of leaving CGEY are given the opportunity to start their own spin-out under certain conditions.

The advantages are clear. CGEY keeps its talented consultants who have their own vision on technological and market developments, and at the same time the spin-outs provide new concepts and products that can be the innovative carriers of CGEY's future. Thus, spin-out management is also a way to keep pace with technological developments and changing market conditions.

Infopulse

Itself a spin-out from the start, Infopulse is a medium-sized ICT company based in The Netherlands that was founded at the beginning of the 1990s. Structured closely after a venture capital firm, its purpose is to use its headquarters resources to leverage portfolio firms.

As a network organization, Infopulse primarily aims at creating an environment in which ICT companies can operate optimally. Every company that is part of it must have a clear product/market focus. The parent company feeds the different entities with its resources while guaranteeing their independence and individual identities. This is Infopulse's key success factor for being able to operate flexibly in both local and global markets.

Because Infopulse believes in spin-out management as its main growth vector, it does not pursue alliances, mergers or acquisitions. Organic growth is its paradigm. Even in the mid-term, Infopulse envisages only spin-outs and is not interested in any other growth mechanism. It believes in the concept of self-guiding organizations with their own decision-making power and the freedom to develop their vision and strategy. Its goal is to establish a world-wide network of such independent and locally operating Infopulse organizations.

For quite some time, it has been practicing its spin-out business model outside European borders. An important part of the software development is carried out in the Ukraine and India. It is also active in North and South America. All twelve Dutch and foreign spin-outs are managed by local employees. Senior managers own a substantial number of the spin-outs' shares. In practice, this means that a spin-out is able to decide on its own future while sharing assets and customers with the other spin-outs.

Infopulse Electronic Commerce, the oldest of these spin-outs, provides high-tech solutions to complex e-commerce problems and develops comprehensive, customized B2B software and applications. Infopulse Business Integration is an e-procurement spin-out, whose main product is a flexible e-procurement solution that supports the purchase of products and services via internet.

The focus of the small think tank Infopulse e-Novations is on developing innovative internet concepts such as Eurohealthnet, a portal for health and nutrition products in Europe. The biggest spin-out of the group is Infopulse Financial Markets, which develops software solutions for such financial institutions as the Dutch ING Group. Thus, Infopulse's products and services range from software components used for automated dealing on international stock markets to solutions used to automate processes in dealing rooms.

The methods relevant to spin-out management in Infopulse are somewhat similar to those deployed by independent venture capitalists. Without providing a detailed anatomy of a typical Infopulse spin-out management program, the following activities can be distinguished:

- *Creating the deal flow* - inviting or actively scouting for technologies or investment opportunities.
- *Opportunity selection* – testing opportunities against some sreening criteria that reflect the objectives of the spin-out

management program; besides financial criteria, there is often an "investment charter" that defines the technology or business interest.

- *Due diligence* - the detailed review of the business plan and assessment of the management team.
- *Incubation* - if an opportunity is based on a healthy idea, the spin-out must be built around that idea, a common situation in Infopulse.
- *Investing* - can be made in various ways: direct or indirect, through a pooled or dedicated fund, through an investment partnership, and so on.
- *Governance and monitoring* – determines the relationship between the spin-outs and Infopulse after the investment has been made.

From the outside, Infopulse, which keeps a majority interest in each of its spin-out companies, may look like a holding company. But it does a number of things to maintain an overall sense of cohesion among the various businesses. For example, for a little more than 1,5 percent of revenues, Infopulse provides much of the corporate infrastructure the spin-outs need: financial and legal services, administration, risk management, strategy consulting services. In addition, many employees have incentive packages that include stock options in spin-outs other than the one they work for.

This strategy is beneficial for everyone involved. The spin-outs need capital and support skills to develop and commercialize their ideas and products. And the participation of Infopulse provides spin-out projects with credibility and technology sharing. The spin-outs acknowledge the importance and advantages of this innovative business model. However, it is no secret that it has a few disadvantages as well.

For one thing, it is sometimes difficult for the parent company to provide a fast-growing spin-out with the necessary assets, which forces the spin-out to execute many of the supporting activities itself, such as funding. Thus, it may not be able to concentrate sufficiently on the commercialization of a concept - the original reason for its being set-up.

If any of the innovative concepts or products exceed the parent's financial resources, quick growth of the spin-out can be limited. A worst case scenario is for a fast-growing spin-out to become a financial burden on its parent, thereby requiring additional external funding.

4BB

The Dutch company 4BB was founded in 1997 by four partners and represents a cooperation between different ICT companies, each with its own area of expertise. The former employees of a large ICT company were unable to realize their innovative ideas there, so they spun out 4BB, which consists of three types of organizations: IT firms, business consulting firms, and "back offices".

The IT and consulting firms are responsible for business-oriented IT consultancy, application management and maintenance, infrastructure (including management and maintenance), software products (of-the shelf and tailor-made), and development projects, while the back offices support the other two in implementing their activities. 4BB has its own training center, marketing, communication, and recruitment companies, and an employee benefits organization.

4BB believes in intrapreneurship. Like Infopulse, it has used spin-out management since it first went into business. By combining the assets of its different organizations, 4BB tries to profit from having the characteristics of a small and large company at the same time, limiting the disadvantages of both.

Distinctive treatment of customers and individual employees is the leading principle. The limited size makes it easier to be innovative and adaptive and helps create a positive and intimate working climate. This is an important competitive asset in the crowded employee market for attracting and keeping talented people. 4BB is very much aware of the added value of this asset.

4BB co-owns a diverse array of spin-outs. For example, Transtrack is a specialist in the field of ICT-solutions for tracking and tracing valuables and cash processing and management. E-norm, a medium-sized spin-out, develops, implements, and integrates e-business solutions based on interactive technologies. Blue Willow, also mid-sized, is a specialist in developing software solutions for businesses and not-for-profit organizations.

The investment charter is 4BB's most direct way of narrowing its vast number of investment opportunities down to those that contribute to its strategic objectives. The company works with a charter that is derived from a definition of the current scope of the business. The approach is similar to the one Infopulse uses to determine the appropriateness of spin-out investment opportunities.

A 4BB spin-out has a maximum of 50 employees. There are no cumbersome procedures or hierarchies, just one CEO with a maximum of 49 colleagues. This structure is most fruitful for developing and implementing new ideas. If the firms grow and exceed 50 employees in number, a new spin-out is automatically created. 4BB has a 70 percent share in every spin-out; the other 30 percent is available to the management and employees. To date, 4BB has been able to finance its 30-plus spin-outs on its own.

4BB's approach to ensuring that strategic objectives are achieved is to incorporate optimal conditions for strategic success in the design of its spin-out program. The optimal program depends first on specific, clear, and flexible strategic objectives and, second, on the investment charter. A clear and unambiguous charter can prevent resources from being dedicated to opportunities that do not add to 4BB's strategic goals. Finally, the governance of the spin-outs provides further opportunities to support the strategic dimension of the program, such as by engaging the already established spin-outs as "sponsors" of new ones.

Innovative approach

All of the companies discussed here are active in launching spin-outs. The parent companies are involved in setting up new companies or separating existing ones. Every single company has its own objectives, business scope, budget, and market penetration strategies. The different spin-outs are conquering their own markets or market segments. The parents are carefully checking new ideas and concepts on their commercial feasibility.

The leadership of the parent companies enhances horizontal synergy among the spin-outs. However, there is no pressure on any subsidiary to establish these relationships. Spin-out managers are free to decide whether such relations are to be established. The parent, though, is actively involved in recruiting the spin-out managers, who ultimately determine the success of the firms.

Dell, CGEY, and 4BB prefer to recruit managers from their existing companies. Infopulse first develops new technologies and concepts, then recruits managers through an external channel. The leaders of all four of these companies act as active coaches for the spin-out managers.

For Dell, CGEY, Infopulse, and 4BB, translating spin-out management into a business model reflects their organizational philosophy. Spin-outs lead to the development of innovative products.

In fact, the entire model is innovative, with the following advantages:

- There is greater speed in the product development process and the time-to-market of new products and services. The absence of hierarchical structures makes it easier for spin-outs to focus on the wishes of existing or new customers.

- Management and employees are more motivated when they are offered part of a spin-out's shares; they become more commited to its performance.

- The parent company can keep its talented employees, who might otherwise have left the company.

- The parent company profits from access to new products at the beginning of their life cycle, as well as new clients, new networks, and the horizontal synergy effects initiated by spin-outs.

- Companies usually become more transparent when spin-out management is implemented, which makes them more attractive to external financial suppliers – provided that the spin-outs are not burdened with the non-transparent old performance systems and strong, internal culture, and that financial suppliers are educated about the spin-out management concept.

It is important also to note the disadvantages – or better, the challenges – encountered with spin-outs. I refer here to four interesting ones:

- What ultimately links a group of different spin-outs? In practice, successful spin-outs are the initiators of new ones ("Success breeds success"). Nevertheless, aligning the different strategies becomes more difficult as the number of spin-outs grows. The question then arises: What is the added value of the parent company if spin-outs are able to perform without its help? If that value is not sufficient, break-up could be imminent. The business model is successful only if the parent provides enough added value to the spin-outs.

- Companies that implement spin-out management usually face a capital market that is unaware of the concept. Financial suppliers often do not know the ins and outs of the model and thus may not provide enough resources to the parent. Traditional financiers have difficulty measuring the stability, let alone performance, of the spin-out; because it remains a framework for independent operating firms, it lacks integration. This is why they must be thoroughly educated about the model.

- The spin-out often uses the reputation or brand of the parent company at its inception. So it is important for the parent to be aware of the risks it is taking if the spin-out fails. In other words, the parent should be careful in using an intangible asset that it has carefully built up over the years if the asset could be damaged by spin-out failure in a very short time.

- Finally, new business models are often difficult to manage. For the leadership of an existing company, the concept of spin-out management could be too much of a threat to the existing mental framework and strong management culture. This is even more the case when implementing spin-out management.

Pros and cons

Spin-out success is determined by carefully weighing these various pros and cons and then making deliberate decisions. Managers are sometimes tempted to look only at the advantages, which is a mistake. Both sides of the coin must be considered and acted upon. The examples discussed here may be a source for guiding business decisions on whether or not to spin out.

References

[1] See: P. Evans and T.S. Wurster, "Blown to Bits: How the New Economics of Information Transforms Strategies", Harvard Business School Press, Mass., 2000.

[2] C. Christensen, "The Innovator's Dilemma: When New Technologies Cause Great Firms to Fail", Harvard Business School Press, Mass., 1997.

[3] See: P. Drucker, "Innovation and Entrepreneurship", Harper & Row, New York, 1985; E.B. Roberts, "New Ventures for Corporate Growth", Harvard Business Review, July-August, 1980; R.P. Nielsen, M.P. Peters, and R.D. Hisrich, "Intrapreneurship Strategy for Internal Markets", Strategic Management Journal, Vol. 6, pp. 181-189, 1985; R.A. Burgelman, "Managing the Internal Corporate Venturing Process", Sloan Management Review, Winter 1984; R.A. Burgelman, "Managing the New Venture Division: Research Findings and Implications for Strategic Management", Strategic Management Journal, Vol. 6, pp. 39-54, 1985.

[4] See: Z. Block and I. MacMillan, "Corporate Venturing: Creating New Business Within the Firm", Harvard Business School Press, 1993; R. Schuyt, M. Melford and F. Vrancken Peeters, "Corporate Venturing Provides New Growth Opportunities", Het Financieele Dagblad, November 7, 2000 and P.K. Jagersma, "Corporate Venturing: The Downside", Het Financieele Dagblad, November 20, 2000; I. MacMillan and R. McGrath, "Corporate Ventures", Financial Times, October 16, 2000.

[5] See: P. Anslinger, D. Carey, K. Fink and C. Cagnon, "Equity Carve-outs: A New Spin on the Corporate Structure", The McKinsey Quarterly, Number 1, 1997; P. Anslinger, S.J. Klepper and S. Subramaniam, "Breaking Up is Good to Do", The McKinsey Quarterly, Number 1, 1999; P.K. Jagersma, "International Venture Management", chapter 5 in P.K. Jagersma, "Internationalization", Inspiration Press, Brussels, 1998; P. Anslinger, S. Bonini and M. Patsalos-Fox, "Doing the Spin-out", The McKinsey Quarterly, Number 1, 2000.

[6] The Economist, "The Net Imperative: Survey Business and the Internet", June 3, 2000.

[7] See: P.K. Jagersma, "Internationalization - From economies of Scale Via Economies of Scope to Economies of Skills", Inaugural lecture at Nyenrode University, 1997.

[8] See, for example, G. Hamel, "Leading the Revolution", Harvard Business School Press, Boston, Massachusetts, 2001.

[9] G. Hamel, "Bringing Silicon Valley Inside", Harvard Business Review, pp. 71-84, September-October, 1999. See also: T. Elder, "New Ventures: Lessons from Xerox and IBM", Harvard Business Review, July-August, 1989.

[10] See P.K. Jagersma, "The Fokker-Dasa deal", Veen Publishers, Amsterdam, 1994.

[11] See, for example, P. Evans and T.S. Wurster, "Blown to Bits: How the New Economics of Information Transforms Strategies", Harvard Business School Press, Mass., 2000; P.K. Jagersma and D.M. van Gorp, "New Business Models", Holland Management Review, January-February, 2001.

[12] C. Shapiro and H.R. Varian, "Information Rules: A Strategic Guide to the Network Economy", Harvard Business School Press, Mass., 1999.

[13] M. Porter, "Strategy and the Internet", Harvard Business Review, March 2001.

[14] R. Kaplan and D. Norton, "The Strategy Focused Organization", Harvard Business School Press, Mass., 2001.

[15] G. Hamel, "Bringing Silicon Valley Inside", Harvard Business Review, pp. 71-84, September-October, 1999.

[16] See for new venture divisions: R. Plompen, H. Hendriks and A. Kok, "Ventures: Investment in Innovation", KPN-Studieblad. November - December, 1999; G. Risk and S. Milius, "Apple Computer-Strategic Investment Group", Stanford University Case Study, 1995; Anonymus, "Philips External Venturing", Philips Mondial, February 2000; H. Chesbrough and S. Socolof, "Creating New Ventures from Bell Labs Technologies", Industrial Research Institute, March-April 2000; B. Hunt and J. Lerner, "Xerox Technology Ventures", Harvard Business School Case Study, 1998.

[17] W. Powell, "Neither Market Nor Hierarchy: Network Forms of Organization", Research in Organizational Behavior, Vol. 12, pp. 295-336, 1990.

[18] Z. Block and I. MacMillan, "Corporate Venturing: Creating New Business Within the Firm", Harvard Business School Press, Mass., 1993.

[19] See for example: P. Anslinger, S. Bonini and M. Patsalos-Fox, "Doing the Spin-out", The McKinsey Quarterly, Number 1, 2000.

[20] G. Pinchot, "Intrapreneuring", Harper & Row, New York, 1985.

6

Vertical and Horizontal Synergy in MultiBusiness Multinationals

Charting the performance of enterprises is a popular pastime for scientists and consultancies. The performance of a company is determined to a considerable extent by the industry in which it is active. Studies have shown that the nature of the industry accounts for approximately fifty percent of the maximum profitability feasible for a company [1]. This is an interesting fact: industries, first and foremost, determine the profitability of businesses.

The implications of this empirically determined phenomenon are far-reaching. Indeed, enterprises wishing to successfully expand their activities by crossing borders will have to do so in profitable industries. During the internationalization process a lot of companies rely too heavily on their own products, availability of managers and opportunities presenting themselves on a foreign market. The fact of the matter is that everything starts from the profitability of the industry in which the company wishes to be active abroad.

A company's competitive position also determines, to a great extent, whether or not it is successful. On average, about one quarter of a company's potentially feasible profitability is determined by the distinctive position it occupies versus its competitors [2].

The nature of a distinctive position in comparison with the competitors is determined, to a considerable extent, by whether or not the company has specified skills [3]. Gary Hamel and C.K. Prahalad have devoted a bestseller, *Competing for the Future*, to the phenomenon "competencies" [4]. The quintessence of their argument: a company's sustainable competitive position is not determined by one or several "core activities", but by unique "core competencies". These two "performance roots" have been the constant source of research throughout the last decades and Harvard professor Michael Porter owes the greater part of his guru status to them [5].

Recent research has shown, however, that a firm's maximum feasible profitability is, furthermore, determined to a considerable extent by the degree to which a company manages to realize vertical and horizontal synergy [6].

Contrary to the aforementioned industry and competition research, research regarding vertical and horizontal synergy in companies in general and MultiBusiness Multinationals - multinational firms consisting of several foreign subsidiaries - in particular, is still in the early stages [7].

Horizontal and vertical synergy

Since the 1990s, the Ashridge Centre for Strategic Management in the UK ("Ashridge") has been giving the vertical and horizontal synergy issue flesh and blood. Ashridge occupies itself, in particular, with studying the role of corporate centers (or: head offices) of large multinational companies [8]. Ashridge focuses, primarily, on charting the relationship between the role of a multibusiness company's corporate center and its degree of diversification. The relationship between corporate centers and business units is also often researched.

In the Netherlands, too, researchers increasingly have been paying attention to the role of the corporate center of large multinational diversified enterprises and the phenomenon of vertical and horizontal synergy [9]. However, little is known about the impact of internationalization on the role of corporate centers. The degree of internationalization co-determines the nature of the role of a corporate center and the way in which it deals with foreign business units, i.e. the orientation of a corporate center.

The question I would like to answer in this chapter follows from the above: What is the relationship between the degree of internationalization, the role of a corporate center and the orientation of a MultiBusiness Multinational's (MBM's) corporate center?

Furthermore, I am interested in the direction of causality - which parameter (degree of internationalization, corporate center role, corporate center orientation) is directive with respect to another one? I will answer the research question with the aid of a diverse and sizeable research population.

In this chapter, the following subjects will be addressed:

- Internationalization as a growth process.
- The different "generic" and "specific" roles of a MBM's corporate center.
- The four different orientations of a MBM's corporate center.
- The central research question: what is the relationship between the degree of internationalization, the corporate center role and its orientation?
- Some lessons to be learnt.

Internationalization as a process

In its initial stages, internationalization is often seen as a continuation of what is happening at home [10]. Market research and international market segmentation are hardly considered issues of importance. Often, for instance, products are mainly exported on a trial and error basis. They are developed and manufactured for the home market, and, therefore, rarely adapted to foreign circumstances. Firms assume implicitly that foreign markets show, first and foremost, similarities rather than differences [11].

Export is seldom an option for the providers of services [12]. Service companies have to sell their products immediately in a specific market - the production of services takes place simultaneously with their consumption, because they are not kept in stock, have short distribution channels and become obsolete very fast.

Companies investing abroad have four growth options [13]:

- international start-ups;
- international alliances;
- international mergers, and
- international acquisitions.

In this context, the word "experience" is a key factor [14]. For example, setting up an international start-up from scratch may sound exciting, but quite often turns out to be a bridge too far. International experience is often a scarce commodity and sometimes confused with experience on product level. The lack of international experience calls for an adequate growth strategy. Therefore, companies lacking international experience often prefer to engage in different kinds of cooperative ventures [15].

Cooperation with local and third enterprises enables companies to expand their playing field internationally by running relatively few risks at a relatively low price and in a relatively short period of time. This strategy allows them to benefit from the experience that local and third companies gained in a specific foreign market. Companies benefit from sharing the burdens and the profits of internationalization.

When internationalizing industrial firms continue to export, they increasingly make use of the "threshold value strategy" [16]. Whereas, in the beginning, export is quite often managed in an uncoordinated and non-focused manner, after a while it is approached in a more selective manner. The adage is: first operate with success in one or some export markets and then work to expand activities to other, often neighboring markets. Firms will only export to new foreign markets if they have crossed a certain "threshold value" in terms of experience in tackling specific export challenges.

In time, companies initiate more and more international activities. Research has shown that the macro-economic conditions influence this trend in a somewhat peculiar way [17]. A lot of firms continue to internationalize their business scope, regardless of whether or not they are confronting an economic boom or bust. The realization of economies of scale is a high priority on the managing boards' agenda [18].

Furthermore, internationalization is reflected in a rising flow of cross-border acquisitions and joint ventures [19]. The central issue with regard to the acquisition of, or cooperation with, foreign companies is that candidates for cooperation or takeover have sufficient experience in working in local or global markets.

In this stage, consolidation and integration are the "magic bullets" for a continuously growing company with cross-border activities [20]. Especially in recent years, global

155

companies have started to capitalize on their international experience. This policy has resulted in stronger emphasis on autonomous growth strategies and in divesting non-core activities.

The management of many MBMs has drawn the conclusion that the cost advantages of economies of scale do not always counterbalance disadvantages, such as coordination and control difficulties. This phenomenon, to a great extent, determines the split-up of various large MBMs [21].

Today, many global companies are capitalizing on the advantages of "economies of skills" via the implementation of modern ICT architectures. Internationalizing firms can profit from the international exchange of experiences and skills gained on foreign markets. Companies operating solely on the domestic market lack this opportunity; which is the ultimate difference between a company operating at international scale and one operating solely in a domestic market.

Role of a corporate center

Corporate centers can be found in all kinds and sizes. Some MBMs have enormous corporate centers. Dutch DSM is an example of a large MBM with a sizeable corporate center. Financial services MBMs, such as ABN AMRO, ING and Fortis, too, have big corporate centers.

MBMs with small corporate centers are often diversified. They have a diverse array of business units that have little or nothing in common. It is difficult for a corporate center to add value to a multicoloured palette of business units that serve a variety of customers in various geographical areas or product markets. This explains why MBMs fanning out in all directions often opt for smaller corporate centers.

Nevertheless, the negative correlation between the size of a corporate center and the degree of diversification has not been demonstrated unambiguously. Divergent models appear to be used [22]. The corporate centers of American MBMs, for instance, are, on average, twice as big as those of MBMs from France, Germany, the UK and the Netherlands.

It is difficult to provide an unequivocal explanation for these differences. The volume of the domestic markets of the MBMs might possibly explain some of the differences. The bigger the domestic market, the less the need to organize specific corporate center activities in business units. In that case, the most obvious thing to do is to offer guidance from one managing board or to lend support via all kinds of staff services emanating from the corporate center.

Therefore, the process of internationalization seems to influence the size of corporate centers of MBMs established in smaller and internationally oriented countries, such as the Netherlands, Sweden, Switzerland, and Belgium. Furthermore, the size of a corporate center can also relate directly to the added value provided to subsidiaries/business units. However, so far no study has demonstrated unambiguously that there is a direct positive link between the size of a corporate center and the degree to which a corporate center adds value to business units.

In general, it can be argued that a MBM corporate center has two "generic" roles, i.e., to realize [23]:

- *Vertical synergy.* Vertical synergy refers to the realization of vertical added value by a corporate center to its business units. This concerns, for example, formulating a company-wide strategy based on a vision, as well as corporate goals and policies. A corporate center can also provide added value with regard to corporate restructuring and portfolio management (i.e., acquiring enterprises and divesting ones). Furthermore, a corporate center can bring about a certain "esprit de corps". Additionally, in specific circumstances, the managing board may be better equipped to take decisions such as complex acquisitions or alliances, and negotiations with national or transnational (political) authorities [24].

- *Horizontal synergy.* Realizing horizontal synergy requires ensuring horizontal added value [25]. This means that a corporate center creates the ideal conditions so that business units are given the opportunity to realize added value through joint activities. Horizontal synergy relates to bringing about economies of scale, economies of skills and economies of scope through collaborating domestic and foreign subsidiaries.

In addition to generic roles, I distinguish four "specific" corporate center roles [26]:

- The "initiation" of new activities resulting in additional sales and profit (for example, through a new start-up).
- The "allocation" of financial and human resources - the oxygen of MBMs – among domestic and foreign subsidiaries.
- The "coordination" of domestic and foreign subsidiaries' activities to enhance firm-wide competitive advantages.
- The "integration" of various domestic and foreign activities. For instance, jointly performing, in one laboratory, different R&D tasks that are in line with each other.

The specific roles of a corporate center follow from the aforementioned generic roles. The roles "initiation" and "allocation" concern vertical synergy. The roles "integration" and "coordination" concern horizontal synergy (see box 1).

Box 1 Generic and specific corporate center roles		
Generic role:	Vertical synergy	Horizontal synergy
Specific role:	Initiation	Integration
	Allocation	Coordination

Orientation of a corporate center

Executives have a specific view on international challenges –
a "management orientation." Well-researched management
orientations are [27]: ethno-, poly-, regio- and geocentrism.

An ethnocentric corporate center orientation is used by
MBMs with limited international experience. They engage in
cross-border activities primarily through an "export" or
"international department". This nationalistic orientation is
developed in the home country and simply extrapolated at
international level. The adage is: what works inside a home
country will also work outside it.

Polycentrism stands for initiating activities whereby the local
environment is the starting point of strategic, tactical and
operational decision making. Foreign subsidiaries operate
relatively independently from one another: Each has its own
agenda and has a hands-off relationship with the corporate
center in the home country. Polycentrism is a synonym for a
country-by-country approach.

In the case of a regional corporate center orientation
(regiocentrism), most decisions are based on a regional basis.
Regional factors are decisive in the decision- and policy-
making process. MBMs with a regiocentric corporate center
orientation attempt to capitalize on regional economies of

scale, scope, and skills. The rise of regional trade blocks, such as the European Union, Nafta, Mercosur, and Asean, is a fertile breeding ground for this corporate center orientation.

With regard to the geocentric corporate center orientation, it is not a region that acts as the point of departure for decision and policy making, but the entire world. The world is seen as one entity ("global village") in which similarities are more important than differences.

Research

In selecting the research population, I used Fortune's "Global 500" (2003 edition), Business Week's "Global 1000" (2003 edition), and the Financial Times' 2003 top 500 of European, American and Japanese enterprises. A key criterion for selecting companies was the requirement that they were global players. Furthermore, they had to have clearly distinguishable domestic and foreign subsidiaries. Finally, sufficient data had to be available on all subsidiaries.

I was looking for Multibusiness Multinationals meeting the aforementioned three criteria; ultimately, 347 enterprises qualified as such. They were active on an international scale, were built up around several distinguishable domestic and foreign subsidiaries, and sufficient data were available on the subsidiaries. Based on this, I was able to make reliable and valid pronouncements on the relationship between the degree of internationalization of business activities, the role of corporate centers and their orientation.

Eventually, I ended up with a highly diversified portfolio of MBMs - starting from companies that only deployed a limited number of international activities in a few countries, to enterprises realizing the bulk of their sales via a multitude of foreign subsidiaries.

In this study, I was interested in the experiences and opinions of executives at corporate centers and general managers of foreign subsidiaries. Eventually, 226 members of managing boards, 89 senior staff executives (such as strategy directors), and 173 (former) general managers of foreign subsidiaries were interviewed.

Internationalization versus the role of a corporate center

The degree to which a firm is active on an international scale determines, to a great extent, the role a corporate center plays; The internationalization phase – "initial," "growing" or "mature" - determines the role of a corporate center and not vice versa. In some respects, this result shows similarities to Chandler's well-known "structure follows strategy" paradigm [28]. Indeed, a corporate center can be conceived as a specific structure.

Environmental conditions force a corporate center to adopt a certain role (see box 2). Eventually, it tries to respond to developments, such as internationalization of its business scope. The interviewees were strikingly unanimous in their views on the direction of the causality.

Box 2   Degree of internationalization versus role of corporate center

| | **Internationalization phase of MBM** | | |
	phase 1 [Initial]	phase 2 [Growth]	phase 3 [Mature]
Role of corporate center			
Vertical synergy			
1. Initiation	yes	weak	no
2. Allocation	yes	weak	weak
Horizontal synergy			
1. Integration	weak	yes	yes
2. Coordination	no	weak	yes

Legend
Yes: there is a direct connection
Weak: there is a weak connection
No: there is no connection

Initial stage

Executives of internationalizing companies are of the opinion that a corporate center should initially only "allocate" and "initiate." The first priority in this stage is to make the right decisions in terms of where, how and when to start new foreign activities.

Against this background, the necessary means need to be mobilized and allocated - more specifically the financial resources and the employees in terms of skills and capabilities. In other words, a corporate center "allocates" tangible and intangible assets.

In this stage, a foreign subsidiary usually lacks money and human resources. The organizational structure and business model are simple and the commercial pressure high. There is a shortage of time and attention for issues such as transferring employees from existing, for instance, domestic business units to new ones that operate in similar markets. There is a clear "one-on-one" relationship between the corporate center and its foreign subsidiaries.

In this stage, everything is focused on serving foreign customers as effectively as possible [29]. This requires a certain type of management - managers showing local initiative as well as keeping a keen eye on the firm-wide interests and guidelines.

The emphasis lies on realizing vertical added value through a corporate center. Vertical synergy limits itself to making available means, such as human resources, general managers, and financial resources. A corporate center does not interfere in the day-to-day activities of a foreign subsidiary, but keeps an eye on the budget.

Growth stage

The corporate center of a MBM with several new foreign subsidiaries that have already shown some growth will increasingly interfere in the local initiatives of its foreign subsidiaries. This may seem remarkable because foreign subsidiaries have survived the start-up phase, and, therefore, should be deemed able to continue to do so.

However, after the start-up phase, foreign subsidiaries will have to deal more and more with corporate center systems, processes and guidelines. There is no longer only control via short-term financial goals (the budget). More frequently than before, corporate centers interfere in the decision-making of the foreign subsidiaries. According to the interviewed general managers, foreign subsidiaries regularly find themselves stuck between, on the one hand, the dynamics of the foreign market that claims all the attention and time of a general manager and his colleagues, and, on the other hand, pressure emanating from the corporate center to conform to the working methods of the company. In practice, this means adopting all kinds of procedures, codes, and guidelines.

The interference by the corporate centers often leads to obstruction from the foreign subsidiaries involved. As a rule, general managers dislike the formalities imposed on them from the home country. During one of the interviews, a managing board member put is as follows:

> "This is actually a typical 'chicken-and-egg' problem. If we allow the foreign subsidiary to go its own way in this fast-growth stage, we lose grip on it once and for all. After all, we have chosen to appoint 'heavy weights' who have to look upon the subsidiary concerned as their own enterprise. Unfortunately, they also behave that way vis-à-vis the corporate center. The foreign general managers go in all directions, except ours. That is why we weave a 'web of rules and procedures' around the general manager and his management team. There is simply no other way. Especially in this stage, it is impossible for us to steer foreign subsidiaries in an 'informal' manner. We have no choice but to straitjacket the subsidiary, because if we don't, we fail in integrating the foreign subsidiary in the group."

Internationalization often goes hand in hand with friction between foreign executives and their managing boards, and, therefore, with corporate centers. In practice, general managers who show initiative and make foreign subsidiaries successful, try to accomplish as much as possible on their own. They are fully aware of the fact that asking for additional support in the form of, for example, finance, will lead to a stifling relationship based on a multitude of formalities, rules and regular consultations. Furthermore, emotional issues, such as "pride", "self-esteem" and "desire to be the boss without outside interference", often play an important role. Therefore, in this stage, the centrifugal forces with regard to the corporate center are stronger than the centripetal forces.

Only a small minority of corporate centers have mastered the art of communicating with managers of foreign subsidiaries. The majority, however, seems to use institutionalized financial standard methods to (I quote a board member) "keep a grip on our foreign business" [30]. This chief executive continues:

> "For us, such financial methods are an ideal instrument to establish the performance of any arbitrary foreign subsidiary. The financial reports serve as point of departure for all kinds of discussions. We primarily communicate on the basis of such financial reports. Discussions with general managers have to be based on facts embedded in financial reports."

This comment is typical of many other chief executives. Furthermore, most foreign subsidiaries are lumped together, and are, therefore, not perceived in a differentiated manner. Most corporate centers lack a "custom-made policy" for their foreign subsidiaries that is tailored to local conditions. "Situational leadership" is a rare commodity. General managers argue that non-differentiated management of corporate centers is the breeding ground par excellence for disruptive conflicts. It explains to a large extent why the relationship between corporate centers and their foreign subsidiaries is often far from optimal.

In this stage of the internalization process, there is a strong urge on the part of corporate centers to get a grip on the growing foreign subsidiary. "Integration" is the name of the corporate center game. The primary goal is to prevent particularly successful foreign subsidiaries from steering courses that are too independent.

Mature stage

In this stage, it is less difficult for corporate centers to manage the relationship with foreign subsidiaries. The most troublesome general managers have already left of their own accord or have been replaced by general managers who "dance better to the corporate center tune".

A great number of general managers get tired of (I quote a former general manager) "fighting with corporate center executives" and simply decide to leave. Other former general managers said: "They never listen to us anyway", "Eventually, you're fighting a losing battle, no matter how tough you are", and "You are tied hand and foot by the tight financial goals", or:

> "The fact of the matter is that you are constantly squeezed between the loyalty to your colleagues in the subsidiary and the ambition to eventually become a member of the managing board. It is a very personal 'battle', a battle - because that it is how I have always experienced it - with a political dimension. It is almost impossible to discuss it with anyone. This is what makes leading a foreign subsidiary so difficult. You are deprived of a sounding board and the managing board most certainly isn't acting as such. It lacks knowledge and is obviously not objective."

Managing a foreign subsidiary is often a breathtaking task. The biggest financial successes are realized in this stage. Therefore, corporate centers need to appoint the right general manager at the right point in time. He/she will eventually be the decisive factor when it comes to success or failure. Or, as a strategy director put it:

> "We realize that we often need self-willed and obstinate general managers to actually come up with tangible results. This is even more the case in the initial and growth phase. General managers must be willing and able to walk straight through brick walls. They have to steer a course of their own. They have to be creative and, in my opinion, that is often at the expense of the relationship with the corporate center, in other words, with us. However, it is

my opinion that as soon as a foreign subsidiary has made it through the minefield, the start-up and growth phases, the need for structure and stability only grows. We then no longer need 'entrepreneurial' general managers but ones who 'really' manage. Managers we can bank on - in good times and bad times. Such general managers have to be available and able and willing to engage in a constructive dialogue with the corporate center. At this point, we do not need entrepreneurs, pure and simple."

During this phase, economies are often realized through integration and coordination of activities of various foreign subsidiaries. Harmonizing the strategies of these subsidiaries begins to bear fruit. According to the interviewees, the integrating and coordinating role of corporate centers offers a lot of added value. Sharing best practices, various operational and supporting activities, and jointly purchasing different resources and semi-finished products, may result in sizeable cost and revenue advantages.

Internationalization versus the orientation of a corporate center

The managers interviewed agreed almost univocally that the ethnocentric corporate center orientation does not exist, and that there is actually no such thing as a geocentric corporate center orientation.

The majority of managers feel that ethnocentrism is simply outdated. One general manager of a foreign subsidiary put it as follows:

"The idea that you can just pick up and transfer the practices used and the experience gained in the Netherlands to another country, is nothing but a lack of foresight. Perhaps that was possible four hundred years ago, but today you can no longer literally hold a gun against the head of your business partners or customers. Today, in international business, it all begins and ends with adaptive capabilities."

When it comes to doing business on an international scale, empathy is the name of the game. According to the majority of the research population, it is the most discriminating character trait between poorly and well-performing international general managers [31].

Box 3 Degree of internationalization versus orientation of corporate center

	Internationalization phase of MBM		
	phase 1 [Initial]	phase 2 [Growth]	phase 3 [Mature]
Orientation of corporate center			
1. Ethnocentrism	no	no	no
2. Polycentrism	yes	yes	yes
3. Regiocentrism	no	yes	yes
4. Geocentrism	no	no	no

Legend
Yes: there is a direct connection
Weak: there is a weak connection
No: there is no connection

According to one chief executive,

> "Ethnocentrism is at odds with the necessity to listen to your local foreign customer. Especially in international business, you have to be willing to understand the customer and to respond adequately to its wishes and needs. An ethnocentric corporate center orientation actually does the opposite."

In an era in which everything centers around a customer-based attitude, ethnocentrism has fallen out of favor with the research population. They are of the opinion that a polycentric corporate center orientation is the most effective. Local challenges have to be looked at from a local perspective.

Many managing board members find it difficult to make the change from a polycentric to a regiocentric corporate center orientation. Most of them said that, as a rule, MBMs with a polycentric corporate center orientation only switch to a regiocentric orientation when the company-wide business domain is fundamentally restructured around geographic regions. According to the study, this is often the result of market developments, political developments, such as the rise of regional trade blocks, or the arrival of a new chief executive.

Idealism and realism appear to intersect in a geocentric corporate center orientation. In this case, the point of departure for business policy is the world, but in everyday practice it shows that even global players with a big portfolio of foreign subsidiaries adapt to a great extent to local circumstances [32]. To summarize: Polycentrism is the most prominent corporate center orientation throughout all stages of internationalization.

Orientation versus role of a corporate center

It did appear from the interviews that the role and orientation of corporate centers are closely intertwined, but that the direction of the causality cannot be determined unambiguously (see box 4).

Box 4 Orientation versus role of corporate center

Orientation of corporate center

Role of corporate center	Ethno-	Poly-	Regio-	Geocentrism
Vertical synergy				
1. Initiation	no	yes	yes	no
2. Allocation	no	yes	yes	no
Horizontal synergy				
1. Integration	no	no	weak	no
2. Coordination	no	no	weak	no

Legend
Yes: there is a direct connection
Weak: there is a weak connection
No: there is no connection

MBMs with a polycentric corporate center orientation are characterized by a firm-wide policy based on the principle that foreign subsidiaries have to be organized and managed on a stand-alone basis. According to one chief financial officer, bringing about horizontal synergy is:

> "not an important role for our corporate center. In our company we still look at international challenges from the perspective of the local market. We try to adapt to local market and political circumstances to the best of our abilities. Being a sales-driven organization helps. The emphasis lies on the creation of added value for local customers and less on using and spreading knowledge built up in the Netherlands and in other countries. In a sense, we fail to share the know-how available in our organization. We are completely focused on the needs and wants of our [local; PKJ] customers."

MBMs with a polycentric corporate center orientation are usually working on optimizing market and financial performance of individual foreign subsidiaries. They (can) only realize vertical added value. Moreover, a polycentric corporate center exists merely by virtue of doing so.

General managers of foreign subsidiaries, to a certain degree and after proper mutual consultations, accept a proactive attitude on the part of corporate centers. This is interesting, because general managers normally show little enthusiasm for "outside" interference. Nevertheless, one general manager put it as follows:

> "Thanks to our proactive corporate center, I have the feeling that I am not on my own. It is really pioneer work for us in this part of the world. We depend almost completely on our own resources, which can be difficult. This is not Western Europe or North America [the subsidiary was located in Argentina; PKJ]. I find commitment of our Dutch corporate center more important than no commitment at all. Delegation of authority and decision-making power has its downsides, especially in such a remote corner of the world."

Commitment with respect to performance of foreign subsidiaries is an intrinsic part of a polycentric corporate center orientation. Such a corporate center is more or less expected to intervene from time to time. However, according to the interviewees, a polycentric corporate center approach does not comply with company-wide policies aiming to realize productive horizontal relationships among foreign subsidiaries.

Regiocentric corporate centers try to realize both horizontal and vertical added value. For example, a regiocentric corporate center often stimulates the idea of centralizing certain supporting activities in one region. This concerns, in particular, activities such as, legal affairs, corporate communication and human resource management. The joint use, in certain regions, such as Europe or North America, of

IT/IS is also a form of horizontal synergy. In this way, there are ways to benefit from economies of scale, scope, and skills. However, according to most executives and managers, MBMs with a regiocentric corporate center orientation focus primarily on realizing vertical added value.

Lessons learnt

The lessons to be learnt, based on this research study, will be addressed briefly [33].

The advantages of MBM corporate centers are strongly linked to the exchange of valuable experience gained in the global arena. This "management of experience" primarily concerns the productive exchange of experience embedded in various internationally distributed subsidiaries. MBMs can capitalize on this asset.

This global management approach means adhering to certain organizational principles. Firstly, foreign subsidiaries should not be kept on the leash of their corporate centers. The foreign market with its specific local challenges and, therefore, competitive pressure justifies a shift in decision-making power from corporate centers to foreign subsidiaries. Ultimately, they are responsible for successful interactions with local customers, not the MBMs corporate center.

Secondly, effective global "management of experience" also means harmonizing the strategic and operational policies of foreign subsidiaries. This often pays off - especially in the growth and mature phases.

Sharing skills and acquired knowledge leads to economies of skills which increase if:

- The skills are unique vis-à-vis competitors and customers. This makes it possible to gain a competitive edge in various foreign markets.
- The business scope is extensive. The more foreign subsidiaries, the more opportunities to realize economies.
- The foreign subsidiaries have a lot in common with regard to products delivered/services rendered, markets to be worked upon, and technologies used.

Especially in the early stages of internationalization, MBMs view corporate centers primarily as the "mother ship". Corporate centers are the "focal point" that have a grip on the international web of subsidiaries. Consequently, in this stage, the relationship between corporate centers and foreign subsidiaries could be labelled as intensive and embedded in "allocation" and "initiation" efforts.

As a result of more cross-border initiatives, the "mothership approach" becomes more difficult to implement. MBMs increasingly develop into international networks of domestic and foreign subsidiaries – the "network-based" business model. The role of corporate centers begins to change. The focus is no longer only on "initiation" and "allocation", but increasingly on "coordination" and "integration". The emphasis shifts to horizontal synergy instead of vertical synergy. In this new corporate paradigm, there is little room for 'dirigisme'. The enhanced geographic scope requires a shift in the approach of the corporate centers - it changes from a "controlling" into a "coordinating" body.

Policy must be geared towards creating horizontal, in addition to vertical synergy - creating a transparent business model that facilitates the internal transfer of domestic and foreign skills, capabilities and experience. This is the responsibility of a corporate center. The results of this research study show that MBMs still have a long way to go with respect to this important issue. Realizing horizontal synergy is often a rare phenomenon. It is often realized only on the level of support or "secondary" activities, such as the provision of legal services, corporate communication, management development, tax management and ICT management.

According to this research study, the dominant polycentric corporate center orientation frustrates its "integration" and "coordination" role. Horizontal synergy can hardly be achieved with a polycentric corporate center approach. Polycentrism leads to one-sided attention to local developments instead of balanced attention to local and global developments. It also often results in control problems. Managing a (large) portfolio of independently operating foreign subsidiaries is difficult. Each foreign subsidiary has specific views on the local policy to be pursued. Corporate centers often find it hard to steer this centrifugal process in the right direction.

References

[1] H.H. Newman, "Strategic Groups and the Structure-performance Relationship", Review of Economics and Statistics, Vol. 60, p. 417-427, Augus 1978; R.P. Rumelt, "How Much does Industry Matter?", Strategic Management Journal, Vol. 12, p. 167-185, 1991; R.P. Rumelt, Schendel, D.E., and D.J. Teece, "Fundamental Issues in Strategy: A Research Agenda", Harvard Business School Press, Boston, 1994.

[2] M.E. Porter, "The Structure within Industries and Companies' Performance", Review of Economics and Statistics, Vol. 61, p. 214-227, May 1979; R.P. Rumelt, D.E. Schendel, and D.J. Teece, "Fundamental Issues in Strategy: A Research Agenda", Harvard Business School Press, Boston, 1994.

[3] For an overview, see: R.P. Rumelt, D.E. Schendel, and D.J. Teece, "Fundamental Issues in Strategy: a Research Agenda", Harvard Business School Press, Cam., 1994. See also: V. Ramanujam and P. Varadarajan,

"Research on Corporate Diversification", Strategic Management Journal, Vol. 10, pp. 523-551, 1989 and M.E. Porter, "On Competition", Harvard Business School Press, Boston, 1998.

[4] G. Hamel, and C.K. Prahalad, "Competing for the Future", Harvard Business School Press, Boston, 1994. See also: J.C. Collins and J. Porras, "Built to Last", HarperBusiness, New York, 1994 and K. Ohmae, "The Mind of the Strategist", McGraw-Hill, New York, 1982.

[5] M.E. Porter, "Corporate Strategy", The Free Press, New York, 1980; M.E. Porter, "Competitive Advantage", The Free Press, New York, 1985; M.E. Porter (ed.), "Competition in Global Industries", Harvard Business School Press, Boston, 1986 and M.E. Porter, "The Competitive Advantage of Nations", The Free Press, New York, 1990.

[6] M.E. Porter, "From Competitive Advantage to Corporate Strategy", Harvard Business Review, Vol. 65, p. 43-59, May-june 1987; S. Goshal and N. Nohria, "Internal Differentiation within Multinational Corporations", Strategic Management Journal, Vol. 10, p. 323-337, 1989; A. Vizjak, "Exploiting your Synergy Potential: Promoting Collaboration between Business Units", Long Range Planning, Vol. 27, No. 1, p. 25-35, 1994 and A. Campbell, M. Goold, and M. Alexander, "Corporate Strategy: The Quest for Parenting Advantage", Harvard Business Review, p. 120-132, March/april 1995.

[7] See, for example: C.A. Bartlett and S. Goshal, "Tap your Subsidiaries for Global Reach", Harvard Business Review, p. 87-94, November-December 1986; M.P. Kriger, "The Increasing role of Subsidiary Boards in MNCs: An Empirical Study", Strategic Management Journal, Vol. 9, p. 347-360, 1988; C. Lorenz, "How the Discriminating Parent should Behave", The Financial Times, December 5, 1988; J. Murrin, "How to Raid yourself Before others do", The Financial Times, June 22, 1988; J.C. Jarillo and J.I. Martinez, "The Evolution of Research on Coordination Mechanisms in Multinational Corporations", Journal of International Business Studies, Fall 1989 and J.C. Jarillo and J.I. Martinez, "Different Roles for Subsidiaries: The Case of Multinational Corporations in Spain", Strategic Management Journal, Vol. 11, p. 501-512, 1990.

For recent research see: H. Hungenberg, "How to Ensure that Headquarters Add Value", Long Range Planning, Vol. 26, p. 62-73, 1993; S. Goshal, H. Korine and G. Szulanski, "Interunit Communication in Multinational Corporations", Management Science, Vol. 40, No. 1, January 1994; B. Pursche, "Creating Value from Horizontal Integration", In Vivo, p. 9-13, October 1995; M. Goold and A. Campbell, "Desperately

Seeking Synergy", Harvard Business Review, p. 131-143, September/october, 1998; K.M. Eisenhardt and S.L. Brown, "Patching: Restitching Business Portfolios in Dynamic Markets", Harvard Business Review, p. 72-85, May/june 1999; R.A. Burgelman and Y.L. Doz, "The Power of Strategic Integration", Sloan Management Review, p. 28-38, Spring 2001.

[8] See, for example: A. Campbell, M. Goold and M. Alexander, "Corporate-level Strategy: Creating Value in the Multibusiness Company", John Wiley & Sons, 1994 and M. Goold and A. Campbell, "Strategies and Styles: The Role of the Centre in Managing Diversified Corporations", Basil Blackwell, Oxford, 1987.

[9] For an overview, see: P.K. Jagersma, "Corporate Strategy, Synergy and the Multinational Corporation", Holland Management Review, Vol. 19, Winter 2003.

[10] See: J. Johansson and J.E. Vahlne, "The Internationalization Process of the Firm: A Model of Knowledge Development and Increasing Foreign Commitments", Journal of International Business Studies, p. 23-32, Spring/summer 1977.

[11] J.M. Stopford and L.T. Wells jr., "Managing the Multinational Enterprise", Basic Books, New York, 1972.

[12] D.R.E. Thomas, "Strategy is Different in Service Businesses", Harvard Business Review, Vol. 56, p. 158-165, July/august, 1978; M.M. Habib and B. Victor, "Strategy, Structure, and Performance of U.S. Manufacturing and Service MNCs: A comparative Analysis", Strategic Management Journal, Vol. 12, p. 589-606, 1991.

[13] See: W.G. Egelhoff, "Strategy and Structure in Multinational Corporations: A Revision of the Stopford and Wells Model", Strategic Management Journal, Vol. 9, p. 1-14, 1988.

[14] See: J. Johansson and J.E. Vahlne, Ibid.

[15] M.K. Erramilli, "The Experience Factor in Foreign Market Entry Behavior of Service Firms", Journal of International Business Studies, p. 479-578, Third quarter 1991.

[16] P.K. Jagersma, "Globalization of Dutch Service Companies", Ph.D study, Tilburg University, Tilburg, 1993.

[17] P.K. Jagersma, Ibid.

[18] P.K. Jagersma, Ibid.

[19] F.J. Contractor and P. Lorange [ed.], "Cooperative Strategies in International Business", D.C. Heath and Company, 1988.

[20] P.K. Jagersma, Ibid.

[21] See: D. Sadtler, A. Campbell and R. Koch, "Break-up!", Capstone, Oxford, 1997.

[22] See: ACSM, "Effective Headquarters Staff", The Headquarters Fact Book, Pearson Education, 2000.

[23] See: H. Hungenberg, Ibid.

[24] See, for instance: M.P. Kriger, "The Increasing Role of Subsidiary Boards in MNCs: An Empirical Study", Strategic Management Journal, p. 347-360, 1988.

[25] A. Vizjak, "Exploiting your Synergy Potential: Promoting Collaboration between Business Units", Long Range Planning, No. 1, 1994.

[26] P.K. Jagersma [ed], "Multibusiness Corporations", Inspiration Press, Brussels, fourth edition, 2003.

[27] H.V. Perlmutter, "The Tortuous Evolution of the Multinational Corporation", Columbia Journal of World Business, No. 2, 1969.

[28] A. Chandler, "Structure follows Strategy", MIT Press, Boston, 1962.

[29] P.K. Jagersma, "International Venture Management", Chapter 5 of P.K. Jagersma, "Internationalization", Inspiration Press, Brussels, 1998. See also: P.K. Jagersma, "International Corporate Venturing", Het Financieele Dagblad, November 2000.

[30] R.S. Kaplan en D.P. Norton, "The Balanced Scorecard", Harvard Business School Press, Boston, 1996 and R.S. Kaplan en D.P. Norton, "The Strategy-focused Organization", Harvard Business School Press, Boston, 2001.

[31] P.K. Jagersma and D. van Gorp, "International HRM: The Dutch Experience", Journal of General Management, Vol. 28, p. 75-88, No. 2, December 2002.

[32] Also see, Akio Morita's (co-founder of Sony) adage: 'Think global, act local' For more information, see: A. Morita, "Made in Japan", E.P. Dutton, New York, 1986.

[33] For a more extensive discussion, see: P.K. Jagersma [ed.], "Multibusiness Corporations", Inspiration Press, Brussels, fourth edition, 2003.

7

The Hidden Cost of Doing Business

Managing Business Complexity

If strategy is the art of gaining a competitive edge, what's the secret of sustaining it? Consider Nestlé, Toyota, Philips, BT and Porsche, all notably well-managed companies, all examples of enduring competitive excellence. Each operates in an industry where innovations can be quickly copied by competitors. All are strategically nimble. But where they really shine is in execution. Their competitive edge is consistent operational effectiveness through effective complexity management.

Environmental issues often lead to dynamic challenges which are inherently difficult to resolve (box 1). Nestlé, Toyota, Philips, BT, Porsche and many others build reinforcing global growth engines while simultaneously managing or removing the 'frictional forces' (bottlenecks within business processes) that restrict profitable global growth. Through this approach, they literally add more 'fuel to the fire'. Managing or removing complexity is essential to prevent a global growth engine from stalling.

Box 1 From 'uniformity' to 'complexity' era

'Uniformity era'	Major changes	'Complexity era'
simple business model	fragmenting customer preferences	increasing diversity in customer needs and wants
limited information	information explosion	information overload
one-product/-approach	new distribution channels (e.g., internet)	multi-channel approach
efficiency/low-costs key	new competitors (e.g., China, India etc)	productivity is key
sales-driven firm behavior	'added' value becomes center of gravity in business policy	stakeholder orientation
market 'available'	cut-throat global competition	market 'searching'
unsophisticated buying procedures	'educated' customer and supplier	sophisticated buying procedures

Even today, many global companies dream of coming up with a brilliant new strategy that will lift them permanently above the dreary grind of head-to-head competition. Some pursue this dream like alchemists in search of the Philosopher's Stone. Yet in most global industries, new strategies are easy to emulate, if not for competitors, then for share hungry new entrants. Operational effectiveness via complexity reduction, not fancy strategic footwork, will decide who wins.

The 80/20 rule, a core concept in strategy, tells us that one-fifth of almost anything typically accounts for four-fifths of the value or cost. The message: focus on the big-ticket items and forget the chickenfeed. However, this is fatal for executives in today's complexity-driven global businesses. It is just those companies that excel in that last 20 percent that consistently make out in difficult times. The world's best companies share a single distinguishing characteristic: close and consistent attention to complexity management (i.e. 'the last 20 percent'). Managers of global companies need to be skillful 'putters' as well as strong 'drivers'.

Complexity pays?

As a result of continual pressure for international growth, most companies have both expanded their product lines significantly and indulged in what appears to be ever promotional activity in an effort to stimulate customer interest and gain share.

Not so long ago, markets admired the company that could stretch its brand across everything. One of the consequences of all this activity has been an enormous increase in the complexity of their businesses which tends to increase the fixed costs of conducting business. This complexity manifests itself in many forms affecting everything from the day-to-day operations of the business to senior management's strategic plans. Economies of scale, scope and skills appear to be wiped out by 'economies of complexity'.

According to a recent research study by Nyenrode University among 65 chief executives, senior managers and other corporate leaders around the world, many global companies have expressed serious concerns about their capability to successfully manage complexity and, for example, have striven to simplify their business, retrenching to a stable portfolio of core products and processes (box 2). Depth, rather than breadth is what markets and shareholders crave.

For global companies like Philips, single-mindedness seems to be the key to success. They prefer simple monomaniacal business models. However, others like UBS have attempted to manage complexity through information systems, advanced management structures, operational procedures, and decentralized group decision making. Only a few have come to grips with the challenge: they have learnt to manage a complex business in simple ways. It's a public secret that for many chief executives break-ups and demergers are a relief, a final chapter in a complexity reduction race.

Box 2 About the research

This chapter presents the findings of a project to study the complexity management activities and strategies of 20 global companies: Siemens (Germany), Porsche (Germany), Volkswagen (Germany), Ford (USA), IBM (USA), L'Oréal (France), BP (UK), BT (UK), ING (Netherlands), Royal Dutch Shell (Netherlands), Philips (Netherlands), Sony (Japan), Canon (Japan), Toyota (Japan), Santander (Spain), Zara (Spain), Fiat (Italy), Nokia (Finland), Nestlé (Switzerland) and UBS (Switzerland).

This chapter is based on a survey of 65 managers of the aforementioned global companies, executed by the Center for International Business of the Universiteit Nyenrode. Interviews with senior management were combined with the study of public and company files. The managers interviewed included a.o. (Executive) Vice-Presidents, Country Managers, General Managers, Managing Directors, COOs, and CEOs.

Over the next few pages, I will attempt to portray the increasingly complex environment which global companies face and argue that some approaches will allow solutions to the growing complications of dealing with the trade; ones that will avoid the drastic ultimate solution once suggested at a Communist Party Conference by Vladimir Kabaidze, General Director of the Machine Building Workshop who has been reported as saying,

"I can't stand this proliferation of paperwork. It's useless to fight the forms. You've got to kill the people producing them."

The origins of business complexity

Nobody ever thought that running a huge global company was easy. Take Siemens. Even Siemens' managers were surprised, when they looked into how complex its global operations had become. Around the world, for example, for reasons of local regulation, Siemens was offering not one medical device (e.g., an MRI scan) but numerous versions of it. To handle all this, Siemens' back-office needed 11 different computer systems. Siemens has since launched an ambitious project to reduce its complexity by 60 percent, and to cut the number of computer systems to one or two. The goal is to save approximately $450 million a year. Global companies like Siemens have a tremendous opportunity in making quantum leaps in complexity reduction.

Complexity is a by-product of managers' daily decisions - decisions which are influenced by many factors rooted in a company's internal and external environment. But although additional fixed costs - of which complexity costs are a part - may not matter during fast growth phases, they are unacceptable in the slow growing markets of today, especially in many European countries. Fixed costs do not decline along with sales. And the share of costs concerned here is substantial: in the course of various studies, I have found that around 25 to 35 percent of costs is complexity-driven. Therefore, managing complexity is vital. The challenge for management is to effectively capitalize on complexity management.

Managerial decisions generate complexity in terms of the number of 'challenges' that a global company has to handle. Each of these can relate to either physical materials or bits of information. All of these challenges are generated by the multitude of decisions managers make every day about the company's activities. It is often difficult for global companies to make complexity cost/benefit trade-offs because their decentralized and empowered decision-making is split between many managers in different divisions or groups, business units, and departments.

Each manager or group of managers does its best with the challenges it receives, and throws its own decisions 'over the wall' for the next manager or group of managers to cope with. In the end, decisions are made which add complexity without creating offsetting customer, supplier or competitive benefits. It is the exponentially expanding interaction of all these strategic, tactical and operational challenges and decisions that constitutes complexity and leads to severe reductions in a company's global competitiveness. Therefore, complexity management cannot be enacted by the stroke of a manager's pen. It takes persistence and perspiration on the part of everyone, all the time.

A few years ago, Boston Consulting Group (BCG) has calculated that, while market concentration in Britain, as measured by the market share of the top five banks and insurers, has risen from 22 percent in 1990 to 39 percent in 2004, banks' and insurers' expenses as a proportion of premiums have gone up from 29 percent to 36 percent. In the Netherlands, France, and Switzerland, due to a diverse array of local alliances, mergers and acquisitions, the top five controls (in 2004) a bigger slice of the market, compared to 1990, but their expense ratios, too, have risen. For banks and insurers, complexity management is an important agenda item for the years to come. Banks and insurers that can successfully manage complexity will gain a competitive edge.

The BCG results are both interesting and important for managers: the experience curve phenomena (more volume leads to more experience, and, therefore, lower costs) could be derailed by increasing complexity. The experience curve phenomena is self limiting; i.e., because productivity growth depends on an exponential increase in volume. Sooner or later volume fails to keep up with historical productivity growth. As a consequence, productivity growth slows.

Furthermore, as the search for volume continues into ever smaller niches of the market, complexity costs rise. According to my study, complexity costs have reversed the experience curve trend in many industries (examples are banking, automotive and media). Some believe that the continuing evolution of technology can overcome the inherent slowdown in the experience curve, but according to the research, this does not appear to be uniformly the case (box 3).

Box 3 Quotes from the executive suite

Many experts call for a broadening of businesses's strategic perspective. There is often a tendency to focus on far strategic horizons while overlooking immediate operational complexity related pitfalls (Mr M. Lafforgue, Executive Vice-President Production and Technology, L'Oréal (France)).

We have to eliminate complexity as much as possible. In practice, this means that we need not too much structure and hierarchy. Too much structure and hierarchy hinders effective decision-making (Mr Dr W. Wiedeking, CEO Porsche (Germany)).

We are convinced that when business grows more and more complex, structure becomes progressively less effective as a device for unifying our global organization or insuring smooth teamwork (Mr B. Verwaayen, CEO British Telecom (UK)).

We report and continue to report on complexity. We take it very seriously. It has been given a permanent place on our management agenda (Mr C. Espinosa de los Monteros, Director Zara (Spain)).

However, while some companies (e.g., Ford) in mature industries have suffered slower productivity growth, or even productivity decline as a consequence of increasing complexity, others such as BP, Goldman Sachs and Porsche seem to manage dramatic improvements in productivity and profitability.

In the face of growing cost problems, more and more global companies are now taking steps to identify, understand and reduce complexity costs. The good news is that excessive complexity costs can be reversed and prevented. Armed with a thorough understanding of complexity costs and with a knowledge of the critical benefits valued by customers and other stakeholders, managers have to rethink decisions in all areas of a company's value chain.

Basic approaches

There are basically two approaches to managing business complexity costs: simplification and reconfiguration. The interviewed global executives argue that reconfiguration (59 percent) is preferable to simplification (41 percent) but add that a combination of the two is often more effective.

Complexity can be reduced by discontinuing products, services and/or processes whose complexity costs are higher than the profit contribution they generate, or operationally by, for instance, increasing standardization (i.e., simplification) (see also box 4).

Box 4 Operational simplification strategies

Specific actions which simplify the operational business model are:

• shift customers to standardized products;

- select and concentrate on important customer segments;
- link product launch to discontinuation of old products;
- reconfigure the production process - eliminate stock pools and consolidate activities to achieve economies of scale and scope;
- limit design changes and introduction of new variants;
- automate business processes where economically feasible;
- simplify and streamline administrative procedures, and
- improve commonality of parts/product modularity.

Zara, a global fashion retailer, headquartered in Spain, successfully standardizes most of its products (and sales, communication, and distribution strategies), except for their color, which is added at the last minute in response to the latest tastes. Focusing variety on a few features seems to be the name of the game at Zara (its main European competitor, Swedish Hennis & Mauritz, follows a similar competitive strategy).

Simplification of support functions like HRM, ICT, Corporate Marketing, Legal Affairs, and Procurement can be realized through a disciplined analysis of the value of such support activities. Typically, according to my study about 20-25 percent of support costs can be saved by eliminating low-value activities. The key factor for success, however, is to ensure that new products or services (and/or business processes) are optimized *before* they are launched. Remember Sun Tzu's adage: 'Every war is won before it is ever fought'.

Complexity stems from fundamental causes that cannot always be eliminated. The hard reality is that the business world in which we must work is often beyond our comprehension. However, 'reconfiguration' may provide a means to seize the opportunities of complexity - opportunity to deliver greater value to trade and consumer by finer, more targeted segmentation.

In other words, we accept that some increasing complexity is inevitable in an era of disaggregation of needs and wants and we reconfigure the value chain to better handle it. According to the interviewees, to manage increased complexity through reconfiguration requires at least one or more of the following strategies: managing assets more flexibly, building new information systems, developing people with adaptable skills, and decentralizing decision-making.

Approaches like these can substantially reduce the costs of complexity and make the revenue contributions for product and promotion variations more attractive.

Box 5 Simplifying complexity while retaining breadth and depth – a management consultancy perspective

Much management consultancy work is aimed at simplifying the business model, i.e., chopping marginal products/services, focusing on high-priority customer groups, streamlining the information system, and reducing the overhead that has grown as the business model became increasingly complex. This approach has often resulted in turnarounds and much improved profitability.

But the approach is not without its dangers. A large global company may well never be as cost-effective as a small 'shop'. Eliminating smaller customer groups may mean opening up natural niches for competitors. And ruthless product/service line pairing can discourage product innovation and improvement. In the extreme, businesses can be simplified until they atrophy or fall prey to more focused competition.

An alternative for (especially larger) global companies is to create a business model that enables the global company to manage complexity effectively by:
- Designing products/services that are modular and share common parts in order to gain both external and internal shared economies of scale.
- Replacing labor with capital where new (information and communication) technologies can add flexibility and save operating costs.

- Ensuring that overhead does not grow to the level required by the most complex component of the business but rather in genuinely shared across the business model.
- Pricing products/services to capture the value-added inherent in the breadth of the product/service line and the level of customer service provided.

Simplifying complexity while retaining breadth and depth of product and service is not a strategy applicable to all global companies. Clearly, such a competitive strategy requires comprehensive organizational thinking and perhaps unconventional organizational structures, systems, procedures and skills. But for certain larger global companies, developing a business model that possesses this capability may well be the key to long-term success.

Simplicity = complex

Complexity is popping up on the radar screens of global companies all around the world. It is a hidden cost of doing business which in many cases has created a many-headed monster for management. Mergers, alliances, acquisitions, the rise of 'hot spots' like China, Russia and India, the internet and globalization in general adds to the complexity.

Excessive complexity typically grows over many years and fossilizes into structures, cultures, systems, and personnel that are not easily altered but over time the impact on the way the company does its business can be profound. My study shows that companies need a clear (not complex) label if they want to please shareholders, investors, and other stakeholders. Simplification or reconfiguration to reduce complexity can have a major impact on global competitiveness by simultaneously lowering costs, improving customer benefits and cutting response times.

Coping with complexity requires continuous efforts to identify and eliminate complications that add no value. Management has to analyze the global company and its

189

environment to flush out the hidden linkages between costs, activities, and the decisions that generated them. Ideally, this complexity analysis should be extended to include major suppliers and important customers. By involving these stakeholders, the management team will not only gain a better understanding of the total industry costs of complexity, but will also win the stakeholders' commitment to, for instance, complexity reduction. 'Complexity value analysis' has to be the name of the 'complexity management game'.

Part III. Global Strategy and Competition

8 Innovate or Die

9 International HRM - The Dutch Experience

10 Competing with Pirates

11 Strategic Marketing and the Global Banking Industry – Elements of Excellence

12 Redefining the Paradigm of Global Competition – Offshoring and Outsourcing

8

Innovate or Die

You may once have been able to hone your competitive edge by streamlining operations and slashing prices. No more. Today, innovation is central to growth. The "Triad" (i.e. the United States, the European Union, and Japan) gets more than half of its economic growth from industries that barely existed a decade ago. This suggests that innovating must become the most urgent concern of corporations everywhere.

Unfortunately, that sense of urgency is not widespread. Innovation is still an underexploited path to success in the global business community. Perhaps this is because becoming innovative isn't easy, and there is no one-size-fits all recipe for making every company more innovative.

Successful and unsuccessful innovations

The findings of a recent study suggests that innovative global companies have a number of common characteristics. That study, which consisted of 178 interviews with senior executives in 62 global companies (including Sony, Corning, Philips, Bang & Olufsen, Apple, IBM, Nokia, 3M, Porsche, Siemens, Unilever, Microsoft, Nike, and DaimlerChrysler), led to a compilation of case histories of 319 successful (product, service and/or process) innovations as well as 67 unsuccessful innovations.

The results of my study suggest that innovation can be a path to success for those global companies that implement ten strategies. If any of these ingredients is missing, continuous innovation is very unlikely to occur.

Set an innovative vision

Setting clear innovation aspirations is key. Setting an innovation vision requires identifying the likely source and nature of major innovation opportunities, understanding likely key success factors by type of innovation and market position, and targeting appropriate company aspirations for innovation. Top management aspirations have to invoke innovation throughout the organization and across the global business system.

Canon provides a good example of common aspirations. The company explicitly wanted to become "The No. 1 in imaging and information products for private use". Driven by this vision, Canon created a rich portfolio of products backed by consistent in-house development of core technologies.

Ultimately, "dream-driven" aspirations drive innovation. For example, Sony's innovation aspiration is "to provide products and services that 'pluck at the heart-strings' and to contribute to the happiness of mankind and development of society." Motorola wants "to create the platforms upon which whole new global industries will be born."

The aspiration that drives Hewlett-Packard is "to create information services products that accelerate advancement of knowledge and fundamentally improve effectiveness of people and organizations." What does this "dream" mean? It means HP wants to offer solutions that enable customers to link equipment into networks, offer printers with high-quality color at breakthrough prices, and apply HP technologies to fast-growing areas like multi-media.

A great innovation vision provides a broad road map, but leaves room for creativity. It has to generate a "find-a-way" mentality, a tolerance for ambiguity, and a willingness to destroy what exists. Wealth creation results from moving toward the innovation aspiration.

Develop and manage a superior innovation process

Innovation is a continuous process, not an isolated event and must be managed carefully. Superior management of innovation is necessary if a company is to build a process that enables it to launch high-impact innovation with minimum cost and maximum quality at highest speed of development. Therefore, each company has to identify, in a systematic way, how the innovation process operates and can be managed rather than assume it is at the whim of creative genius.

Successful management requires setting sensible priorities. Assessing the potential impact of ideas or projects through a rigorous approach is a key activity. And a thorough assessment program helps global companies avoid wasting resources on low-impact ideas or concepts. Assessments should consider product mix, developability, and manufacturability – three key dimensions of successful product development. Product mix considerations determine the revenues; developability considerations determine risk, time, and investment; and manufacturability considerations determine cost and quality of the development process.

An innovation process that is developed and managed successfully generates high-potential ideas, produces high-quality and high-impact product lines quickly and economically, and eventually strengthens company market position.

Institutionalize innovativeness

Institutionalizing innovativeness is key to achieving continuous innovation. A global company has to establish the right culture to nurture and sustain the innovative spirit and, therefore, institutionalize innovativeness.

Institutionalizing innovativeness is, first and foremost, about building a creative environment. This requires recruiting and developing exceptional people from diverse backgrounds. The ideal employee is a highly inventive person who has a firm grasp of the global competitive marketplace. Continuously innovative companies pay careful attention to the development of such employees, recognizing that the ability of a workforce to make the best of inventions may be a company's best competitive advantage.

In addition, the innovative environment constantly challenges current practices and prunes projects aggressively. It also rewards success lavishly, tolerates occasional failure, and punishes repeated failure.

Nike has built such an environment. "Just do it!" is not just a slogan, the philosophy is embraced and practiced internally. Nike has a history of giving people a chance to accomplish something. It is a very competitive environment but with safety nets: People who fail "honestly" get another chance.

By itself, innovation is not enough. A truly continuously innovative global organization not only creates new products, processes, or services, but also destroys those that no longer serve the purpose of the organization. This is akin to the Schumpeterian concept of creative destruction and is essential for the global organization's long-term survival.

Benchmark against best competitors

Smart managers study innovation outside their companies as well as within it.

Corning, for example, analyzes successful innovations in its industry and similar industries to identify success factors. Based on this analysis, Corning defines key innovation skills, organizational levers that stimulate innovativeness and facilitate an innovative environment, and weaknesses in the innovation process.

Many Japanese companies set themselves the task of outperforming a leading rival – an attitude vividly captured in Sony's "BMW" slogan: "Beat Matsushita Worldwide". German automaker Porsche benchmarks its product-generation skills against rivals. Toshiba tracks both the technical and the managerial accomplishments of its employees vis-a-vis competitors. Getting close to the competition is not just a goal at these companies – it's an ingrained cultural trait.

The advantage of this approach is that it dispels the myths about innovation and brings it firmly into the domain of challenges to which managers can respond. By analyzing their global and local competitors, companies can enhance their success rates.

Drive innovation from the top

Machiavelli, a management guru of his day, understood organizations' hostility to innovation. Four centuries ago he wrote:

> "It must be remembered that there is nothing more difficult to plan, more doubtful of success, nor more dangerous to manage

than the creation of a new system. For the initiator has the enmity of all who would profit by the preservation of the old institutions and merely lukewarm defenders in those who should gain by the new ones."

Innovation is not a random thing. Top management has to identify and nurture innovation and actively champion the ideas of others. Genuinely original ideas are magnets for opposition, so the CEO must be a vocal advocate of innovate strategy. At Gucci, top management gets personally involved to keep bureaucracy out of the way. Gucci's leaders put time and resources into rethinking: where to innovate, how to innovate, and what competencies are needed?

Top management involvement is key for refining ideas and concepts and for deciding optimal resource allocation. Screening ideas using such levers as top management involvement helps to prioritize ideas to be developed further. John Patterson, founder of NCR, devised more than a century ago a scheme for paying employees for their ideas, hoping to turn his company into a "hundred-headed brain."

Becoming innovative usually requires:
- a wake-up call (top management realizes there are compelling reasons to become innovative);
- an initial success (creation of an innovative idea with winning potential), and then
- a lengthy change management program to weave innovativeness into the organization.

When a CEO fails to lead this process, innovation will not take place.

Develop commercialization skills

Innovation is always a risky undertaking. External risks stem from the uncertainty of future customer needs, market developments, and competitors' modes of attack or counterattack. Internal risks stem from the introduction of new concepts, products, or processes and the major changes they might necessitate in a company's organization.

Moreover, opportunity costs may arise if a global company is late to the market with its "new" offering. Innovation efforts often fail if these risks are not managed well during the commercialization phase.

Among the questions to ask about the commercialization of innovations are:

- How valuable is the innovation?
  - Where do we create value?
  - Where can we capture value?
  - How much of the created value can be captured?
  - At what cost?
  - By when?

- How can we best position the innovation for commercial success?
  - How will we deal with remaining uncertainties?
  - How will we address potential roadblocks to commercialization?
  - What kinds of relationships should we seek with other players in the industry?

Correctly assessing commercialization risks allows a company to custom-tailor its approach to innovation. Ignoring the process is to invite failure. In fact, faulty commercialization is the reason why most unsuccessful innovations fail. Some companies wait too long, hoping for clear signals of market changes. Others underestimate how long it will take to launch new products in response to an existing competitive threat. Still others do not fully exploit different new product entry strategies. Finally, too many companies overestimate price sensitivity in launching innovative products and do not put sufficient emphasis on preparing sales channels or finding partners to open new markets.

Focus on the customer

Innovations generally follow an S-shaped curve – the innovation is taken up slowly at first by a few customers ("pioneers"), then by a rapidly increasing number of "early" and "late followers," finally by a few "laggards."

Unfortunately, pioneers often go bust before they make it to the enticing middle section of the curve, where diffusion is increasingly rapidly. Inventors are convinced that there is a market, but often the "established" market is miniscule, or even non-existent. Consider the fate of Philips, which invented and introduced the laser disc before there was an "existing" market. The "established" market was too small. For those who wish to avoid Philips' fate, timing is key. They must launch products before customers know they need them but not so far ahead that the customers are not interested.

Successful innovative companies focus efforts on improving value to the customer rather than on advancing technology. For example, Bang & Olufsen's ideas come from matching what global customers want with what the technical people can do. Other cases illustrate the same point: Innovation is based on superior understanding of customer needs.

Even so, it is often necessary to proceed in the face of initial resistance. When the first digital mixing consoles were introduced in audio studios, most suppliers of analog equipment were convinced that there would be no demand for the new equipment. Digital technology provided no real advantage in terms of traditional performance measure, like signal-to-noise ratio, phase clearness, or transparency. It took a detailed understanding of the sound studio business to make clear what the true advantage of digital consoles were: studio utilization could be doubled.

With digital, the storage and retrieval of individual sound engineers' complex individual control settings became possible. Different engineers could now work in shifts without any cost in long set-up times. In addition, new ways of shaping sound were realized and became standard. The companies, like Sony, that came out with digital equipment first, understood this very well and out-performed those, like Studer, that stuck to analog technology for too long.

Take a team approach

Lone-wolf inventors are a vanishing breed because breakthrough innovation is like a marriage between what is needed and what is possible. Bill Hewlett and Dave Packard aside, successful innovators make liberal use of project-based teams to realize cooperation across functional boundaries. The team, not a lone inventor, is "the hero." Logically, then, the environment in an innovative global company must be very interactive.

In fact, innovative companies are built on multiple high-performance teams that pursue concrete objectives. Team members are selected based on their will and skill match with the team objectives. In global companies like Nokia, teams are evaluated annually. These periodic assessments allow Nokia to continuously enhance the innovative team skills to achieve the team objectives.

In innovative companies, there is a great deal of cross-pollination, between divisions and between geographical regions. At Philips, for example, the top management team, human resource development systems, and external (academic) people networks function as key supporting mechanisms to the team approach.

Become obsessed

At the heart of innovation is a passion for testing new ideas and putting them in force. Innovative companies put their heart and soul into producing innovative products, processes, or services. At 3M, innovation is led by top management, realized through idea generation and commercialization, but motivated by passion.

While competitors have adopted some of 3M's tricks, tools, and strategies, it's hard to copy the DNA that has been percolating since the 1920s. Even today, more than one-third of 3M's sales come from products and services introduced within the past five years.

Those global companies that develop a culture of innovation can use it to maintain a competitive edge. By the time their imitators have caught up, the thing they have caught up with may no longer be the best, because the innovator has moved on again. Both Apple and Bang & Olufsen, for instance, have used continual innovation to compete against larger rivals.

Develop a passion for change

Innovative corporations are motivated by change because they recognize that it is the root of all innovation. So to ensure a continuous stream of innovation, a company has to be obsessed with change. Unfortunately, too many companies have created a change-averse environment and have yet to perceive the importance of sharpening change management skills.

In fact, most companies are dominated by a diverse array of "change-avoiding committees." A member of such a committee usually learns to use the vocabulary of the pussyfooter. "It would not be prudent at present"; "the idea is a bit premature"; "having tried that before"; and "research has shown ....." Building innovation into the global company's DNA is a long-term task that requires major organizational change.

Innovation pays

As traditional sources of competitive advantage erode, more and more global companies must either innovate or die. Innovation is a very complex undertaking, but it is manageable and not inherently random by nature. Several important lessons can be learned from the success of innovative companies.

The innovation process requires a tailored corporate strategy and dedicated execution. Companies that have clear innovation strategies (e.g. Apple, Microsoft, Starbucks, Bang & Olufsen) have found that innovation pays. In fact, innovative companies are financially more successful than others. My database shows that "pioneers" and "early followers" have a larger average return on investment than "late entrants" and "laggards".

However, my research also reveals that there is no magic bullet – no single innovation strategy that will dramatically boost the pace of major innovation. Successful innovators understand that they do not manage innovation. Instead, they oversee a portfolio of innovation strategies.

Being a winner means getting every bit of the innovation game right, not just doing one bit perfectly.

References

Clifford, D.K. and R.E. Cavanagh, "The Winning Performance", Bantam Books, New York, 1985.

Drucker, P. "Innovation and Entrepreneurship", Harper & Row, New York, 1985.

Foster, R. "Innovation. The Attacker's Advantage", Summit Books, 1986.

Hamel, G. "Reinvent Your Company", Fortune, June 12 2000.

Markides, C. "Strategic Innovation", Sloan Management Review, Spring 1997.

Quinn, J.B. "Strategies for Change – Logical Incrementalism", R.D. Irwin, New York, 1980.

Quinn, J.B. "Managing Innovation: Controlled Chaos", Harvard Business Review, May-June 1985.

Wolpert, J.D. "Breaking out of the Innovation Box", Harvard Business Review, August 2002.

9

International HRM

The Dutch Experience

The management of an internationalizing company is not seldom "mentally programmed" [1]. Management usually is highly experienced, but the question that should be put again and again is rarely put. That is the question whether management of such companies also possesses the experience suitable to face current and future international pitfalls.

Managers on the whole lack mentality, experience and skills to benefit from the increasingly difficult and quick changing international challenges. Therefore, the international environment tends to be for these managers an insoluble crossword.

This chapter will explore in more depth international HRM policies implemented by a variety of international companies based in The Netherlands. On the basis of the findings of this research study, I argue that international success is first and foremost determined by a high quality international HRM policy. At the end of the day, internationalizing begins and ends with the "skills owners", the organization's individual employees in general and its international managers more specifically.

The survey was conducted by the Nyenrode University Center for International Business. In total, 218 top executives of global Dutch companies representing different sectors were interviewed. Of these, 142 were managing directors or central management/managing board members and 76 were personnel directors, HRM managers and other company staff whose primary responsibility it is to formulate and implement international HRM policy.

The 218 staff members were active in 142 companies. The scope of the survey was a representative cross-section in both nature and composition of the Dutch economy. Respondents were employed by companies active in dominant sectors of the Dutch economy: agriculture, industry and business services [2].

"Internationalitis" virus

Internationalization can be, as part of an overall strategy, a tool to achieve a specific growth objective. Unfortunately, internationalization is often depicted as 'the' medium for growth or - worse yet - as an objective *per se*. This is perhaps due to the fact that companies, which do not grow, become extremely vulnerable in a fierce competitive environment.

"Move or perish" seems to be a company's slogan number one in today's quick changing international environment. However, internationalization should be part of a well thought out overall growth strategy. It should not be seen as the solely possibility for growth nor be the result of a copy-cat strategy derived from what competitors do.

It is true that many companies have become vulnerable due to the fact that they failed to internationalize. They simply have been unable to face the fact that in recent years competitiveness has become not only boundless but also without boundaries. In this context internationalization, for many companies, has become a necessity rather than an option shrouded in broad and flexible margins. Consequently, the subject should and fortunately has high priority in board meetings of many small, medium-size and large companies.

However, just putting it on the agenda is not enough. Internationalization should be part of a clear formulated growth strategy and learning process. Accumulating experience in managing international activities is a complex matter. Many times the mark is overstepped. This does not have to be fatal if failures become part of a learning process.

Failures are usually, for a variety of - mostly political - reasons, brushed under the carpet. The higher echelons of the researched companies rarely make the effort to learn from their international debacles. The latter are rarely mapped out systematically and constructively with the purpose of employing them in the context of excellent management development systems for young, rising talent. It is precisely in this way that the managers of today could provide the managers of tomorrow with a valuable economic commodity called a solid "sense of reality": an effective serum against international bloopers.

The double-edged blade of their international operations often cuts international companies. As a rule, building a local branch from scratch in any geographic market requires time as well as financial and management resources. Acquiring or allying with foreign companies virtually always results in clashes of national and corporate cultures leading to adverse consequences for the integration (full or partial) of the company's business processes. Internationalization consumes a vast amount of time and attention and the final outcome is always highly uncertain.

In The Netherlands, the "internationalitis" virus fells not only many small and medium size companies, larger companies too are sensitive to the idea of doing business with a global dimension and its related intangible (status-enhancing) effects.

A word of caution is required. As a rule, an international blunder will have radical impact on a company's reputation. And it is precisely that reputation, which international-going companies use as their currency. In the future, international competitiveness - also on Dutch soil - will increasingly be decided primarily by a company's intangible assets such as reputation, expertise and skills, and only secondarily by its tangible assets.

The most important question obviously is: What tool does a company primarily need to ensure international success? My answer would seem self-evident, namely a high-quality international professional and people development policy. In fact, this is a rather weakly developed feature of the global companies I examined for this research study. From the results of this study, I find that in The Netherlands there is a lack of experience of international professional and people development policy. This policy refers not just to having enough (talented) people or attending seminars and export-training courses. What I do mean by professional and people development policy will be elaborated below, by presenting a broad range of factual findings from my research study.

The unpleasant truth is that the majority of researched companies make insufficient time available for attracting, training, developing, exciting and retaining high quality employees capable of making a positive contribution to internationalization of their operations. This is an issue (the term 'challenge', I feel, is overly optimistic in this context) mainly in smaller and medium size companies.

As a rule, pressure on senior staff with international experience is so high that they simply lack time for coaching internationally active junior staff. This time is, sadly, not even available for the most talented juniors. This leads to a fatal course of events, which will ultimately result in rapidly diminishing loyalty of any internationally active junior staff. The end-result is job-hopping on an ever-increasing scale.

International business is first and foremost a people's business. Moreover, I argue that global companies focusing more on 'business' than on 'people' are turning their backs to the future. The results of my research study show that such companies are currently dominating the economic environment in The Netherlands.

Status quo of international HRM in The Netherlands

It is striking in the context of international HRM to notice that less than seven percent of positions at managing board level is held by non-Dutch nationals in the top 1000 of Dutch companies. Consequently, the typical extent of internationalization of managing boards is zero to low. This is in contrast with the fact that these companies acquired an average of 38 percent of their turnover in 1999 outside The Netherlands. I conclude from this that international HRM policy will require a drastic change at upper echelon levels. This is in alignment with the findings of my study.

Considering the intended tone of this chapter, I will focus on the following survey results, all contributing to my conclusion that a fundamental new approach to international HRM is required - especially for large (Dutch) companies.

Poor international human resources policy

To the question: "Does your company implement an explicitly international HRM policy," 65 percent answered in the affirmative and about one third in the negative. Of those managers answering in the affirmative only one quarter held that this concerned "a high-quality international HRM policy." In other words, only about one in six international companies based in The Netherlands implements a high-quality international HRM policy - a share that can only be regarded as low.

Lack of skilled managers

To the question: "Do you feel that your international managers are sufficiently qualified in terms of skills to handle the challenges they will be facing in the future?," 45 percent answered "Yes" and 55 percent "No". In other words, over half of the interviewed (top) line and HR managers feel that, in terms of skills, their international managers are insufficiently equipped for the near future.

Box 1 Key issues to be addressed with regard to international HRM

According to the interviewed managers, the following key issues (in random order) should be addressed with regard to an international HRM policy:

- To develop and retain young, international trained (candidate) managers as the (future) core of an international company.
- To develop the appropriate skills to compete successfully in global and local markets.
- To develop, and refine over time, internal and external training courses aimed at enhancing or developing international skills.

- To persuade central management of the importance and necessity of commitment for international HRM.
- To align international HRM objectives (functional objectives) with strategic objectives (company objectives): international HRM objectives should always be part of an overall/generic company strategy.

Insufficient training

To the question: "Do you invest adequately in off-the-job training for international managers?", 37 percent answered "Yes" and 63 percent answered "No". Consequently, close to two thirds of the interviewed managers are of the opinion that insufficient investment is made in training for international management.

Insufficient focus on developing, expanding and/or redefining skills

To the question: "Is your company (focused on) consciously working on expanding and/or refining the skills required for international management positions?", 22 percent of sampled management answered "Yes" and over three-quarters answered "No".

Misdirected focus of international HRM policy

The majority of all communication between a company's head office and any given international manager relates to local adaptation issues of the international manager. The researched companies attempt as much as possible to resolve problems on site, thus providing the impression of an organization attempting to deal with the consequences of non-optimum preparation rather than implementing a professional approach towards the cause (sub-optimum preparation).

Ergo, the researched companies in The Netherlands fail to prepare sufficiently when doing business with an international dimension. The preparation phase is usually quite short - the proverbial crash course still being a prominent feature - or skipped altogether. In itself, this makes sense. After all, more often than not companies have to respond to sudden commercial opportunities. They simply underestimate the associated requirements to provide adequate, let alone accurate, attention to managers responsible for successfully handling international challenges.

National HRM policy dominates *international* HRM policy

In terms of attention afforded, talented employees with international ambitions are subordinate to talented young employees with national ambitions. HR departments of any of the researched companies provide more intensive coaching to managers with a national focus than they do to managers with international responsibilities. This finding gives reason to worry about the success of the internationalization efforts within the researched companies.

Another remarkable finding indicated that also, in the near future, managers with a national focus would probably receive more coaching than international managers. Needless to say this is remarkable, as many of them are active on the global market and there is a strong tendency to increase these activities.

The conclusion that can be drawn from this is that coaching of managers is primarily focused on national oriented managers located in the parent country, The Netherlands.

Management skills are frequently generalized

Dutch HR managers often work with blueprints of HRM policies. This makes sense, as standardization is sometimes necessary. However, for international managers this is virtually impossible. International managers operate in very specific circumstances and not one country resembles the next; even in the European Union, for example, differences between national cultures of countries are extensive. By applying standardized tracking, assessment and reward methods, international managers inaccurately receive a standard label.

Basically, an international manager's functioning cannot be standardized. Therefore, companies operating on the international market need to apply a highly individualized approach to international HRM, especially where it concerns coaching and developing of international managers.

Box 2 Qualities of an international manager

In the survey population's opinion, the prime qualities of an international manager - in descending order - are:

1. Mental flexibility: be open to local cultural and other influences (legislation, work habits, work ethic, and so on).
2. Convincing commitment to company objectives without such detracting from effective realization of local objectives. Loyalty will lie, when push comes to shove (in the event of potential conflict of interests), at all times with the parent company and not with the local activity.
3. Perseverance (specifically in situations requiring much adaptation).
4. Strongly developed empathic qualities when dealing with a great variety of stakeholders (both local and inside the parent country/at head office).
5. Superior substantive (functional) and human (relational) skills and the willingness to continuously upgrade them.

Many regular external training institutes neglect to address the preparation phase of international managers

A considerable responsibility lies with the external training institutes. This applies to the Dutch MBO (i.e. Advanced Education), HBO (i.e. Higher Education) and Universities. It is in these institutes, after all, that the preparation of international managers starts - not at the company gate or in-house.

Potential international managers must be educated in the profession, because international business is and will always be a matter of expertise. Doing business in an international context is an aggregate of "daring", "doing" and "thinking". A great many external training institutes are insufficiently equipped to meet this need. Most training courses do not come close to matching the actual (often quite specific) needs of individual international managers. The level of external training courses in The Netherlands is frequently dubious.

According to the interviewed managers, The Netherlands has been clearly remiss in this respect. Most of the talented (candidate) international managers are sent by their companies to attend renowned international management institutes (i.e. Insead, IMD, London Business School, and so on). The genuine international talent is being trained not in The Netherlands but abroad.

International mobility among young Dutch managers is declining rapidly

In recent years, it has become increasingly difficult to acquire extra international manpower. Many young managers have their reservations about an international career. The home situation (often double income) throws a long shadow, affecting the decision of young talented people whether or not to make their way in an international career.

According to the interviewed managers, the favourable economy in The Netherlands at the time also played a significant role. Why go far to earn an income when the local streets are paved with gold? For this very reason, promoting international mobility among managers requires systematic attention to implementing a high quality international career development policy. In this respect, many of the interviewed managers were still on a quest for the Holy Grail.

Exact benefits created by expatriates are seldom identified. Expatriates are expensive, but add to control from the corporate center over the company's internationally dispersed activities: they are the proverbial "extended arm" of the corporate center. Continuously rotating such employees is one way of reinforcing the (corporate) identity of a global company. This also allows the company's organizational culture to be more or less imposed and institutionalized in the various countries. This may result in enhancing the breeding ground for international synergies.

Box 3 Selection criteria

The following criteria - in descending order - are used by HR managers (supporting staff) or line managers (directors/managing board members) to select employees for international positions:

1. Functional skills (based on content).
2. Relational competencies (including linguistic skills).
3. Step/activity/phase as part of the Management Development of the manager in question.
4. Expertise with regard to market, buyers and other stakeholders.
5. Expertise regarding the parent company (more specific its systems, processes and procedures).

Too many internationally oriented companies have yet to become learning organizations

A prime condition for a company's global success is to grow into a "learning company". There must be a willingness to learn continuously, beyond national and industry boundaries, and there must be a capacity and a willingness to apply lessons learnt throughout the company.

A global climate of learning implies a free exchange of lessons learnt. This will bring about a more intensive and high quality dialogue among the various managers from around the world. Moreover, there will be no need to re-invent the wheel locally all over the world.

Managers who can deal with global issues need many qualities, e.g., high degree of empathy, receptive to other cultures, open to change, linguistic skills, knowledgeable of specific international market segments and industries, a talent to establish and function in partnerships, and - possibly most important - extreme physical and mental endurance. This last aspect, especially, is often overlooked. On the global market rises are rapid and drops are perhaps even more rapid.

Box 4 Barriers to international HRM

According to the survey results, I identify the following, in descending order, as threats to a high-quality international HRM policy:

1. The spouse/partner objects because of own career or preference for a different (more stable) life. As a result, too few (potentially attractive) managers aspire to an international career.
2. Talented managers are at an increasing distance from the center of power (they are both geographically and "psychologically" far from the decision-making center – the head office). Talented managers abroad may, therefore, feel "side tracked".

3. The financial impact is major: having individuals gain international experience costs the company a great deal of time and funds (in other words, human capital loses out to financial capital).
4. It is often a difficult process to fit returning expatriate managers into a company's structure and corporate culture again. Many companies are anxious about this other side of the international HRM coin. Many talented international managers proved to be incapable after prolonged secondment abroad of settling down in the parent country. Ergo, sub-optimum management behavior during a significant portion of the remaining career.
5. The added value of the international manager is impossible to rate directly: the infamous "rating syndrome" of HR managers. It proves virtually impossible to make cost/benefit analyses. Seconding international managers abroad is therefore difficult to objectify and thus difficult to justify.
6. There is insufficient commitment from companies' central management for international HRM projects (a "company mentality" issue).

From the above is clear that the present course of events in international HRM is food for serious thought. The survey results warrant the conclusion that the researched companies in The Netherlands must invest much more in their own international human capital.

This means attracting (recruitment and selection), training, developing, (on-the-job training), exciting (offering challenging career development tracks) and retaining (final result of the four preceding activities) of international managers. This should be done in the knowledge that to deploy managers in a variety of geographic locations is not a sinecure.

An alternative

The results of the survey lead to the question "What are the success factors of an effective international HRM policy?"

I elaborate on the following issues that play a key role in developing a successful international HRM policy, as a prerequisite for the success of an internationalization process:

Awareness of the importance of international HRM

Successful international HRM policies of global companies start with the awareness at central management level that HRM is the cork that keeps them afloat. This would seem self-evident. The results of the survey, however, suggest otherwise. According to many top managers - especially HR managers - there is still a big gap between ornamental narrative and sorely needed action. Line management (i.e. managing boards) and support staff (HR management) prove to communicate poorly on aspects of international HRM. International HRM is and continues to be a relatively isolated staff activity.

Alignment of international HRM and strategic objectives

A second condition for a successful international HRM policy is to realize an explicit link between international HRM objectives and strategic (company-wide) objectives. International HRM objectives must always be embedded in the company-wide objectives, i.e. be part of a company's overall strategy. International HRM objectives were, according to the interviewed managers, often "stand-alone" objectives rather than "interlinked" objectives (interlinked with the strategic company-wide objectives).

Sufficient, adequate and high-quality tools for gaining expertise and experience

A third prime success factor aims at realizing an adequate mix of off-the-job and on-the-job training courses, so that sufficient expertise and experience can be gained to face international challenges successfully. Many companies lack awareness in terms of the impact international HRM has on their global operations. As a result, many companies lack the breeding ground required to make cross-border activities a success.

An intangible critical success factor is the proper mentality generated from the awareness that international HRM is of crucial importance not only to the company's long-term continuity but also its short-term profitability. In this respect, the researched companies in The Netherlands still have a long way to go.

Another striking finding is that in-house training programs are too few and lack a proper level of quality. Most of the researched companies have outsourced training courses directed to enhance international business skills of managers.

Basically, implementing a successful international HRM policy comes down to providing a selection of tools to the international employees, allowing them to focus on gaining expertise of and experience in a variety of international issues. This would typically be a mix of training courses conducted by the company and by external institutes, in addition to planned rotation of international employees around the globe to serve in different countries facing different macro- and meso-economic challenges.

The future

International companies should aim for a planned international HRM policy rather than - as is frequently the case - implement the prevalent policy of ad-hoc decisions.

Companies operating in an international economic environment should realize that by implementing a successful international HRM policy they benefit from substantial economies associated with exchanging (multi-deployed) skills gained by employees in various countries. International companies implementing a successful HRM policy specifically seek these economies of skills in a three-pronged approach:

- *First, flatten the organizational structure.* What is to be achieved is an exchange of expertise and experience among various internationally dispersed groups/divisions/units of the company. This exchange of experiences and information will be faster and more convenient in a flat organization.

- *Second, facilitate the exchange of information and experiences through high-quality systems and processes.* In this context, I do not refer to IT architecture alone, but also to the company's performance and remuneration systems. This exchange of information must be encouraged. Ultimately, it should be mirrored in the pay cheque of employees (answering the question: what is in it for them?)

- *Third, create a mentality of continuous learning within the company.* The degree to which economies of skills will be realized is largely determined by the willingness to learn from one another and exchange local and international experiences.

The phenomenon of economies of skills manifests itself particularly via mutually dependant and, more important, mutually committed organizational units and individual managers exchanging - first and foremost - information about (potential) customers, products, processes, technological and market developments.

The difficulty of attempting economies of skills is that many international employees are required to undergo a mental somersault. Companies will need to think much more actively about developing the global company and about cross-pollination opportunities. This is hard, because day-in day-out international employees and managers are focused on the "external" environment (customers, competition, suppliers, and so on) rather than on the "internal" environment (other groups/divisions/units including their colleagues). For most of them, keeping the focus of attention solely on the external environment is self-evident; because that is where "the moment of truth" will be, that is where the sales and the margins are generated. In doing so, we tend to overlook that a global company has both external and internal customers. This is a matter of communicating vessels. Internal customer focus will encourage external customer focus.

Extremely important is the ability to think global. Employees need to be good "mental travellers" and should possess "global sense". This refers to having a grasp of global economy issues and being able to translate consequences into the impact on a specific company and it's industry, as well as its competition and customers.

International managers must be able to "think global and act local" [3]. This may be difficult to accomplish, as most managers are locked inside their nationalistic boxes. To think global in an international company is extremely important, because it facilitates free exchange of people, resources and information. But, frequently, it is extremely difficult to introduce global thinking (often referred to as a "global mindset") into companies unused to it.

Resolving international HRM issues is, according to many managers, not simply a sufficient but rather a mandatory condition for achieving global success. There is now, virtually without exception, increasing awareness of this need. For good reason, managing directors are increasingly engaged in HRM aspects. A company that is incapable of internationalizing its HRM policy is also incapable of internationalizing business activities such as production, marketing, finance, and so on. This growing awareness has been a constant feature of this survey.

The researched companies are, furthermore, increasingly of the opinion that what determines a person's international management role is based on competencies and skills rather than on his/her passport. This, also, may be regarded as a positive development in international HRM. It proves to be a slow but quite definitely evolutionary process. For now, a corporate center of a Dutch multinational company staffed with a variety of nationalities is a thing of the future.

In the course of this survey I have come to conclude that (candidate) international managers should be provided with tools allowing them to gain expertise and experience in a variety of international issues and circumstances. However, international managers cannot simply be made. Much of their make-up, after all, concerns individual character traits such as curiosity, boldness and mental flexibility.

An international manager must, first and foremost, be capable of making the somersaults. Many (candidate) managers lack that capability, and their employers are unwise to invest in them. From my research, it appears that quite a few HR managers are actually still convinced that international managers can be made, without giving attention to the individual character traits as a prerequisite for any training or education program.

In the future, speed and not size will be decisive for competing successfully in a global market. Large will not be eliminating small, or vice versa. Rather, fast will be eliminating slow. It is for precisely this reason that smaller companies - frequently faster movers – will potentially benefit from geographically expanding their operations, embarking on high-risk, cross-border business. I am quite prepared to posit here that those unwilling to take risks internationally will be running high risks on today's highly competitive global market. And, this has clear implications for the competencies and skills of a company's executives, managers and employees.

References

[1] G. Hofstede, "Cultures Consequences", Sage, London, 1980.

[2] Interviews took approximately 90 minutes. A semi-structured format used some 15 questions as the basis of its substance and procedure. This provided participants ample opportunity for discussion, and resulted in extensive exploration of the relevant issues. All interviews were taped, allowing their interpretation to be made subsequently.

[3] Late Akio Morita, co-founder and former CEO of Sony, introduced in the 1950s the slogan "Think global, act local". Also see: A. Morita, "Made in Japan", E.P. Dutton, New York,1986.

10

Competing with Pirates

The liberalization of air services provided a significant boost to the development of no-frills airlines. America's best known no-frills airline is called Southwest Airlines. Southwest Airlines is an American icon. The Dallas based company is one of those responsible for the fact that the American and world-wide aviation industry looks completely different now.

The success of Southwest Airlines is based on a very simple principle: transporting passengers over relatively short distances at very competitive airline rates. The traditional high-cost airlines in America and Europe alike cannot compete with that. They risk losing much of the intra-American and intra-European connecting traffic that feeds into their lucrative long-haul networks.

The low-cost strategy of carriers such as Southwest Airlines has a solid basis. Southwest does not concern itself with meals, in-flight films, design chairs, and various classes (and the corresponding options). All frills have been removed from the value proposition. It is also striking that Southwest Airlines does not make use of the hub-and-spoke system so highly praised by other airlines. Instead, Southwest uses the point-to-point flight concept, offering rates that are at least 60 percent cheaper than those of the direct competition.

Southwest uses plastic boarding passes (re-usable) and ever since its foundation has looked for secondary airports in smaller cities and less congested airports in major cities (or in the vicinity of major cities). On top of that, a Southwest Airlines plane is, on average, only idle for 20 minutes at any airport compared to the average of 45 minutes for the traditional airlines. Last, but surely not least, the Southwest Airlines fleet consists of Boeing 737 airplanes (only one type of airplane) and therefore the company benefits from economies of scale, scope and skills.

This is the pioneering recipe of the most successful airline since the Second World War. It is this simple concept of a short-haul carrier that inspired the development of other discounters world-wide and thereby imperilling the existing giants.

The Southwest Airlines success really began to stand out in the late 1980s. Whereas the major American colleagues such as American Airlines, United Airlines and Delta Airlines are losing billions of dollars, Southwest Airlines performs well in terms of relative and absolute figures. Southwest Airlines remained profitable throughout the Gulf crisis, a unique feat in the highly competitive aviation industry. And all this with a very modern fleet (average age seven years) – not with a fleet of dumped leftovers.

With its competitive behavior, Southwest Airlines creates a completely new market sector within the aviation industry and is, therefore, a "first mover player". It has cashed in on the corresponding advantage for many consecutive years. Ever since its foundation (in 1971), Southwest Airlines has refused to compete directly with colleagues for market share and margin, but opted deliberately for the development of a completely new market sector. They choose to stimulate new demand, rather than to take shares from major carriers. Not market penetration, but market development [1].

L'histoire se répète

It took some time for the first low-cost airlines to appear in Europe. In itself this is remarkable, because a lot of regional commuters have been active in Europe from time immemorial. But the regional airlines in Europe have been nothing but smaller versions of their major counterparts for quite some time. In essence, they make use of the same business model as the "national flag carriers" and that does not enable them to distinguish themselves in the game of move and countermove.

European flag carriers, in general, and KLM and British Airways (BA), in particular, encountered quite a lot of problems in the early 1990s with the rise of British Midland. British Midland, founded by Sir Michael Bishop, initially profited from less bureaucracy which manifests itself in a lower cost structure. British Midland lets the traveller share in the lower costs – the tickets become cheaper. Its competitors were consequently forced, after some time, to reduce their prices too.

The appearance of British Midland makes it increasingly clear that the flag carriers will have to concentrate more and more on the long-haul routes. Smaller no-frills airlines focus on the shorter routes. British Midland was the first to jump into that gap, followed by companies such as Ryanair, Virgin Express and EasyJet.

The changing institutional environment is an important reason for the rapid expansion of no-frills air travel in Europe. All mutual air routes between the European Community countries were liberalized as from January 1st,

1993. From that time onwards, a level playing field was created for no-frills airlines. The airline rates are no longer embedded in all kinds of "bilateral" agreements reeking of monopoly between national carriers. Nothing much happened in Europe initially, particularly because the early 1990s were difficult years for nearly all airlines. The years before and after the Gulf War did not provide fertile soil for no-frills airlines.

The first company to introduce discount flying on the European continent was EuroBelgian Airlines Express (EBA Express) operating from Brussels. EBA Express is owned by the City Hotels hotel chain. Passengers can fly from Brussels to Vienna, Barcelona and Rome (and back) for about 150 Euros. EBA copied Southwest Airlines' strategy. Speed and punctuality are the value propositions created by EBA. They only fly one class, serve the passengers with half the staff and only provide one non-alcoholic drink per passenger during the flight.

Several Southwest Airlines clones started to appear after some time in Europe. Ryanair and EasyJet set the ball rolling, followed by the cheap subsidiaries of flag carriers such as Lufthansa, Alitalia, BA and KLM. As a rule, the Southwest Airlines business model is copied: one type of airplane, no meals or basic meals, no papers; drinks, however, are available, but not for free, no business lounges, booking is simple via the Internet and paper tickets are issued rarely or never.

Richard Branson, owner of the Virgin Group and Virgin Atlantic Airways, is yet another example of a business man who, halfway through 1995, fell under the spell of the possibilities low-cost airlines had to offer. The continuing liberalization is the last push he too needed.

Once again, Branson's timing is excellent. Branson became active in the no-frills market sector in 1996. In April of the same year he took over EBA Express for $57.3 million. It has 12 Boeing 737s and in 1995 the company transported 1.3 million passengers. Virgin Express, the new name of the low-cost company, copies the Southwest Airlines business model, exactly the way Ryanair and EasyJet do. It focuses on point-to-point flying: flying from A to B without transfers.

Expectations cage

Hub-and-spoke companies such as KLM, BA and Lufthansa have struggled a long time with the business model used by Southwest Airlines, EasyJet and Ryanair. It is certainly not easy for the flag carriers to combine two completely different business models. The point-to-point system, in particular, is hard to combine with the hub-and-spoke system.

A lot of traditional companies have tried over the last five to ten years to bring both business models under one umbrella. It is hard to chart true success stories. Nevertheless, the urge to link these business models is strong. This primarily has to do with the financial success of the low-cost companies.

Traditional airlines such as United Airlines, number two on the list of the major airlines in the world, still threatened to go under a little while ago. The reason being, among other things, the arrival and the aggressive growth of the low-cost companies. Stephen Wolf, former CEO of United Airlines, feels that Southwest Airlines was responsible, to a great extent, for the problems United Airlines had to face, especially from the early 1990s onwards [2].

When it became clear that the disciples of Southwest Airlines were not exactly nine-day wonders, the establishment decided to start up its own no-frills companies as a part of its own business operations. As from that moment, they also started to take participating interests in airlines operating on a regional basis.

By the mid-1990s British Airways had participating interests in Deutsche BA and TAT and had founded CityFlyer Express for the same reason. KLM tried initially, from the mid-1990s, to join the battle with the no-frills companies via Air UK and its participating interests in Transavia and Martinair. It nevertheless became clear that the existing "traditional" regional companies did not show the required fighter mentality. The creation of KLM's Buzz and British Airways GO is an indication to that effect. Neither company proved to be a decisive success.

The no-frills companies make an important contribution to the dynamics of the competitive struggle. Competition with the major giants is not direct but indirect. This has proven to be an interesting competitive strategy. Lower rates have resulted in increased transport flows. The Southwest Airlines strategy proved this. Low prices have a "pull effect".

Major companies are moreover forced to re-examine their provision of services and to start up or buy up low-cost companies. Various studies conducted by, among others, Dutch market research leader NIPO and the independent Dutch magazine, *Zakenreis*, have shown that service becomes increasingly less important and that efficiency, precision and punctuality take the upper hand.

The hub-and-spoke model, which is so time-consuming for the passenger, is also increasingly coming under fire. The transfer system offers passengers many alternatives (no matter how crazy your idea, there will always be a traditional airline that can get you where you want to go), but it also costs the passenger a bundle (including the enhanced risk of delays).

The rise of the no-frills companies has led to a lot of flag carriers outsourcing or selling their arrival routes. After hiving off catering, maintenance and hotels, the flag carriers are increasingly reverting to their real core business: offering mobility over long distances. These routes create the economies necessary to afford the expensive sales, organization and marketing apparatus.

The strength of the no-frills airlines is also their weakness: the focus is on a very specific value proposition and a business model meticulously constructed around it. The high degree of focus and the distinctive character of the no-frills companies has contributed to the fact that it is very hard to copy the business model. The experience of the last 30 years has taught us that no traditional airline ("flag carrier") has succeeded in imitating Southwest Airlines. The Southwest Airlines business model may be simple in theory, but it is strikingly difficult to clone in practice.

The lack of flexibility is the other side of the Southwest Airlines business model cum suis [3]. The strategic flexibility for instance, is low. It is difficult to switch from a point-to-point business model to a hub-and-spoke business model. In addition, no-frills companies often have an outspoken corporate culture. The fact that they compete with the establishment creates a tremendous sense of cohesion. That makes them inflexible from a cultural point of view. Taking over other airlines that are, for instance, responsible for (expensive) long-haul flights is a tricky business for a low-cost company and, therefore, not to be advised.

Low costs can make or break the business model of Southwest Airlines, Ryanair and EasyJet: If the cost advantages in comparison with the traditional players were to disappear, the low-cost companies would be left penniless and then things would look grim for them. Experience shows that, after a certain time, costs rarely continue to drop, but rather tend to rise.

There are limits to low costs: In time, planes have to be renewed, employees grow older (and, therefore, more expensive), and the mutual atmosphere (i.e. culture) is often put under pressure as the companies grow (with the consequent impact on productivity), cheap airports tend to increase prices in time, almost without exception, and rising kerosene prices often hit the low-cost companies harder than the traditional flag carriers (which use more efficient, younger planes). However, the sustainability of the competitive edge of low-cost companies remains remarkable.

Traditional companies such as BA, Air France, and KLM are imprisoned in the "expectations cage". Passengers have high expectations with respect to the service on board of a flag carrier. If passengers can no longer enjoy a hot meal and read a national or an international newspaper, many would give up.

In the meantime, the price breakers continue their steady advance. It appears that increasing numbers of business people make use of their services. Businessmen are left in peace and quiet on short-haul flights – a modern "first class" treatment, in fact. The parade of meals and drinks does not materialize. Flying without frills has thus touched all layers of the social fabric [4].

Business model strategy

Initially, the low-cost companies did not compete with the traditional airlines. They restricted their efforts only to creating a demand where it did not yet exist: market development instead of market penetration.

This is an important recommendation for low-cost start-ups: competing with low costs is not suicidal provided you expand (develop) the market as a start-up. Direct competition with existing parties for existing customers (market penetration) with a low-cost strategy is generally doomed to failure. The triangle "market penetration – low costs – start-up" rarely results in success.

In mid 2003, the low-cost airlines in Europe had a market share of about 10 percent, but their market share has been growing fast since then. According to the figures of the trade journal, *Airline Business*, there is still room to manoeuvre in the United States, too, where the low-cost companies are now firmly established (the low-cost companies had a market share of about 28 percent in the United States in mid 2004).

It would be interesting to find out whether the business model of the low-cost airlines could be stretched. Can low-cost airlines also be successful in bridging long(er) distances? Not long ago, Southwest Airlines went down this road. Southwest shows that the business model also works for somewhat longer distances, although the results are less spectacular than on short distances. Certain additional costs have to be incurred for longer distances. Consider, for instance, the costs related to catering, higher maintenance (due to the longer-haul flights), cleaning activities (requiring more time and, therefore, more costly), which prevent the plane from taking off within 20 minutes. It is also increasingly important to offer passengers comfort on longer flights (good seats and more leg room).

What have the traditional carriers done so far to reduce the threat posed by the low-cost companies? Firstly, they have tried to perfect their own hub-and-spoke system via all kinds of alliances. Such alliances allowed them to compete directly with other high-cost companies by simply forcing a direct competitor out of the market through a cooperation agreement. Flights and services under each other's flag are offered via such constructions and via intricate and dense hub-and-spoke networks.

The alliance strategy has had little impact on the cost side of the margin and that is exactly the domain where the no-frills companies reign supreme [5]. Today, traditional flag carriers are still not able to offer the same low-cost service at the same low price with the same margin as the low-cost companies.

It is pretty hard for the traditional carriers to ignore the low-cost airlines, which primarily fly short distances, because the latter in particular foul up the "feeder function" of their hub-and-spoke system. For their intercontinental flights, the traditional companies depend on the supply of passengers who often have to be flown in from everywhere and, therefore, have to be flown to a central hub. Each traditional airline needs a critical mass of passengers to turn the intercontinental flights – and consequently their complete business operations – into a success. A properly functioning "feeder function" is imperative.

It is, however, difficult for a flag carrier to compete directly with a low-cost airline on these short distances, because their cost structure is inherently less favorable. In addition to the above, the anti-trust authorities are really alerted when a major traditional player suddenly starts selling tickets below cost price (i.e. "predatory pricing"). Some time ago, the European Commission left no doubt that predatory pricing will never be approved by the anti-trust authorities.

The financial outlook for the flag carriers is rather bleak. How will traditional carriers compete in the future with such low-cost carriers?

The first question they have to ask themselves is: what exactly is the key to the success of the low-cost airlines? On first sight, the answer to this question seems self-evident: their low costs. But what lies at the basis of those low costs? Low-cost companies enjoy a number of cost advantages over their traditional competitors:

- *First of all, the business model is cheaper.* The value proposition is geared towards offering one core product: offering punctual flights from A to B without transfer. All frills have been removed. Such a philosophy simplifies process management. Internal business processes are a lot simpler and, therefore, easier to manage. In addition, it takes fewer hands to bring simpler processes to a favourable conclusion.

- *Low-cost companies employ cheaper employees and consequently incur lower labour costs - an important cost factor in the aviation industry.* Flag carriers have suffered from their employees' high wages and powerful unions. A pilot working for a low-cost company often only makes half or two thirds of the salary his colleague flying for a traditional carrier earns. The ground personnel and the other flight crew members make considerably less than their colleagues working for traditional hub-and-spoke companies. Some low-cost airlines manage to push up labour productivity to high levels despite the lower wages. In spite of a relatively low average income, the average Southwest employee shows a considerably higher level of productivity than his colleague working for any major traditional airline [6]. In addition, a lot of low-cost airlines still use second hand planes and outsource many activities to cheap suppliers.

- *Low-cost airlines offer an 'empty' product: the flight.* All extras have to be paid for. Some low-cost airlines deviate from this philosophy to a certain extent, but in essence the philosophy is to "annoy" the passenger as little as possible with services and products. If any food or drink is offered at all, then preferably cold and not fresh snacks, because warm meals and fresh products have to be used on the same day. Business Class and First Class are irrelevant, because they are not a product the passenger flying with a low-cost company wants. In addition, the above classes also take up a lot of extra seat space. For that very reason, the low-cost airlines often offer many more seats per plane.

- *A last major cost saving factor is the refusal to participate in different kinds of computerized booking systems.* As a rule, passengers buy their tickets directly from the low-cost companies (over the phone or via the Internet) and therefore bypass expensive intermediaries. Ergo: lower costs.

The fact that low-cost airlines are constantly seeking ways to reduce their operational costs contributes to their strong position in terms of cost. Thinking in terms of and working with, low costs is a "way of business life" and, therefore, an integral part of the business culture.

Strategies for traditional players

What are the strategies available to traditional carriers to play the competitive game with the low-cost companies?

- *A first alternative for traditional carriers would be the "cloning strategy".* However, experience shows that the traditional players have a lot of difficulty in making a low-cost business model profitable. The "multibusiness corporation" concept – running several different businesses grafted onto different business models, alongside each other – has not yet been properly introduced in the aviation industry [7].

- *A second strategy traditional carriers could deploy is cooperation instead of competition between the low-cost and the flag carrier.* The low-cost company would then primarily take on the feeder function and the transport of the price-conscious passenger, whereas the flag carrier would concern itself with long distances. In this scenario, the flag carrier would have a guaranteed cheap and reliable feeder function, whereas the low-cost carrier can count on a definite number of passengers and facilities (to be agreed upon properly after mutual consultation). The disadvantage of such an alliance concept is that the passenger must not have any objections to different service levels (no service whatsoever versus proper service). Furthermore, the flight schedules would have to be coordinated meticulously. Both parties would also have to act according to the letter of the agreement and not be forced, over time, to launch into the operations of the colleague-partner [8].

- *A third strategy the traditional carriers could turn to is to get a grip on the slots and the gate capacity of minor airports.* In other words, the traditional carriers could make their networks denser and fly from a greater number of primary and secondary airports to several destinations. The low-cost companies would no longer have access to an important source of their competitive edge (cheap secondary airports) and the passenger would have a choice of several destinations at the same time [9].

- *A fourth strategy consists of taking over low-cost airlines.* Again, this entails a few unavoidable risks. To start with, the anti-trust authorities would have to agree to such a strategy. Secondly, both parties would have to be able to link up, both in terms of infrastructure (IT/IS, route networks, and so on) and culture.

237

- *Strengthening and (re)building the core business is the fifth possible strategy for the traditional carriers* [10]. Their branding, in terms of safety, comfort on long-haul flights, and the possibilities of flight connections is still worth a lot to business and other travellers interested in some of the frills making life on-board more comfortable and exciting.

- *An "obvious" strategy is to treat the customer as a king.* All too often, today, passengers still have to be grateful for being "allowed to fly with a flag carrier." This requires a change of mentality. Only the rare flag carrier – e.g. Singapore Airlines – knows how to offer its passengers the necessary high-quality services and overall service. Pampering passengers is a serious trade.

The future

The key to a future sustainable competitive edge – and the sweet fruits to be reaped afterwards – is optimizing the relationship with the customer.

It is a true relief to fly with the no-frills companies because they do exactly what the customer expects them to do: no hustle, check in and go. If the flag carriers fail to please the customers the end will come fast. That means that they have to show a real interest in the customer and his/her needs and wishes. Making up lost ground turns out to be a pretty difficult task in practice.

References

[1] For an elaboration of this strategy see: B.J. Nalebuff and A.M. Brandenburger, "Co-opetition", Doubleday, New York, 1996.

[2] In Fortune (August 22nd, 1994), Wolf observes that the $ 1 billion dollar UAL lost in 1992 would have been a profit of $ 700 million had it not been for the competitor from Texas.

[3] See for an excellent discussion of the subject 'flexibility ': H.W. Volberda, "Building the Flexible Firm. How to Remain Competitive", Oxford University Press, Oxford, 1998.

[4] The influential Dutch magazine *Zakenreis* (issue 930; January / February 2001) wrote some time ago that more than half of all Virgin Express passengers are business travellers.

[5] For a detailed discussion see: P.K. Jagersma, "Global Strategy", Inspiration Press, Brussels, 2000.

[6] Fortune, "Is Herb Kelleher America 's Best CEO? ", May 2nd, 1994.

[7] See: P.K. Jagersma [ed.], "Multibusiness Corporations ", Inspiration Press, Brussels, 2001.

[8] See: P.K. Jagersma, "Global Strategy", Inspiration Press, Brussels, 2000.

[9] See: "Alliance Management: The KLM/Alitalia Case", Chapter 14.

[10] See also: C. Zook and J. Allen, "Profit from the Core: Growth Strategy in an Era of Turbulence", Harvard Business School Press, Boston, 2000.

11

Strategic Marketing and the Global Banking Industry – Elements of Excellence

It is not news to even the most casual observer of the financial services industry that these are challenging times for financial institutions. The pace of change and the growing complexity around are breathtaking. The information technology revolution, globalization, increasing buying sophistication and significant demographic changes are driving forces behind these changes.

For CEOs, the implications are far-reaching: an exponential growth in information availability and use, new parts of the globe opening up, rapidly fragmenting demand, a proliferation of sales channels, shortened product, project and process life cycles, and intensified, often price-based competition.

These trends are all the more challenging because many banks are emerging from a period dominated by cost-cutting, downsizing or delayering. In other words: after a prolonged period of internal focus, banks must again concentrate on external issues, and put strategic marketing at the top of their agenda. In this chapter, I will touch on the following issues:

- the four development stages of strategic business marketing;
- excellence in strategic business marketing;
- the methodology and the main results of a survey conducted among global banks, and
- the banking industry's strategic marketing challenge.

The four development stages of strategic business marketing

Strategic business marketing (also known as strategic industrial marketing or strategic business-to-business marketing) is the strategic marketing of products and/or services for transformation or "consumption" by businesses.

Strategic business marketing has developed over time. We can identify four main eras of strategic business marketing [1]:

- the sales era (from World War II through the 1950s);
- the product/service era (the 1960s until the late 1970s);
- the customer era (the early 1980s until the mid-1990s); and
- the needs-driven era (starting in the mid-1990s).

Each era has different driving forces, requires different key strategic marketing skills and is characterized by different strategic marketing hallmarks.

Sales era

The sales era was a time of booming primary demand: the industrial base expanded rapidly and companies like IBM set the standards for the sales function that we still apply today.

It also witnessed the development of the now traditional four Ps of the marketing mix - Price, Product, Promotion and Place.

The four Ps framework had several advantages. It was easy to apply, served as a powerful communication tool, and was an effective instrument for solving marketing-related problems. In those days, the four Ps framework was first and foremost a consumer marketing tool. Strategic business marketing at that time was in essence synonymous with knowing "how to win friends and influence decision makers". When strategic business marketers used the four Ps model, they generally focused on the two core Ps, i.e. Pricing and Product.

Product/service era

As the level of (mainly domestic) competition increased in the 1960s and 1970s, new strategy tools were needed. Brand marketing came into fashion. Executives were generally 'product champions' who knew a great deal about the products they sold.

P for Packaging became increasingly important in this era, especially for industrial and retail companies. In financial services, packaging stands for adding value beyond the basic product by providing certain additional services. Differentiation became a way to deal with the fragmentation of markets and their segments.

Customer era

The growing importance of market research was the most prominent feature of the next era, the 'customer era'. Market research became an important competitive medium as customer markets became increasingly fragmented and growth in primary demand slowed, resulting in a more competitive playing field.

Knowledge about the 'Position' of a company in its own industry, and about the relationship between it and its customers, became an important strategic asset. Companies used competitive analyses to determine their market position vis-à-vis their competitors, and market analyses to establish their position vis-à-vis their existing and prospective customers. 'Strategic marketing' became an important topic: understanding and responding to customer buying behavior using such strategies as segmentation.

Needs-driven era

The last era, the 'needs-driven era', has only just started and is marked by an often flat primary demand, rising customer sophistication, cut-throat competition, an explosive growth in the amount of information available and used, and an increasing number of strategic alliances and acquisitions, some of them across borders.

The essence of strategic business marketing in this environment today consists of creating and developing new (often global) markets and/or businesses, sometimes with strategic partners. The main components of this process include:
• identifying unfulfilled customer needs;
• being proactive in pricing and product development strategies; and
• managing (strategic) information efficiently and effectively.

The people working for the companies in question are responsible for the breadth, depth and quality of customer relationships. This adds two more Ps to the six Ps of the third era: Partners and People.

Elements of excellence

Era four-type companies in the banking industry, such as Citigroup and ABN AMRO, provide us with best-practice examples in the field of strategic marketing skills. In essence, front-runners like these know how to add and maximize value. Their focus is not only on getting the aforementioned basics (the eight Ps) right, but also on the attributes that drive customer choice, knowing how to limit costs and how to innovate extensively:

- *Best-practice strategic marketing specialists are dyed-in-the-wool customer marketers.* They have an intimate knowledge of the attributes that drive customer choice and they induce changes to affect the customer's choice. For example, they promote product messages as well as relevant corporate messages in a highly targeted manner.

  They have strong pricing skills and know how to manage these skills, both strategically (controlling price levels, setting value-based prices) and tactically (offering discounts) [2]. Best-practice strategic marketers determine which customers or prospective customers are attractive, when and why. Then they choose which ones to serve, and vary the mix as circumstances change.

- *Second, successful strategic business marketers keep their costs low for the value they choose to provide.* They decide where to pitch the value they deliver to customers by consciously considering their current and potential cost position and their unique assets and skills. Successful strategic business marketers do not just cut costs in-house, but also use non-traditional, marketing-oriented cost-reduction tools, such as strategic partnerships with customers.

- *Third, successful strategic business marketing specialists shape the industries they compete in.* This requires aggressive innovation. Whenever possible, it also involves global scope (which means building an understanding of international customers) and building a flexible and focused skills-based organization capable of continuous improvement. The 'industry shaper' understands how his industry is structured and what strategic options and channels will make it most profitable. He takes a broad view of his competitor and of the products or markets that make up his competitive arena.

Needless to say, many companies still have a long way to go before they reach this high skill level. Many still focus on price to influence customer choices, and operate at the mercy of the demand flow. These companies merely react to changes in the industry, and define their business by the product they make. They look no further than selling and sales support, continue to hold customers at arm's length, rarely innovate, and generate only marginal revenue from new products. They confine themselves to building strength in domestic markets only, wait for others to invent new channels, continue to rely exclusively on their own business systems, and ignore the opportunities provided by cross-border strategic alliances and acquisitions. They will not be competitive enough for tomorrow's global markets.

Strategic business marketing in the banking industry

In general, the banking industry is still a long way from strategic business marketing excellence. Most banks are still in the second era, focused on professionalizing their basic product tailoring and their customer classification skills. Their aim is to become excellent sellers of excellent financial products and services. Most banks are product-oriented instead of customer-oriented: they focus on their own needs, the needs of the seller.

Thus, learning how to create strategies aimed at understanding and adding value to customers is a key issue. Banks have to develop focused strategies to identify, segment and exploit customer needs that could offer promising potential. Formulating such strategies is a tough job, implementing them may be even tougher.

Implementing a focused strategy means choosing between different alternatives that are often all attractive, for example selling the same product with two different technologies/distribution strategies to different customer segments which are both profitable. Commitment to a strategic choice is a key success factor here, given the inherent shortage of financial and/or managerial resources.

Some banks, such as Banco Santander and HSBC, excel in making these choices. What distinguishes them from the pack?:

- They understand and use need-based market segmentation principles.
- They know how to monitor customers' explicit and implicit desires and wants as well as competitive activity.
- They possess a corporate culture where strategic marketing plays a key role, and use concepts providing unique value to the customer.

In short: they have a strong customer orientation.

Scope of study

Over the past few years, attention to strategic issues has increased dramatically in the banking industry. For many CEOs, strategic marketing has become a key area of corporate strategy. Markets are changing rapidly, and the management task of exploiting the changes is becoming increasingly difficult.

The era of drifting along relying solely on experience and intuition appears to have passed. Customers are making increasingly varied and higher demands, and banks that fail to respond are ruthlessly punished by the market. There is no room anymore for improvisation; a strategic approach to market issues is imperative.

This chapter is primarily devoted to strategic (business) marketing. Moreover, the chapter is mainly concerned with wholesale banking, where in practice strategic business marketing is used most. Little attention is paid here to retail banking or investment banking. While investment banking is playing an increasingly important role in the global banking industry, coverage of its strategic marketing aspects would demand specific research, which has not been carried out.

The key to attaining competitive advantage is satisfying the explicit and implicit needs of the customer. Most banks have also found themselves faced with the need for greater cost control. These two major pressures can easily end up in conflict: on the one hand, there is the externally focused need to improve customer orientation and tailor market offerings closely to customer requirements. On the other hand, there is the internal need to improve operating efficiency by reducing staff while simplifying and standardizing core processes. Resolving the dilemma, and achieving a balance between 'looking out' and 'looking in', is one of the key challenges for (wholesale) banks.

More than two hundred executives (225) from banks in 11 countries (the USA, Switzerland, The Netherlands, Japan, the UK, Germany, France, Spain, Italy, Belgium and Austria) completed a detailed questionnaire. I received information about wholesale products, market segments in the banking industry, the organization of and processes within banks, the strategic marketing mix used, and future trends in the industry. Roughly one-third of the 225 respondents were based in the USA, one-third in the UK, and one-third in Japan, France, Italy, Germany, Belgium, The Netherlands, Switzerland, Austria and Spain.

Methodology

From September 2004 through January 2005, the Nyenrode University Center for International Business conducted a survey on marketing strategies of global banks.

In total 225 top executives (CEOs [9 percent], Board of Directors' members [11 percent], Non-executive Directors [6 percent], Vice-Presidents [23 percent], and Senior Staff Directors (like Strategy Directors) [51 percent]) of 88 banks in 11 countries completed a questionnaire. The questionnaire provided an 'instant picture' of the marketing strategies of the world's largest banks. The scope of the survey was a representative cross section in both nature and composition of the global banking industry.

The survey was conceived as a way of highlighting the major changes occurring in the market place and also identifying the approaches and strategies the more successful banks are adopting to cope with, and profit from, such changes.

Examples of banks participating in the research study: ABN AMRO (The Netherlands), ING (The Netherlands), Fortis (The Netherlands/Belgium), Rabobank (The Netherlands), KBC (Belgium), Dexia (Belgium), Deutsche Bank (Germany), Dresdner Bank (Germany), Citigroup (USA), Bank of America (USA), JP Morgan Chase (USA), Wells Fargo (USA), Royal Bank of Scotland (UK), HSBC (UK), Barclays (UK), Lloyds TSB (UK), Abbey (UK), BNP Paribas (France), Credit Agricole

(France), Societe Generale (France), Antonveneta (Italy), Unicredito (Italy), UBS (Switzerland), Credit Suisse (Switzerland), Mitsubishi Tokyo Financial Group (Japan), Mizuho Financial Group (Japan), Sumitomo Mitsui (Japan), Bank Austria AG (Austria), Banco Santander (Spain), and BBV (Spain).

Results

Banks expect the wholesale market to grow. Only 5 percent of my research population thought that the market would shrink or remain constant in the coming years. The majority believed that the market would grow by 1 to 5 percent per year (40 percent of respondents) or 5 to 10 percent per year (35 percent). A total of 20 percent of the respondents expected the wholesale market to grow by 10 percent or more per year.

Banks are less optimistic about the future profitability of the wholesale market. Most executives thought that profitability would shrink (57 percent) or remain the same (23 percent). Only 20 percent of the executives were quite optimistic about profit trends.

Most executives (44 percent) expect a major shift from organic growth towards anorganic growth (growth through mergers, acquisitions and alliances) in their main line of business. A total of 26 percent of the executives expected no change. A total of 12 percent thought there will be a small change in the growth direction (towards anorganic growth). A further 18 percent had no clear expectations on this point.

With regard to the expected value proposition in the coming years (2006 - 2010), 78 percent of the executives expected they would have to offer more customer benefits for roughly the same price. A total of 22 percent of the respondents expected roughly the same customer benefits for a lower or the same price.

To sum up: banks expect to have to pedal harder for the same reward in the future. This emphasizes the need to rethink and revamp marketing strategies. The banks best able to meet the challenges of today and tomorrow will be those that manage the following four strategic challenges effectively:

- Creating a customer focus.
- Updating the product development program.
- Pricing banking products competitively.
- Putting a productive information architecture in place.

Strategic challenges

Managing all the above strategic challenges properly will be the ticket required for admission to the new competitive game. In the remainder of this chapter, I will discuss these strategic challenges in relation to some of the results of my survey.

Creating a customer focus

Identifying and fulfilling customer needs and managing customers more comprehensively are increasingly important activities in the banking industry. According to the survey, almost 90 percent of executives thought that marketing was not or would not be 'just' a support discipline for sales or 'merely' the promotion of banking products and services to customers.

Managing the customer was and would remain the most important marketing activity of a bank. This is in line with other results of the survey, for instance:

- customer satisfaction is the topic most frequently researched on a regular basis amongst banks; and

- building long-term relationships with customers is replacing the traditional attitude of selling to anyone who wants to buy and differentiating market segments on the basis of the products and services offered.

There are two main ways of achieving excellence in the customer focus of a bank: improving the quality of the sales force and forming partnerships with customers. Most banks recognize the importance of training sales people in marketing skills, theories and methods. More than 90 percent of the research population thought that training sales and marketing staff was important (38 percent) or very important (54 percent). Training all other employees in marketing skills, theories and approaches was considered important too. Most banks realize that marketing skills and approaches have to be understood widely, not just in the marketing and sales department, if the entire organization is to be customer-driven.

The need to form customer partnerships, my second approach to creating a customer focus, has been recognized by most banks. Few have actually done it, however. Establishing true customer partnerships can be a sustainable and very powerful supplementary strategy to achieve superior customer satisfaction and loyalty, especially in the more mature areas of the banking industry where they offer an attractive alternative to cut-throat, price-based competition.

Customer partnerships are based on the idea that both companies, customer and supplier (bank), can build core capabilities and use these to achieve superior customer satisfaction. Customer partnerships can add value:

- because each partner can concentrate on its own skills and capabilities;
- by cross-fertilization of ideas between the parties, which also helps to reinforce the relationship; and
- by lowering costs in the value chain of both the bank and the customer.

To create productive customer partnerships, banks need to develop a unique capability-based win-win partnership proposition, as many industrial companies like British Petroleum (BP), Philips and HP have done over the last few years.

Updating the product development program

The development and marketing of new products has been referred to as the 'life blood' of any company [3]. Historically, new product development was always an adjunct to the mainstream of strategic marketing management [4]. Today, with the increasingly narrow premium that can be extracted from 'me too' products, new product development is becoming a critical process in its own right. In the banking industry, it is an attractive alternative to price-based competition. It is one of the most powerful strategies for increasing the profit margin. However, few banks have outstanding track records in this area.

To be an outstanding innovator, a bank has to manage four overlapping elements of effective new product development:

1. Set new product development goals and objectives. The bank should be clear about:

- *The nature of the challenge.* The focus of the effort obviously depends on the combination of the skills of the bank and the assessment of high-opportunity segments.

- *How time-critical new product development is.* The timing of product launch is crucial: new banking products not only have to be new to the bank, but to the banking industry as well.
- *The scale of the expected benefits.* The amount of benefit that can be expected should be established from the start. New product development strategy should be realistic in terms of the expected bottom line impact, yet ambitious enough to stimulate radical thinking.

2. The new product development portfolio has to be balanced by understanding the different types of development which will be appropriate to different market segments and the technologies and skills which will be needed to realize them.

3. The appropriate level of resources to be invested in new product development has to be evaluated against a realistic estimate of returns.

4. Finally, the organization has to be managed. If a bank wants to improve its new product development effectiveness in the long term, not even a clear strategy, a balanced portfolio and sufficient investment will be enough on their own. Long-term innovativeness requires a shift in values and attitudes to new product development throughout the entire company. Banks should consider:

- *Using 'aspiration-based strategies'.* Successful innovators find ways of marrying dream-driven aspirations with industry practicalities by defining an innovation strategy with guidelines that will not hamper creativity, but rather help focus innovation 'bets' on high potential opportunities.
- *Creating a 'heaven for innovators',* i.e., an environment that fosters innovation. This is the way to attract, motivate and retain the type of people who will generate future growth.

New product development is a key determinant of competitive success. Constantly seeking to improve existing products and/or coming up with new ones is one of the characteristics of successful banks.

Pricing banking products competitively

Pricing can be the business lever with the greatest bottom-line impact. It drives the amount of money the bank makes by balancing the costs of supplying the product against the benefits provided to the customer.

My survey shows that the availability of information on all aspects of pricing is increasing. High-level pricing skills are, and will continue to be, more important than ever before, according to respondents. Most banks agree that pricing information is still improving, which, together with a more mature market, has contributed to the cut-throat, price-based competition we now see in many segments of the wholesale banking market.

Most banks can no longer maintain profits simply by raising prices. The key question therefore becomes: what is the best way to manage this crucial business lever? Excellence in strategic marketing is about capturing the real economic surplus by gaining a better understanding of the customers' perception of value.

Wholesale banks should move from cost- or competitor-based pricing to value-based pricing, avoiding under-pricing or the launch of products that customers regard as over-expensive. The three major 'pricing-to-value' questions are as follows:

1. *What product attributes do customers value?* The aim here is to understand how customers value product/price combinations, and what they value about products in particular. This entails gaining a complete understanding

of customers' views, not only regarding 'hard' benefits (e.g., funding advantages) but also 'soft' benefits (such as the image of the bank).

2. *What competing products do customer segments consider as alternatives to banking products?* The aim is to identify customer groups for which similar product attributes and price levels in a range of products/services provide similar (real or perceived) value. Price itself can play a significant role in shaping perceptions and an awareness of some of the behavioral aspects of pricing may be useful, for instance how 'reference pricing' is being used to establish value. Customers evaluate actual prices in relation to reference prices, which are prices they consider fair.

3. *What price optimizes the combination of perceived value and profits?* The first step here is to determine how demand for a product will vary as a function of its price, and the price then has to be set at the level that optimizes profit. An understanding of strategic pricing will ensure that the product/service is not being 'given away' and that, in each case, as much as possible of the total value available to the buyer and seller remains with the seller (the bank). The key is how to decide the exact price to assign to each customer transaction, and how to structure that transaction.

Failure to understand the value that customers perceive in a banking product will, at best, mean that pricing opportunities are missed and, at worst, can result in competitive pricing behavior, which can lead to a spiral of decline and most undesirable price wars.

The losses from price wars almost invariably outweigh any gains (that is, the increase in volume required to compensate for lost profit is unlikely to be achieved), and the much-cited rationale that price wars drive poor performers out of the market is rarely true. This is because price advantages are often short-lived (particularly in commodity financial products), the capacity rarely goes away, and industry shake-outs seldom occur in the financial services industry.

The biggest problem of all is that price competition in general, and price wars in particular, increase customers' price sensitivity, and therefore do lasting damage to price perceptions, i.e., what constitutes a fair price according to customers.

Putting a productive information architecture in place

Information in general and marketing information in particular is a key asset for banks, and is becoming a more important avenue to exploit as sources proliferate and technology advances. However, it is also becoming harder to manage.

Judging by the annual market research budget reported by executives, most banks are aware of the strategic importance of information: the average annual budget for market research five years from now (i.e., 2010) is expected to be four times as high as it was two years ago (i.e., 2003).

Internal and competitor information will become available in ever-greater amounts. But most banks also expect that the quantity of information on customer needs and integrated customer databases will make a quantum leap in the next five years. Five years from now, 91 percent of executives will be using database marketing, compared to 58 percent today.

In general, the increased variety and complexity of information enables banks to radically improve the quality of marketing decisions, provided the risk of information overload can be avoided. Advanced technology allows for more frequent monitoring, finer geographic and demographic cuts and an increased number of relevant and available measures.

The opportunity to design information flows that can support the strategic marketing decision process could therefore be critical for achieving competitive advantage in the future. Learning from strategic marketing information involves identifying patterns and relationships in order to anticipate customer needs and competitive actions and reactions. Accordingly, designing and managing information flows is probably the most powerful management task.

To build a more productive information architecture, banks must activate their 'sensors', i.e. their sales forces, in order to obtain reliable and valid data. The quality of the information used to support marketing and strategic management decisions depends to a large extent on this interface between the bank and its environment.

No middle course

To meet the demands of the new and more complex global environment, banks will have to make the transition from the second to the third or preferably the fourth strategic marketing era. They will have to rethink their strategic objectives, redevelop marketing strategies, redesign the process of strategic marketing and create a new strategic marketing approach. This represents a profound change that must be driven by CEOs and their senior executives.

The theme of banking and marketing strategy is a fascinating and challenging subject. Interesting yet difficult challenges await managers who really want to get grips with this subject. It is difficult to predict the future, but, in the long run, ignoring the fact that the rules of the game have changed can only result in being knocked out of the competition. If you want to stay in the match, you must have the courage to take chances - or risk being eliminated yourself. There is no middle course.

References

[1] Jagersma, P.K., "The Competitive Advantage of Global Banks", Congress organized by Harvard University and London School of Economics 'The Future of Global Banking', Hilton, London, October 2003.

[2] See: Rao, A.R., M.E. Bergen, and S. Davis, "How to Fight a Price War", Harvard Business Review, pp. 107-116, March-April, 2000.

[3] Jagersma, P.K., "Innovate or Die", Journal of Business Strategy, Winter 2002.

[4] See: MacMillan, I.C. and R. G. McGrawth, "Discover Your Products' Hidden Potential", Harvard Business Review, pp. 58-73, May-June 1996.

12

Redefining the Paradigm of Global Competition

Offshoring and Outsourcing

Offshoring is an irreversible trend that is already expanding to include - not only routine processes - but also the core activities of Western service firms.

The beauty of the offshoring phenomenon lies chiefly in the fact that business processes are performed in places with lower operating costs and a supply of qualified employees. There is also the "following the sun" principle, namely that companies can accomplish more by shifting work around the world with the clock.

Offshoring, referred to by some as global sourcing, refers to the development where companies relocate business activities, including the jobs involved, to foreign locations. It is redefining the paradigm of global competition, as companies use it to obtain costs and other, more strategic, advantages such as increasing product quality, entering new markets and following customers.

The impact of this phenomenon on the service sector has remained largely unnoticed. Given the magnitude of offshoring activities in this sector, it deserves to be the focus of attention. Just as service firms should decide on cross-border mergers and acquisitions and strategic alliances, they should answer the question as to whether and how offshoring should be a part of their international growth strategies.

Box 1 Logica

Logica grew from a relatively small, largely UK-based company into a large global IT services company, operating in 35 countries, quoted on the London and Amsterdam stock exchanges and headquartered in London.

In the growth years of the IT market in the second half of the 1990s, Logica and other IT services companies were competing for talent. This resulted in an escalation of pay rates because demand outstripped supply. In order to remain competitive and successful, European IT services companies had to adjust strategies; sometimes drastically. Many of them responded by embracing an offshore strategy and developed their own offshore capabilities in countries such as China and India.

By adopting an offshore strategy, Logica and other IT companies were able to compete more efficiently and better on a global scale. In doing so they redefined global competition.

In this chapter, I will first discuss the differences and common denominators between offshoring and outsourcing, as they are sometimes treated identically; however, they are not purely interchangeable and demand different responses from companies.

Secondly, the four different phases of the offshoring process are discussed and applied to service companies linked to some important lessons learnt. Every phase of the offshoring process demands adequate responses to essential questions and the integration of specific offshoring issues in a firm's strategy. The questions and issues raised in this chapter are not exhaustive, but nevertheless essential for the offshoring process.

Box 2 The research study

The lessons learnt in this chapter are largely drawn from a research study that the Nyenrode Institute for Competition (NIC) executed in 2005.

247 Respondents mentioned having 'offshoring experience' (i.e., 39 percent of the total research population) or 'offshoring plans for the future' (6 percent). The lessons learnt refer to their motives behind and goals achieved with offshoring, types of offshoring they choose for their offshoring activities, their offshored activities, preferred offshore locations and issues regarding managing offshoring activities.

Finally, in the section, 'Conclusions and Recommendations', I make the connection between the different phases of the offshoring process.

Offshoring and outsourcing: what's in a name?

Offshoring and outsourcing are sometimes treated identically, as companies seem to choose them for similar reasons, such as to focus on core competencies, to increase flexibility and to realize cost savings. However, offshoring cannot be regarded as purely interchangeable with outsourcing.

The differentiating issues are the involvement of a third party (outsourcing) and a foreign location (offshoring). Outsourcing always requires the involvement of a third party, offshoring does not per se, as activities can be relocated under direct control. Offshoring always involves a foreign location, whereas outsourcing can be done in the local market as well.

In order to translate these differences in concrete issues in the decision-making approach of companies, I will focus on the offshoring process, i.e. the relocation of value chain (for instance, administrative, product development or marketing activities) or business activities to a foreign location under the direct control of the firm (i.e. captive offshoring) or via a foreign third party (i.e. offshore outsourcing).

At the end of the 1990s, service firms were dominating industrialized economies. This trend is meanwhile mirrored in offshoring, where a shift from manufacturing to services took place as well. Therefore, this chapter focuses on applying the offshoring process to service companies. The process is divided into four phases that will include relevant steps to be taken and important lessons learnt.

The offshoring process: the 4M Approach

The offshoring process, as discussed in this chapter and shown in the flowchart below, is referred to as the '4M Approach'. It is divided into the following four distinct phases:

- 'Making' the offshoring policy;
- 'Mapping' an offshoring profile;
- 'Managing' the roll-out of the offshoring profile;
- 'Measuring' the results of the offshoring process.

Box 3 The offshoring process - the 4M Approach

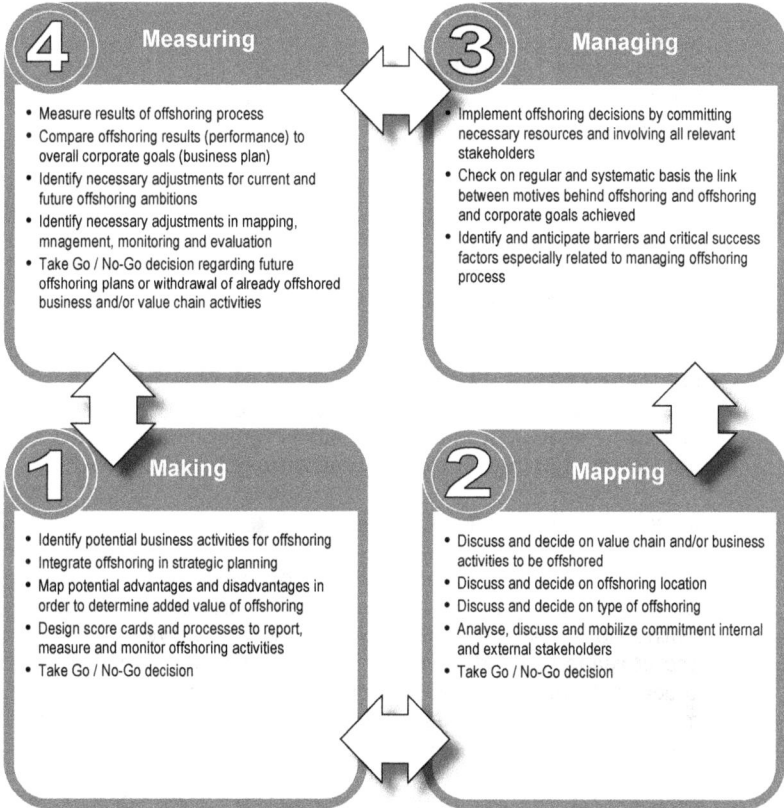

4 Measuring

- Measure results of offshoring process
- Compare offshoring results (performance) to overall corporate goals (business plan)
- Identify necessary adjustments for current and future offshoring ambitions
- Identify necessary adjustments in mapping, mnagement, monitoring and evaluation
- Take Go / No-Go decision regarding future offshoring plans or withdrawal of already offshored business and/or value chain activities

3 Managing

- Implement offshoring decisions by committing necessary resources and involving all relevant stakeholders
- Check on regular and systematic basis the link between motives behind offshoring and offshoring and corporate goals achieved
- Identify and anticipate barriers and critical success factors especially related to managing offshoring process

1 Making

- Identify potential business activities for offshoring
- Integrate offshoring in strategic planning
- Map potential advantages and disadvantages in order to determine added value of offshoring
- Design score cards and processes to report, measure and monitor offshoring activities
- Take Go / No-Go decision

2 Mapping

- Discuss and decide on value chain and/or business activities to be offshored
- Discuss and decide on offshoring location
- Discuss and decide on type of offshoring
- Analyse, discuss and mobilize commitment internal and external stakeholders
- Take Go / No-Go decision

Phase 1: 'Making' the offshoring policy

During the first phase of the offshoring process, the focus is on the motives behind offshoring in order to answer the question as to why a company should relocate its value chain or business activities. Answering this question is fundamental with respect to the preparation of the offshoring process.

This phase demands careful valuation of the (dis)advantages of offshoring for a company. This phase is time consuming and should result in the ability of a company to master the offshoring phenomenon while 'playing' with the facts and figures for example when examining its own value chain.

Imagination is crucial in this phase in order to not just nominate obvious business activities (facilitating and non-core) for relocation. This phase also includes designing the necessary score cards and processes to report, measure and monitor offshoring activities during the offshoring process.

Lessons learnt: motives

Offshoring is often mentioned in connection with lowering costs, and low labor cost countries as the main offshoring destinations. Even though cost-related motives can be a strong reason for offshoring in the early stage (especially for relocating offshore activities via a third party), its importance may decrease over time and should be viewed in combination with other motives and strategic goals.

ABN AMRO, for example, announced, in 2005, that it was offshoring $2,2 billion worth of IT activities, partly to low-cost countries. The company expects a yearly cost reduction of $720 million. The added value of offshoring, however, is not just about saving costs. It also has strategic value, such as the availability of highly qualified employees at an offshore location, and the opportunity to enter new markets.

Offshoring is increasingly used as a strategic tool to respond to developments in a dynamic environment and is thus redefining global competition. The main reasons for choosing offshoring, and important motives behind the offshoring behavior of service companies are: improving quality of services produced, consolidating activities for economies of scale, scope and skills, and accessing certain skills or markets. These motives behind offshoring may be related to the fact as to whether they meet the envisioned strategic goals with the relocation, and may also serve as indicators for the success rate of offshoring activities of service companies.

Motives related to expansion, competitiveness and cost reductions are the most important factors behind the offshore behavior of service firms. On the one hand, motives related to growth in new markets are cost-inducing activities and will most likely not be used in conjunction with cost-reduction motives as reasons for relocating business activities. On the other hand, motives related to competitiveness will likely be used in conjunction with cost-reduction related motives.

Lessons learnt: offshoring activities

When looking at offshoring activities, it becomes clear that activities such as operations, administration, technology/application development, service and sales are frequently offshored by service firms. Activities such as operations, service, and procurement are relatively more often offshored under direct control than via a third party, whereas offshore outsourcing is leading in technology/application development and IT infrastructure. In comparison to manufacturers, service firms more often refer to most of their offshored activities as being part of their core business.

Phase 2: 'Mapping' an offshoring profile

The different steps in this phase are both demanding and time consuming. Mapping an offshore profile refers to deciding on offshoring activitities, type of offshoring and offshore location.

At this stage it is important to find internal support for the offshoring process, for example, with regard to commitment of sufficient financial means and management involvement. This phase also includes contacting relevant organizations, experts and institutes, e.g. ministry of foreign affairs or export promoting organizations or specialized lawyers that can support a company's offshoring process.

Offshoring decisions are more successful when all relevant internal and external stakeholders in the process are involved. In fact the second phase is also a preparatory phase in which many difficult questions have to be answered before implementation can take place.

The decision to relocate activities is an important one because it is linked to, for example, control issues whereas the implementation process is much more related to entrepreneurial issues. Control issues demand clarity regarding the type of offshoring, namely under direct control (captive offshoring) or via a third party (offshore outsourcing) or a combination of both.

In the case of offshore outsourcing, it means that the second phase should be used to draft agreements about transferred responsibility for the relocated activity to a third party. In the case of captive offshoring it should be determined how an activity will be relocated, i.e. whether it is done, for example, by an acquisition or a greenfield. This may involve, among other things, hiring new employees and building a network with stakeholders at the offshore location.

Box 4 Hewitt Associates

Hewitt Associates offshored 300 Hewitt associates to work at their HR outsourcing centre in Krakow, Poland. This centre provides customer service support to Hewitt's HR Business Process Outsourcing (BPO) clients in Europe, as well as pension administration and software development services.

Lessons learnt: entry mode

The choice for captive offshoring or offshore outsourcing is dependent on the mode of entry. Depending on their choice for a specific entry mode, companies will face a variety of specific strategic issues, risks and other factors, which they have to satisfy.

How does the choice of entry mode differ for service versus manufacturing firms? Practice shows that the entry mode strategies differ between the two categories of firms. The entry mode used by the service sector is said to be determined by the level of tradability – whether or not the service can be exported, and subject to certain degrees of physical customer interaction.

For example, storable services and service activities that do not involve physical customer interaction are exportable. However, such operation and standardization of services may be limited due to adaptation needs for different cultures and for physical proximity. There is for example evidence that service firms choose captive offshoring, depending on a firm's business sensitivity to tacit knowledge and intellectual property, and the physical proximity requirement of the activities.

The choice of entry mode is also related to the motives behind offshoring of service firms. Strategic motives may be related to the choice of a specific type of offshoring, captive offshoring or offshore outsourcing or a combination of both types.

The motives of service firms to opt for offshore outsourcing are generally more driven by cost-saving perspectives, as well as perceived increase of flexibility. It is often the preferred entry mode for companies when direct control is not an issue and for back- and front-office work that has a low complexity level and that can be standardized and separated from other activities. However, service firms increasingly offshore their core activities involving high skilled jobs and increasingly opt to relocate these activities under direct control.

Captive offshoring is usually preferred by firms when strict control is crucial, information is sensitive and internal interaction is important. It is also preferred when a company seeks to capture savings and other advantages or when there is a lack of local firms that can provide the required services.

Lessons learnt: offshore location

Motives for offshoring will affect the choice for different offshore locations of service firms. If, on the one hand, cost reduction is the most important motive behind offshore decisions, aspects such as labor costs, housing, electricity, tax and regulatory costs will be taken into account. Combined, they comprise the total financial structure, which will then play a leading role in the decision-making process on offshore locations, followed by issues, such as the political, cultural and business environment and the availability of qualified employees.

If, on the other hand, the rationale behind offshoring is the market, i.e. market potential and international expansion, the aforementioned issues, such as availability of qualified employees, will become leading factors in determining the most attractive offshore location. Some countries, Vietnam and the Philippines, for example, may be the best offshore locations in terms of contributing to a favorable financial structure, but they need improvement with respect to issues relating to business environment and availability of qualified employees.

This, however, is also subject to change because countries develop, sometimes at a rapid pace. Countries like India and China, which used to be referred to as low-cost countries, today score high in some ratings on all relevant aspects, both regarding market and costs.

Phase 3: 'Managing' the roll-out of the offshoring profile

Phase three refers to implementing offshoring decisions. Given the political sensitivity of offshoring, managing the process also means paying extra attention to the consequences of offshored activities; at headquarters, for example, with regard to employees who see their jobs or part of their jobs being moved to foreign locations.

Offshore outsourcing demands that firms think about getting engaged and maintaining an outsourcing relationship with a partner that is responsible for the relocated activity at an offshore location. Captive offshoring includes managing a foreign subsidiary and thinking about how much control is possible and needed to successfully manage this foreign entity.

Both types of offshoring are demanding for the management of service firms. Managing offshored activities can make or break the success of relocated activities and goes far beyond financial implications. For example, successful offshore outsourcing is not about cost-savings, but about establishing a collaborative relationship with a partner in order to create sustainable competitive advantages that go far beyond cost savings.

Lessons learnt: implementing offshoring decisions

Service firms perceive offshoring, in general, as demanding for the organization, management and employees involved. It is an important reason for withdrawing activities and returning them to the country of origin. It is also mentioned by service firms as an important reason for not achieving original goals set at the outset of the offshoring process.

Issues, such as lack of control, insufficient planning, time and capacity, as well as problems relating to human resources and difficult communication also play a role in this respect. Problems relating to the political situation at the offshore location combined with cultural differences and language difficulties are also mentioned as prominent reasons for difficulties in managing the roll-out.

Box 5 ClientLogic Corp.

Formed in 1998 by Onex Corp., a large Canadian investment firm, Nashville-based ClientLogic Corp. is a major provider of corporate outsourcing services. It provides outsourced customer service tasks to corporate clients including Microsoft, Sony and Continental Airlines.

For example, it uses call centres in 12 countries to serve as a client customer service arm by responding to phone and e-mail inquiries and marketing additional services. It also handles customer bills and product rebates via five U.S. fulfilment centres. White-collar workers from ClientLogic have seen their jobs shifted to offshore locations and most notably to India. Through a joint venture it opened for example a centre in Bangalore to supplement its North American and European contact centres. In addition, it has centres in the Philippines and Mexico, and is looking to expand to Africa and Eastern Europe.

In order to manage the process, ClientLogic hired Garner, an outsourcing industry veteran, who implemented a $30 million cost-cutting program to consolidate its North American and European finance, marketing and sales operations. This offshore strategy should contribute towards boosting the company's revenues.

Various outsourcing projects are unsuccessful due to failure to properly manage the relationship between provider and client. Outsourcing projects are nearly always extensive and complicated and often involve moving targets: what applies today can be completely different tomorrow. Only thorough preparation will help to manage outsourcing and offshoring activities successfully.

The most frequently cited success factors for managing offshoring are: qualified employees, knowledge of the market, culture of the offshore location and communication.

Lessons learnt: barriers

From my observations of service firms that are involved in offshoring, it is clear that their perceived barriers influence both the types of offshoring and the preferred offshore locations.

How do the barriers, as perceived by service firms, relate to the choice for a specific entry mode? Companies often prefer entry into similar markets in order to minimize uncertainty and try to avoid perceived barriers such as lack of market knowledge. However, this preference seems to be conditioned by companies' international experience. As companies gain experience, geographical and cultural familiarity are less important.

The barriers, as perceived by service firms, also have an impact on the choice for specific locations. Service firms encounter, in general, fewer barriers in Western Europe and the USA. Also the type of barriers differ according to specific locations. Legal and political issues, for instance, are somewhat more severe in Western European countries and are perceived as less drastic in fast-growing Asian countries. Barriers related to human resources, such as quality of work and availability of qualified employees, are higher in Asia and lower in Western Europe.

Phase 4: 'Measuring' the results of the offshoring process

The pros and cons of the offshoring process should be evaluated during the fourth phase. The aim of this phase is to answer the question as to whether offshoring resulted in added value for a company or not. Evaluation should be done in a systematic manner with specific score cards.

Currently, these score cards are rare but should in any case include a comparison between, on the one hand, objectives that were set at the beginning of the process and, on the other hand, goals achieved or not in the relocation of the business activities. The objectives set and realized this way can be compared and interpreted with a view to determining a future international growth strategy. This phase is, in fact, a firm's mirror in terms of the success of its offshored activities.

Lessons learnt: added value

Offshoring, although perceived by many service firms as an important asset of international growth strategies, is rather demanding on their management. Nevertheless, service firms, in general, perceive it as a successful undertaking that increases their competitiveness in the international playing field.

Offshoring does not always result in financial benefits. Other strategic benefits play an important role in the motivation for continuing offshoring activities. However, far too often, the evaluation of these cost-benefit perceptions is not executed in a systematic manner.

Box 6 Aviva

Aviva, a large UK insurer, established a joint venture, 'Aviva' Life, in India. It offshored 5,000 jobs to India of which the majority belonged to Aviva's non-life operations company Norwich Union. Aviva plans to increase this number by 3,000. Aviva is said to value the performance, the quality of service and operational flexibility this joint venture provides to its business in the UK.

In order to determine the added value of offshoring for service firms, it is important to know which goals they did or did not achieve by relocating their activities, and how they relate to the original motives that served as drivers behind the offshoring process. Cost savings, entering new markets, improving competitiveness, increasing turnover/sales and following important customers/suppliers seem to be important goals achieved. In addition, they also serve as motives for continuing offshoring and relocating new activities to foreign locations.

Conclusions and recommendations

Before taking a decision to offshore, service firms should first have a clear idea what of they are getting into when offshoring their activities. They should also decide on monitoring, reporting and measuring processes.

Offshoring starts at home and is seen by many service firms as a tool to maintain and increase their competitiveness. At the same time, offshoring places major demands on an organization and its management. The organization, management, and employees involved should, and can, prepare themselves for offshoring.

The offshoring process, as discussed, is dynamic and inhibits dependency between the four different phases of the offshoring process. The individual steps, as well as the links between them, deserve and demand ongoing input and monitoring from management.

* Co-author of this chapter: Desirée van Gorp, assistant-professor of International Business (Nyenrode Business Universiteit) and leader of Nyenrode's Competition Practice (NIC).

Part IV. Global Strategy and Reputational Capital

13

Success beyond Success

The 'Golden Triangle' of Continuous Performance
Improvement

The pace of change in today's industries means management
has to go on improving execution continually. As a result,
managers are kept in what seems like a perpetual state of
reassessment and change, with inevitable allied tensions and
challenges. Indeed, you have to be a world class operator just
to survive (see box 1).

My interviews with 48 executives and senior managers
suggest that there is no simple, transferable global success
formula. The kinds of initiatives that are attempted and the
urgency with which they are pursued depend heavily on the
capabilities of the organization, the scope of performance
improvements which the leadership team wants to achieve,
and the time within which they want to achieve them. This
chapter explores a number of performance management
thoughts in greater depth, giving insight of how excellent
companies address Continuous Performance Improvement
('CPI') issues.

'Golden Triangle' of CPI

Crafting a CPI strategy is an analysis-driven exercise, not a task where companies can get by with opinions, good instinct and creative thinking.

Continuous performance improvement – by definition – is a relative notion; It is directed at bridging the gap between the 'theoretical ideal' performance and 'today's real' performance. The 'change gap' – i.e., performance improvement gap – to be expected in any company will naturally be dependent on the amount and pace of change in environmental forces and the ability, willingness, and initiative to change of a companies' management. A systematic screening of the need for business model change on the one hand and the ability, willingness, and initiative of management to effect change, can provide a first indication of where the major potential improvements should be expected.

It can be postulated that performance improvement within a unit or division is easier to conceive and implement than performance improvement between businesses or fundamental improvement of the total business model. Total business model redesign frequently offers the highest potential performance improvement because it is most difficult to effect. It takes a comprehensive change in virtually all elements of the business model to arrive at a totally new level of performance, i.e., a quantum leap. Quantum jumps in performance are almost always conceivable, though not necessarily always affordable in view of the necessary investment.

Box 1 The research behind 'Success beyond Success'

In 2008, I launched a study to determine companies' most important continuous performance improvement (CPI) roots.

The study was conducted from January to September 2008. I conducted 48 interviews with senior executives of (in alphabetical order) Apple, Bang & Olufsen, Condé Nast, Danone, Egon Zehnder, Goldman Sachs, HP, LVMH, Mittal Steel, Merck, Nokia, Pixar, Philips, Porsche, Royal Dutch Shell, Siemens, Richemont (Cartier), Ricoh and Sony. The companies cover a wide range of industries: automotive, financial services, pharmaceuticals, energy, ICT, entertainment, consumer products, among others.

My main subject was continuous performance improvement; but, more specifically, I sought to understand the most important management challenges under that heading. The interviews were open-ended. Between the interviews, I had e-mail exchanges and telephone conversations with participants. I supplemented my core study with shorter interviews involving a range of senior partners of BCG, Booz&Co, McKinsey&Co, and Bain.

Most companies face a new era today as the result of several major changes over the last decade, e.g., an accelerating pace of technological change, traditional industry boundaries are being redefined, unanticipated threats from new entrants, M&A 'feeding fremzy', many potential opportunities versus highly uncertain returns, and an end game in many industries which is far from clear.

Companies have to meet a complex set of new challenges with management approaches that were developed to match a much simpler era. Looking forward to an even more complex environment in the future, the opportunity for management today is to develop new approaches that can match the strategic imperatives of the future.

Continuous performance improvement means constantly searching for a 'better practice', implementing that practice, and then searching for another 'better practice'. Ad-hoc bottom-up efforts can only capture one-time performance gains. Often they are focused on low-hanging fruit. Without the emphasis on continuous improvement, one-time gains are unlikely to lead to further improvements.

The following three categories of performance roots are – according to my research population - undeniably the chief variables of firm and management effectiveness: leadership, business models and people, i.e., the 'Golden Triangle of CPI'.

Continuous performance improvement at world class levels will only occur if all of these levers are focused upon on an ongoing basis, year after year. These three main categories are abstractions, and, therefore, need to be brought down to earth case by case.

Leadership

Since great execution requires breakthroughs along a number of fronts, companies need better leadership at all organizational levels if the execution challenges are to succeed. A successful continuous performance improvement strategy requires leadership throughout businesses in order to piece together best practices and wring out synergies while striving to carry on business as usual and rally the spirits of employees.

Most of the things outlined in a continuous performance improvement strategy will require significant organizational commitment to performance improvement, and, therefore, change across many levels and functions within a company. There has to be strong consensus across the leadership group that continuous performance improvement is required.

Leadership equals a set of actions to transmit the continuous performance improvement strategy onto the organization, create an environment conducive to success, build the necessary skills, and inspire enthusiastic pursuit of the CPI strategy.

For world-class levels of continuous performance improvement to be realized, empowerment, accountability, and support must be deepened progressively and rigour must be locked in to reinforce performance improvement and monitor progress in new directions. Better CPI decisions will be taken the closer the decision maker is to the facts involved, and to the ramifications of the decision made. Because of this, ever deeper empowerment is crucial to continuous improvement.

It is clear, however, that pursuing empowerment does not subtract from the duties of management, but rather adds to those duties the obligation to provide people with the tools to make good decisions, and the obligation to energize them to do so. Given this, leadership style and actions exhibited by managers must constantly evolve, based on their success in developing an empowered workforce. For instance, poor results from bottom-up decisions are a sign that management has failed to develop its people. Leadership is therefore among the most dynamic of performance levers.

Leadership is needed because companies operate in uncertain times. In a more stable, predictable era, corporate direction is likely to be more continuous – incremental change may be acceptable. It is the uncertainty and volatility of the current business environment that demands rapid rather than incremental change in corporate strategies and actions, and, therefore, leadership instead of mere management.

Some will argue, that the degree of uncertainty is such that the best we can do is to be flexible and ready to respond rapidly to the unexpected. But, critical though it may be as an organizational characteristic, flexibility sets no direction. Leadership, on the other hand, clearly establishes both a direction and a destination. It is the star we can steer by as we sail the turbulent and unchartered waters of the future. Leadership is needed as a force for empowering and implementation.

Experience has taught that strategy implementation is a complex and, at times, tough challenge for which no single solution is possible. However, leadership plays a key role in strategy implementation. At a minimum it serves to focus action throughout a business model, inspires and generates enthusiasm and commitment for the tasks ahead. Leadership aids implementation of strategies and actions by focusing thought and action on the agreed-upon strategy, helping ensure that everyone marches to the same drummer.

Leadership aids implementation also by providing both the readiness and the 'aim' – as in 'ready, aim, fire' – for both strategic and operational decisions, helping ensure consistency throughout the decision making process in a company. Through explicit leadership, we clarify what we want to be; It reflects our aspirations and values.

The payoff for leadership is more than a reputation for business statesmanship. Leadership translates directly into improved customer satisfaction and loyalty, greater employee commitment, and increased shareholder value. Leadership is a critical CPI driver, and, therefore, should be recognized as a required skill of every manager. For instance, at Ricoh, a global document solutions' giant, and LVMH, the world's biggest luxury behemoth, managers 'talk' CPI.

Business model

The famous Belgian surrealist René Magritte painted a series of pipes and titled the series "Ceci n'est pas une pipe" – this is not a pipe. The picture of the thing is not the thing.

In the same way, a 'structure' or 'organization' is not a business model. A business model is a term for all the internal structures, mental frameworks, and operating procedures, processes, and practices that determine how work actually gets done in a company. Many of the performance improvement challenges companies face are in fact embedded in their business models.

In business as in politics, today's challenge often has its roots in yesterday's solution. All too often, the management remedy of the past turns into a 'mild headache' for a later generation of managers and executives. It isn't surprising that an organizational device tailored to fit the needs of one period should fail to meet the requirements of a later era. What is odd is that so few companies have bothered to spell out the assumptions underlying their organization structures and management processes so that they can be alert to the need to change or replace them as new challenges arise.

We are in the midst of fundamental changes in management practices. In the past decade, many organizational experiments have been under way in many firms. These experiments were initially triggered by the need to reduce costs. However, it also reflects the impact of information and communication technologies. For example, increased use of ICT and shared databases has, over time, reduced the need for traditional middle management.

Apple, for instance, is always looking for ways to create a more entrepreneurial organization, where employees at all levels are focused on increasing stakeholder and shareholders value. Royal Dutch Shell, Merck and Nokia are experimenting too with novel organizational principles and management processes to accomodate the fast pace of technological change, competition, and the emergence of a knowledge-based economy. The resulting impetus is toward flexible and agile organizational forms which can accomodate novelty, innovation, and change.

However, with some variations, most companies are organized around the 'command and control' model of the 1900's. This business model created many of the concepts that we now take for granted – line and staff, policies and procedures, middle management and so on. It created an environment where problems could be identified by weekly or monthly reports, analyzed by staff, presented to top management, delegated to middle management, and implemented by workers. The 'command and control' business model is a highly refined system predicated on stability and forged by a particular set of technological and market forces. It shaped a strategy of standardized, high-volume production and sales.

The forces shaping today's companies are dramatically different. End-use markets are fragmenting, requiring faster and more targeted responses. Advances in the ability to capture, manipulate and transmit information electronically make it possible for companies such as HP to distribute decision making ('command') without losing 'control'. Workers today are better educated, in short supply, and demanding greater participation and variety in their jobs.

Individually, all these and other changes are dramatic, collectively they shape a new era for companies in business model design. Competitive strength is derived from a '4S approach': the skills, speed, specificity and service levels provided to customers. For example, a few years ago, French icon Danone became increasingly aware of the shortcomings of the 'command and control' model and searched for alternatives. Drawing on all kinds of examples and own insights, Danone synthesized a common set of characteristics for the company. These characteristics contrasted sharply with those of the 'command and control' approach:

- *Customer focus versus supervisor focus.* In Danone, every executive, manager and employee is focused on providing value to their external and internal customers. This contrasts with command and control-organizations where only certain businesses and staff departments or levels of management make understanding and satisfying customers their chief concern. The customer mindset directs that the business model be designed so that data and information from the environment flow to and penetrate the entire organization. Danone is not only aware of their environment, but actively seek information from it. This information can range from a general awareness by employees to formalized customer surveys to product development which starts with an identified customer desire.

- *Continuous performance improvement versus meeting periodically defined objectives and goals.* Great companies are constantly identifying relevant opportunities both within and across businesses and adjusting their actions accordingly. A focus on superior value, excellence, and quality is always present. These companies believe the best of these efforts will be driven by multiple measures, that is, customer value delivery, shareholders value, corporate social responsibility, and employee gain.

- *Team relationships versus hierarchical relationships.* The classic hierarchical structure is no longer the dominant determinant of organizational relationships. Multiple performance-oriented and accountable teams are found at all Danone levels. Employees are organized in teams, cross-trained, and provided with information to enable them to perform multiple roles and to adjust quickly to varying requirements. The formation of multi-disciplinary teams to solve particular performance issues becomes the norm rather than the exception. As a result of this team orientation, decisions become more participatory due to employees' possessing the skills, incentives, solution space, and information to contribute.

- *Flat and flexible structures versus vertical and static structures.* Flexibility means being fast on one's feet, able to move rapidly. As industries become increasingly complex, companies need greater strategic flexibility than ever before. Therefore, a business model must have the flexibility to deliver value and excellence along many dimensions. Companies need new forms of organization that enables greater flexibility to accelerate change. Danone continuously reduces levels and barriers across businesses in order to respond quickly and effectively to internal and external customers and their changing needs.

- *Empowerment versus compliance.* Management will have to spend much more time on clarifying goals and shaping values, and much less on participating in operational decision making and control. Management will need to lead more, and manage less. Every Danone employee looks for opportunities to improve performance and take action without relying on procedures from above to act. However, empowerment is not simply an untargeted increase in individual freedom. By bounding behavior with broader concepts such as shared values, the individual and team has greater opportunity to improve performance.

- *Vision- and values-driven leadership versus control-oriented leadership.* Building a great company requires leaders to shatter expectations that all important directions comes from above and that deviation from prescribed norms will be punished. Employee initiative requires imbuing everyone in a company with a clear, shared sense of purpose – and with values linked closely with teamwork, problem solving and risk taking.

The business model challenge is not on finding ways to divide up tasks more and more. The vital business model issue for Nokia, for instance, is not how to divide but how to unite: how to integrate a global company. The challenge is coordination and integration – how 'it' works. If a business model is viewed only as structure, it will fail. It is too complex. If, on the other hand, it is viewed as a way of adding value to customers, employees and other stakeholders, it may work. Seen from a CPI perspective, Nokia prizes pragmatic business results above structural elegance.

As current and future trends indicate, companies need a flexible and agile organization that can effectively function in environments of continuous and kaleidoscopic, rather than periodic and paradigmatic, change.

Under today's challenging circumstances, it is the intangibles such as management style and shared values that count most toward ensuring CPI, i.e., the human dimension of continuous performance improvement.

People

Achieving and consistently maintaining superior levels of performance depend almost entirely on the ability to mobilize and engage the enthusiasm of people. Motivating and pushing people just to do more is demanding enough. Channeling their extra effort into sustained improved results is much harder. It takes more than just raising their expectations and energy, because activity alone does not translate easily into sustained performance improvement.

CPI is about using the detailed knowledge and experience of people who really know their job. Firm-wide performance improvement starts with the individual employee. After all, who knows what is wrong with it in the first place? You have to use the enormously valuable resource called 'individual'. Ultimately, they add value to customers.

Box 2 Mittal Steels' CPI rollout principles

To implement CPI successfully, Mittal Steel applies five best practice guidelines:

1. *Measurable performance improvement must be the ultimate goal.* There are good reasons for this:
- it provides focus. A clear focus on CPI helps set priorities about which battles are worth fighting and which should be deferred.
- it releases energy. When a performance target means something to employees, they can take action to achieve it.
- it gives room for learning. A focus on CPI results can give employees room for autonomy in how they do their jobs. Employees usually want to perform – they do not need to be told every aspect of how. How CPI results are achieved can increasingly be left to the freedom and creativity of employees involved.

2. *Committed, consistent leadership and active follow-through.* Employees down the line wait to see how senior management act. If senior managers' actions are inconsistent with what they say, it quickly tells down-the-liners how their future is best served – guarding the status quo or embracing CPI. CPI requires committed leadership.

3. *Follow principles to provide discipline.* Any initiative that has a measurable impact on total company performance will need to have managers committed to the CPI-challenge. In turn, there are few better experiences than leading CPI to shape the next generation of leadership. Teams of managers and employees with the right skill mix and mutually committed to the CPI-challenge, will deliver the best results. Teams need demanding CPI goals - low targets easily become ceilings; high aspirations force a clear break away from satisfaction with half measures, underachieving and the status quo. In doing so they build confidence to take on ever higher CPI goals. Furthermore, managers and

employees can be highly motivated by having to deliver quickly. Bite-sized achievements concerning CPI build momentum.

4. *Support CPI initiatives to ensure impact.* Many obstacles inevitably spring up to hamper CPI actions. Getting the right support in place is important during CPI. This involves:
- performance measurement. A performance focus needs measurement systems that gather and disseminate useful data to management in time for them to do something practical with it.
- organizational alignment. Consistent signalling and support for what really counts is essential to make CPI come alive. Each plant must fight to shed the unnecessary 'drag' exerted by 'old ways of doing'.
- people development. In building a CPI mindset, employees need to work with their direct superiors, as well as peers, to translate the overall CPI-challenge into their own role, goals, accountabilities and behavior.

5. *Overcommunicate.* You have to tell employees what is happening and why. Directness in communication is a powerful means to release energy for CPI. Open communication is essential if executives and managers want to continuously engage employees. Listening to feedback and acting on it is a strong credibility builder and motivator.

To take full advantage of the power and capabilities of people, a self-challenging organization should be created that is capable of ongoing renewal and is committed to continuous performance enhancement. The art of 'human' and 'humane' management has to be the name of the game.

'Continuous performance improvement companies' have one characteristic in common – they hold their executives, managers and employees accountable for improving customer satisfaction and productivity, and, therefore, operational excellence.

Management must link empowerment to accountability for results because you can only improve what you manage and manage what you measure. Empowerment alone will not deliver CPI. Accountability drives behavior. Therefore, empowerment must be linked to accountability. Linking empowerment with accountability for results will ensure that CPI is the focus of the bottom-up effort and that everyone, from front-line workers up through senior management, gives the bottom-up effort the appropriate priority.

At both Siemens and Sony, four ingredients form the foundation for successful 'empowerment–with-accountability' programs:

- *Make CPI the shared aspiration.* Empowerment for empowerment's sake does not improve performance, because the investment in the bottom-up processes will be significant, given the value of people's time. The investment must add value to the organization. Therefore, the objective of empowerment must be to improve performance continuously and people must be held accountable for CPI results.

- *Strive for CPI principles.* Without the emphasis on continuous improvement, one-time gains are unlikely to lead to further improvements. Therefore, continuous improvement should be explicitly made a part of the performance expectation. Every employee has the right and obligation to improve the processes on which (s)he works. A continuously improving organization is one that captures opportunities on an ongoing basis while building skills and confidence, instilling a readiness to embrace change, building a performance ethic, and challenging employees to continuously meet or beat the 'best-of-the-best'.

- *Focus on customer requirements.* Bottom-up efforts must improve processes for meeting customer requirements in the most efficient and effective way. This also means establishing key measures to evaluate process performance. Process measures, rather than activity based measures, must be developed to monitor and track performance.

- *Stimulate creativity and innovation.* CPI will be achieved only by stimulating creativity and innovation. The perspective of most employees is often bounded by the area they consider their direct responsibility. They are typically not asked or expected to think of their work in the context of end-to-end processes. Expanding the frame of reference though will dramatically reshape not only their view of their own work but also their view of the customer.

Empowerment does not equate to abdication. Management's responsibilities are by no means lessened as an organization shifts its style from 'command-and-control' to 'engage-and-empower'. Management has an important role to play, even when empowerment is in place. The overall process must be resourced and set in motion with clear direction as to the areas of focus in magnitude of performance improvement expected.

Leaders don't necessarily sit only at the top of organizational pyramids – they are scattered throughout an organization. Markets, products, and technologies come and go, but a company that continually produces leaders at all levels is here to stay because it has people who anticipate and know how to deal with dreams, discontinuities, and deadlines.

Leadership, however, is not a static pose, but an exhilirating partnership. Only the vital interplay of wills between leaders and followers can direct them both toward continuous performance improvement. When 'followership' is effective, behavior at all levels of the organization is both aligned and adaptable, and, thus, the organization performs to its potential. Each company needs such an institutional capacity for followership.

To build a smooth 'followership engine' is one of the most important CPI challenges. In essence, this means embracing specific values, being able to motivate and energize others, and having that infectious enthusiasm to tap people's potential and generate the capacity of the organization beyond what it otherwise would do.

There is no great strategy; there is only great execution. The trick is to make the 'soft stuff' hard, to operationalize it. The main challenge of management at Hollywood box office success Pixar is to move from ideas to CPI. The success of this transition rests on how well Pixar executives and managers really understand their people. The only way leaders achieve high performance is through the work of followers.

However, the people challenge cannot get far without leadership and adequate business models. This is not something added on to the other two. It is the reason for the other two's existence. It is the equalizer between leadership and business models. One- or two-legged chairs do not, of themselves, stand. A third leg is needed. Leadership, business models, and people make up the three equally necessary supports for excellence and, therefore, continuous performance improvement.

No magic silver bullet

It's always comfortable to think there is one single magic solution with regards to big challenges – a silver bullet. However, there are no final victories in life, and the same principle applies to building and implementing a CPI strategy.

Having established a basis to undertake a CPI strategy, companies' must not rest on their laurels. Too many companies wait until something is conspicuously wrong before they're willing to reassess the way they do business.

These days, in many industries, the managements of many companies deserve at least a C-grade just for surviving. The question is: do you have a well-articulated CPI strategy that moves your company forward?

14

Restoring Reputations

The Strategic Value of Sustainable Stakeholder Management

The curse 'May you live in interesting times,' may cause many companies to shudder, but not really great ones. Today, in this most interesting of times, many banks believe they are beset by the curses of uncertainty, complexity, and change. However, what may be perceived as curses can be opportunities as well.

Banks currently face dramatic changes in their environment. The complex environment poses historic challenges for banks. Financial markets and banks will be fundamentally different three to five years from now. The overwhelming question to answer is to what degree will these changes be autonomous and to what degree will banks be able to direct them? What can banks do between now and then to significantly enhance the probability of ongoing success?

According to a recent study, the trick is to build a corporate reputation that is distinctive, value creating, leverageable and embedded in a sustainable stakeholder management approach (box 1). The 'reputations to restore' motto provides the main rationale for banks to build a sustainable stakeholder management mindset. In doing so, they preserve market positions and organizational vitality.

Box 1 About the research

Reputation is a matter of perception. A bank's overall reputation is a function of its reputation among its various stakeholders (e.g., customers, investors, suppliers, competitors, the general public, regulators, politicians, the communities in which the bank operates, etc) in specific categories (e.g., product quality, customer service, financial performance, handling of environmental and societal issues, intellectual capital, etc). Effectively managing reputation involves assessing a bank's reputation among stakeholders. This argues for the assessment of reputation in multiple areas (e.g., financial performance, people management, innovation management, corporate social responsibility, product/service quality, quality of management, competitiveness). Building a name that matters involves maximizing all characteristics.

Our research program started in the third quarter of 2008 and ended at the World Economic Forum in Davos (january 28 – february 1 2009). Our research team conducted 179 in-depth interviews with top executives of global banks; CEO's, CFO's or COO's of global corporations (banks' biggest clients); politicians (mainly senators); top executives of global hedge funds, and executives of the World Bank, IMF, SEC and ECB. We used analytical induction for our data analysis, iterating between data and existing theory. The analysis benefited from the perceptions drawn from personal experiences and firsthand observations. During the study, we viewed ourselves as builders, piecing together many pieces of a complex puzzle into a coherent whole.

Our interviews identified several bits and pieces of information with regards to banks' reputations. There is a very strong consensus across our research population that sustainable stakeholder management is required. The interviewees selected four outstanding 'stakeholder management banks': Santander (Spain), Rabobank (the Netherlands), HSBC Bank (UK) and Nordea (Sweden).

Future leadership in banking will require significant commitment to sustainable stakeholder management. A sustainable stakeholder management approach, as discussed in this chapter, minimizes both perceived and actual risk while insuring that the benefits from the efforts are captured.

Reputational Capital

Reputation has gone from being a buzzword to being a corporate strategy. Reputations provide meaning, direction, and boundaries to people and resources. In banking, there is a real separation between the 'reputation haves' and have-nots. So establishing a favorable reputation is a key element of a bank's strategy.

According to our study, reputation is a crucially important aspect of bank management, but it is an area where understanding could be developed much further. Defining, building and leveraging reputation remains as difficult as explaining the origins of the universe. Reputations have come a long way since their pre-20th century origins. Despite this, or perhaps because of it, the meaning of reputation is not consistently understood. Historically, reputations originated as a way of differentiating products and services, a name that connotes a set of attributes, or a means of communicating a product's benefits (both tangible and intangible).

A corporate reputation is a broad entity which enables a bank to establish a relationship with their stakeholders and encompasses the full range of attributes associated with the underlying product and service experience. Reputations that are sustainable and difficult to imitate by competitors are typically based in the bundling of unique skills, assets and relationships that are difficult for competitors to understand. Ergo: there are no quick wins in reputation management. It is a long-term investment (see also box 2: 'Reputation pays').

A corporate reputation should be developed soundly in order to create the key attributes for success. Therefore, management has to understand the needs of a diverse array of stakeholders, create and position a product or service that capitalizes on strengths within the organization, and design an effective marketing mix to promote the reputation to the target stakeholders. The reputation must then be successfully managed and maintained so that reputation equity is protected.

According to our research, learning to actively manage reputational capital, and the human and intellectual assets it encompasses, may be a bank's most crucial and strategic task because star performers in the banking industry first and foremost deliver superior stakeholders returns. For instance, Dutch Rabobank creates a pervasive profitable growth ethic based on its solid reputation. While our research suggests that maintaining profitable growth in banking is exceedingly difficult, it can be done, and Rabobank, Santander, Nordea and HSBC Bank provide us the clear lessons on how to achieve this challenging objective.

Box 2 Reputation pays

At Rabobank, reputation is of paramount importance, it is everybody's business. Reputation is sought for both products/services, involves every function, and is the 'business of banking'. Rabobank's reputation rests on the notion that, in the long run, a singular focus on reputation will have its own reward. Reputation management is a way of thinking and doing that affects all aspects of the Rabobank organization, including its management style and cultural values (embedded in Rabobank's motto: 'Stakeholder first!').

However, at Rabobank, reputation is not a panacea, nor is it excellence. Despite the importance of reputation management, there are many other important elements of business success. Rabobank thinks carefully about what they want to achieve through reputation in the context of specific business objectives and key activities.

Rabobank's management of reputational capital is a powerful competitive weapon, especially against the background of the decreasing effectiveness of the traditional sources of competitive advantage: product differentiation, cost leadership, and market power. However, to get there requires a massive awareness-building and capability-building exercise.

At Rabobank, there is only one valid definition of business purpose: to create, maintain and leverage a solid reputation. Reputation programs and 'reputation audits' not only contribute to the banks' economic statistics, but to Rabobank's fundamental quality of business life.

At a time when battered investors, customers, and employees are questioning whom they trust, the ability of a reputation to deliver proven value flows straight to the bottom line. However, the things we savor the most are the hardest earned. It is senior management's responsibility to manage the bank so as to develop and maintain a solid reputation. If our discussions with executives and politicians are any guide, there is a growing conviction that superior and sustainable stakeholder management is at least as important a source of long-term competitive advantage as superior strategy or operational effectiveness. Stakeholders are gravitating toward reputations that they sense are reliable, enduring, trustworthy and responsible. The strength of a bank's name depends on how well it has fulfilled its promise to stakeholders over time.

Sustainable Stakeholder Management

An old story tells of a drunk searching the ground beneath a street lamp. "Missing something?" inquires a curious passerby. "My keys," mutters the drunk, gesturing toward the surrounding darkness. "Lost 'em somewhere over there." "Well, why not go over there and look for them?" the passerby suggests. "Think I'm stupid?" retorts the drunk. "It's dark over there. I'm looking where the light is."

301

Banks are challenged by major discontinuities. Adapting to such challenges means change, and managing such change effectively can require approaches, time frames, and efforts that are quite different from 'where the light is best' (business as usual), especially where major change and skill building are called for.

Discontinuities in many areas have created the need for a new business paradigm. Moreover, these changes impinge upon and reinforce one another, giving direction and thrust to the emerging new paradigm. In the wake of such forces, traditional sources of competitive advantage are under assault and new bases for strategic competition are emerging. Notions of operational effectiveness and organization efficiency must be balanced by a new characteristic of success: sustainable stakeholder management. Factoring the notion of sustainable stakeholder management explicitly into banks' strategy formulation and implementation efforts will significantly improve the robustness of banks' reputations. Rabobank, Santander, HSBC Bank, and Nordea are delivering strong financial performances by applying sustainable stakeholder management precepts.

The current situation in the banking industry calls for a view on management, where management has to be engaged in a pro-active dialogue with stakeholders to really understand the true drivers of present and future industry performance. This strategic dialogue must be bifocal, attending both the long-term objectives of banks and the immediate operational issues that need to be resolved.

Banks that aspire to grow earnings profitably in future markets must apply strong stakeholder management skills. They must transform from 'distributors of products and services' to 'stakeholder managers of solutions', if they want to capture this potential. According to our research, most banks do not yet fit the profile of a true 'stakeholder manager' (box 3: 'Seven characteristics of stakeholder management capabilities').

Box 3 Seven characteristics of stakeholder management capabilities

From 'traditional banking strategies'	*To* 'stakeholder banking strategies'
Banking is a numbers game: 'knocking on lots of doors', i.e., don't leave any stakeholder out	Banking is a precision game: 'identifying and knocking on a few of the right doors', i.e., undertake indepth dialogue and partnering with selected stakeholders based on both 'feeling together' and analytics
Not having a rigorous process for listening to stakeholders and extracting the implications	Execute market research and invest in the rigor required to determine implications and priorities
Support activities undertaken by marketing department alone	Leveraging understanding of how actual stakeholder behaviors drive value
Business mainly based on product and price	Doing business through a satisfying stakeholder 'experience'
Make decisions based on standard financial analysis and anecdotical evidence with regards to customers, suppliers, and competitors	Make decisions based on a detailed, fact-based understanding of stakeholder satisfaction drivers and the relative importance of potential stakeholder experience elements
Reponsibility starts and ends with senior management	Give front-line employees the responsibility and authority to do what it takes to satisfy stakeholders
Measure, evaluate, and motivate based on volume and cost	Drive performance measurement, evaluation, and motivation from stakeholder satisfaction requirements

---

Sustainable stakeholder management is an approach in which banks seek to build long-lasting and close partnerships with stakeholders or stakeholder segments in order to encourage them to concentrate a disproportionately high share of their value with them. Banks have to pursue this objective by developing and continuously updating a deep understanding of each stakeholder's' present and future needs, and by tailoring the choice, delivery, and communication of their value propositions to these needs as closely as is feasible.

Although stakeholder management is important, relatively few banks have a sharp understanding of the ingredients for success. Stakeholder management champions' Rabobank and Nordea follow several rules:

- *They use the information they gather to serve their stakeholders better.* Excellence in banking flowes from understanding how to deliver what stakeholders need. While sustainable stakeholder management can be used as a tool to improve a bank's impact, its real power is as a lever to help banks expand by acting on insights about stakeholder needs. Particularly in areas where they can provide distinctive offerings and build loyalty over time.

- *They build stakeholder partnerships, not databases.* This means using data to identify valuable stakeholder actions that will affect value drivers.

- *They are willing to treat stakeholders differently.* Many banks fail to treat some stakeholders better than others despite value ten times greater. Stakeholder management champions differentiate.

- *They compete with partnership competences, not financial capital.* Stakeholder management champions recognize that competitive advantage is based on intangible assets, i.e., understanding stakeholder behavior, identifying ways to serve stakeholders better, and, above all, building enduring partnerships with stakeholders.

Stakeholder management is so basic that it cannot be considered a separate function. It is the whole business seen from the point of view of its final result, that is, from the stakeholder's point of view. In essence, sustainable stakeholder management is about shaping and guiding the stakeholder dialogue to build long-lasting, competitively advantaged relationships. It is a commitment by stakeholders and banks, regardless of size, to a long-term valuable relationship based on trust and on clear, mutually agreed advantages.

Developing and implementing a successful stakeholder management strategy requires a keen understanding of the basic tenets. At Nordea and Santander, basic beliefs of sustainable stakeholder management are:

- *A successful stakeholder management approach will focus on delivering satisfaction across the entire stakeholder experience.* A comprehensive understanding of the whole stakeholder experience helps clarify who the stakeholder is and develops real insight into what stakeholders need and want.

- *Capturing the benefits from a stakeholder management approach requires rigorous targeting of investments to 'move the needle'.* Which specific elements drive stakeholder satisfaction with the experience is not always obvious. For each element, the key drivers can be discerned (e.g., product/service quality, ready on time, good attitude of employees, knowledgeable organization, fast follow-up). At Nordea and Santander, the return on stakeholder satisfaction is determined by the balance of investment and results achieved.

- *Successfully implementing a sustainable stakeholder management strategy requires fundamental changes in how the organization thinks and acts.* Banks that generate high levels of stakeholder satisfaction have translated the insights into actions which are very different than those banks that are less successful at satisfying stakeholders. For instance, Santander and Nordea make decisions based on a detailed, fact-based understanding of stakeholders' satisfaction drivers, give front-line employees (e.g., account managers) the responsibility and authority to do what it takes to satisfy stakeholders, and drive performance measurement, evaluation, and motivation from stakeholder satisfaction requirements.

If stakeholder management skills will be increasingly important and if there are some 'secrets' to building them, how can banks address this need? HSBC developed a systematic approach that incorporates these secrets. Their approach starts with clarifying the stakeholder value proposition, that is, a statement of what benefits an identified target group of stakeholders will receive at what relative cost. A bank's strategy, which should embody the value it proposes to deliver to its stakeholders, determines the core skills it needs.

Next, HSBC is explicit about the few institutional skills their bank as a whole must possess to deliver this stakeholder value proposition. The trick is to focus on a few genuinely core skills, those with the most leverage and central to the ability to execute the strategy. That means first assessing how strong each of these skills is relative to what's needed and to how good competitors are, as well as estimating the value of strengthening them. Doing this helps banks know which skills to build first. It also helps them explain why they are important.

Third, for each core skill, HSBC identifies the one, two or three essential jobs that must be performed brilliantly. Ultimately, success depends on the success of pivotal job holders in delivering value to stakeholders. Because these jobs are positions that directly affect the delivery of value to stakeholders they are usually close to the front-line. Identifying these jobs requires close analysis of banks as stakeholders see them. HSBC is clear about the stakeholder management skills required by their strategy, the nature of the essential jobs and the behavior required of them.

Fourth, HSBC designs the infrastructure (e.g., information systems, decision-making procedures, management style) needed to influence, support, and empower the pivotal job holders to move toward the desired behavior. Management cannot expect superior execution of a sustainable stakeholder management strategy unless all this infrastructure is properly aligned to help build and sustain stakeholder management skills. This step lays the groundwork to 'make it happen', and requires the most time.

Stakeholders expect to be treated as they want to be treated, and that implies the bank understands how they want to be treated. Building institutional stakeholder management skills is typically a two- to three-year undertaking. However, competence-based competitive advantages offer banks substantial impact on performance and are difficult for competitors to replicate. They put a bigger premium than ever before on developing human capital.

Moving to become a winner in today's banking industry involves identifying stakeholder management competences which are essential to boost a bank's performance, then developing a program to build, sustain and leverage them. Done well, such a program can help make a bank a real winner. At Santander, HSBC, Nordea and Rabobank, these skills became the essence of the bank. They not only enable them to execute their current strategies; their strength will provide the basis for their next strategy when the current one reaches its limits.

Stakeholder mindset

Banks are facing a challenge unlike anything they have had to deal with in recent memory. The banking industry has changed dramatically in the last two years, making it difficult for old management approaches to work effectively. And as stakeholder pressures intensify, and sources of differentiation dry up, the relative value of a solid corporate reputation increases. Excellence in stakeholder management has clearly been instrumental in building a strong reputation.

There is no short-cut to making a bank stakeholder focused. Scale and scope need not be an insuperable barrier to stakeholder management if there is focus, commitment to sustainable stakeholder management, and leadership for organizational change. Unfortunately, too many banks are unwilling or unable to systematically determine the role of stakeholders in their strategy and aggressively pursue the required organizational changes. Amid all the pressures and distractions, it's easy for banks to set other priorities, or to mistakenly assume that merely putting together a new marketing strategy is enough. It is, after all, hardest to become stakeholder-minded when competitive pressure is least. It is easiest to achieve when it is already too late.

To make sustainable stakeholder management a 'way of life', it must not be seen as a separate project but as 'how we do things in this place'. The real challenge is how to build a stakeholder mindset and how to rollout it at a pace that will be sufficiently fast to stay ahead of the pack. Great stakeholder management, however, is not something you can simply invoke or turn on or off. Stakeholder management at world-class rates will only come about through persistently pushing the right levers of stakeholder performance. The road not taken can be very expensive.

15

Managing Reputation Equity

The most critical and strategic asset that a global company possesses is its reputation. Reputational capital is a vital strategic resource. Reputations reflect a firm's relative success in fulfilling the expectations of multiple stakeholders. They are crucial because they 'work' for global companies.

Building a reputation has become a major concern of global companies in industries as diverse as engineering, chemicals, ICT, FMCG, financial services, management consultancy, and retailing. Interest in corporate reputation has never been higher. It has become a corporate strategy in recent years (box 1).

Box 1 The value of reputations to global companies

1. A reputation can add value to a product beyond its physical attributes in a way that is sustainable over time.
2. A strong reputation can convince a customer to buy one product/service in preference to another.
3. A reputation can be a platform for launching new products and/or services.

4. A good reputation will be given more support by a diverse array of stakeholders (e.g., high-reputation businesses attract high-caliber people).
5. A good reputation can be resilient in the face of one off threats – if it is managed well.
6. A good reputation raises entry barriers to competitors.
7. A reputation is used by customers as shorthand for a set of desirable attributes/values and, thus, by companies as a way of rapidly building trust.

The things we savor the most are the hardest earned. It is senior management's responsibility to manage the global company so as to develop and maintain a solid reputation. Reputations aren't listed on balance sheets, but they can go further in determining a company's success than a new product, sales or channel strategy. Good reputations are essential because of their potential for economic value creation, but also because their intangible character makes replication considerably more difficult. Strong reputations have the power to loft sales and earnings.

The strength of a reputation often depends on how well it has fulfilled its promise to customers over time. It also plays an important role in attracting the best employees, suppliers, and financial stakeholders. For instance, in global investment banking and global strategy consultancy, a great reputation acts as a powerful magnet to potential employees (e.g., MBA students), helping to attract the best and brightest and keep turnover rates low.

Traditionally, reputations were expected to have a limited lifecycle. However, there is no reason why they should not live longer if they are developed soundly, maintained well and then leveraged carefully. And although the actions of all employees are reflected in a corporate reputation, management and the board of directors in particular can have a significant effect on corporate reputation. A reputation must be successfully managed and maintained so that 'reputation equity' is protected [1]. A useful instrument for this is the 'reputation improvement plan'. The reputation improvement plan is an effective tool to focus managers and employees on the tasks required to continually review and improve a reputations' progress.

What is a reputation improvement plan?

A reputation improvement plan is a critical document for the board of directors. The process of producing it forces management to think through the issues related to a particular reputation and how to address them. The document itself summarizes the reputation's competitive position and guides the implementation of strategic initiatives.

A reputation improvement plan is the document that details the future objectives, strategies and plans for a corporate reputation. The plan and the process of producing it lie at the core of the activity of great global firms, e.g, Goldman Sachs, Boston Consulting Group (BCG), Skadden, Google, Apple, McKinsey & Company and Egon Zehnder.

In companies that do them well, reputation improvement plans are typically produced annually, prepared by the board of directors with significant input from stakeholders (e.g., important customers), revised in a series of iterations with management before being agreed, and linked to other functional plans (e.g., operations, sales, R&D) ensuring that all the company's activities are focused on achieving common goals.

In practice, reputation improvement plans vary enormously in terms of structure, format and content. There is no 'right' way of producing a reputation improvement plan but this chapter summarizes what content should ideally be included. It has been derived in part from the prior experience of global companies such as BCG, Egon Zehnder and Google, and in part from my own experience as a non-executive director.

It is important to remember that reputation improvement planning is just one component of the process. The other components are:
- implementing the plan;
- monitoring progress (the process of measuring whether the plan is achieving its goals); and
- auditing the corporate reputation's situation (i.e., the auditing process comprises identifying a global company's reputation-related problems and/or opportunities and evaluating different, for instance, marketing, levers. This analysis then provides input into the reputation plan).

And, although the focus is often on the document, it is the process of drafting, discussing, agreeing and using it that is important. The document facilitates discussion and decision-making and can then be used as a guide to action.

Box 2 Purpose of reputation improvement plans

1. To review the long-term objectives and strategy of a corporate reputation in the light of the previous year's developments.
2. To propose an action plan for the corporate reputation for the next financial years covering all relevant elements.
3. To provide a detailed rationale and supporting information for the proposed course of action.
4. To establish clear measurable objectives to enable tracking by senior management.
5. To input a perspective to the strategic plan.
6. To ensure that at least once a year the corporate reputation is subjected to detailed analysis and review.

What goes into a reputation plan?

In this section, we go through the ideal components of the reputation improvement plan, explaining for each component what should go into it and why it is needed.

1. **Summary**.

   A reputation improvement plan starts with a brief description of the proposed plan summarized on one page. It provides a concise summary of a corporate reputation's current position, key threats and opportunities, and strategies for the forthcoming years. It is often appended to the full plan although its prime use is as a stand-alone summary for key managers and pivotal job holders. A 'one pager' provides a quick overview for busy management. Furthermore, it is a useful format for cross-functional communication.

2. **Overview**.

   A brief overview of the corporation's reputation improvement objectives for the coming budget year(s). What financial resources are required and how will they be employed to achieve the reputation improvement goals? Such an overview sets the context from which senior and junior management will read the plan.

3. **Role of reputation in the company**.

   This section gives a brief description of a reputation's role in the global company's overall portfolio of activities. Does a reputation fit into the company's overall business scope? This would at a minimum state the corporate strategy for the overall global company, outline where a company's reputation fits into the overall corporate

313

strategy, and where a reputation is in 'cash generation terms' (i.e., invest or not?).

4. Current corporate reputation position.

All reputation review and improvement processes will have to start with an analysis of a company's current position with regards to its reputation.

This section provides key information on the global/local market, company products, global/local competition, marketing mix, and macro environment. It is essential that this section is focused on vital information. The purpose of the 'current corporate reputation position' section is to provide the key background information necessary to understand and evaluate the reputation objectives, strategies and action plans that follow. The aim is to get the leadership group and management team to agree on the, for instance, shortcomings of the global firm's current reputation and on the need to change, rather than simply work harder at what they are doing.

For instance, in a recent study for a global investment bank, I found that they had an inadequate understanding of their clients and their real needs. I initiated a market research program that led to a proper client segmentation and the reputation being more consistently positioned to meet target customer needs.

The competitive situation gives details of major global and/or local competitors and their activities and performance. Although the content is situation specific, it should cover much or all of the following for each key competitor: reputation positioning, overall company strategy, short-term company goals and long-term aspiration. A competitive reputation analysis is a vital element in understanding the reputation's positioning versus competitive reputations and how this might change due to competitive developments.

Many global companies (particularly in services markets) offer similar product performance (e.g., banks, insurers, law firms, ICT companies, and management consultancies). However, they may offer very different levels of perceived value to customers. The difference is the intangible value added by reputation. Hence, this is a critical success factor that requires meticulous and consistent management.

5. Opportunities, threats, strengths, weaknesses and issues.

This component of a reputation improvement plan is about the opportunities and threats facing the corporate reputation (external factors) together with an assessment of strengths and weaknesses of the corporate reputation (internal factors) leading to a statement of the key strategic issues for the corporate reputation (over the term of the plan). They should be written so as to suggest some possible actions that might be taken and ranked so that the more important ones are focused on.

In short, global companies need to use the findings of the analysis to define the main issues that face the corporate reputation. Next steps should indicate how the issues are going to be resolved.

6. Corporate reputation lessons learned.

What key reputation lessons were learned over the course of the last years and what will be the learning agenda for the next years? This will range from insights into customer behavior to experience of the effectiveness of different marketing levers and their impact on the corporate reputation.

A key to success is the extent to which global companies can learn from experience. It will be critical to develop this capability. Many of the leading global company's are moving towards this kind of learning strategy.

7. Reputation objectives and strategy for the long-term and short-term.

This section is about the corporate reputation targets for the next 3-5 years (long-term), the next twelve months (short-term), and, a statement of the long and short-term strategy to achieve the objectives.

Reputation objectives will be derived from the global company's overall objectives and ambitions. They allow global companies to aggregate plans and see if they will satisfy stakeholder expectations. This will include details of how the corporate reputation will be positioned against target competitors and clients in 3-5 years' time.

Objectives should encompass both market measures (e.g., reputation ranking versus competition) and client perception (e.g., client awareness, perceived benefits and weaknesses of the reputation). Such objectives give management measures that can be assessed directly against their knowledge of the market and are thus less abstract than mere financial metrics.

Management should check that the set of reputation objectives meet certain criteria. Each objective should be stated in an unambiguous and measurable form with a stated time period for accomplishment. Furthermore, the mix of objectives should be internally consistent, stated hierarchically – if possible – with lower level objectives being derived from higher level ones, and, the objectives should be attainable, but sufficiently challenging to stimulate maximum effort.

As a rule of thumb reputation objectives should be thought of as being the 'what', the strategies as the 'governing thought' of 'how' to achieve the 'what'. The action plans are then lower level tactics stemming from the 'how'.

In developing a reputation strategy, there are a multitude of possible choices. Each objective can be achieved in a number of ways. Each of these corporate reputation strategies can in turn be achieved in a number of ways. By going down the path of each objective and strategy, the manager can identify the major strategic alternatives facing the firm's reputation.

What should be contained in the 'strategy section'? First and foremost: the target market. The target market is who you want to persuade (to buy products or services) through your corporate reputation. Furthermore, the 'positioning strategy' is what a company wants the customer to believe about its product/service and how they should use it. Both strategies vary enormously from short-term tactical strategies (e.g., promotional support and competitive responses) to long-term reputation development (e.g., external image building and internal identity building).

8. Rationale, action plan and options.

By now the plan has defined the corporate reputation's current position, the threats and opportunities facing it and its roles in the global company's business scope. In the light of these circumstances a set of objectives and strategies has been developed from any number of alternatives.

The task now is to explain the rationale for proposing the suggested course of action. The rationale should detail:

- How the objectives were set and why they represent a challenging, but realistic target given the market context and the resources requested.
- Why the overall reputation strategy is the best approach for achieving the aforementioned objectives.
- Why certain action plans best deliver against the strategies. Action plans are typically detailed plans for the next year(s) outlining the timing of key events with the associated costs, including media bursts, client events, and market research studies; and
- What options were considered. An option is an alternative scenario based on pursuing a different set of objectives. This should include a rationale for why each option might, or might not, be worth pursuing. It allows management to see the incremental effect of the proposed plan against possible alternative choices.

Such a rationale allows management to see the logic behind the selection of one course of action over another which should quickly highlight flawed thinking. In practice it is difficult for management to understand the reasoning behind the selection of one course of action over another. Consequently, if is often difficult to determine whether the logic underpinning the plan is sound and whether the plan represents the value maximizing approach.

9. **Financial statement and special resource requirements**.

This is essentially a projected (expected) financial statement, based on the action plans outlined. It is the bottom line for senior management. Analysis of the financial statement often highlights plan anomalies and key issues. Higher management will review the budget and approve or modify it. Once approved, the budget is the basis for operations.

This section also outlines any special resource requirements in terms of staffing (for instance, dedicated marketing support personnel), unique skills and funding (e.g., major cash injections) that will be critical to the achievement of the reputation improvement plan. This flags any special requirements so that management can confirm its approval.

10. **Controls**.

The final section of a reputation improvement plan outlines the controls that will be applied to monitor the plan's progress and what deviation from the plan will trigger a response.

Risks that could affect the plan should be highlighted and, if possible, quantified. Good control sections also include contingency ('what if?') plans. These outline the steps that management would implement in response to the top three or so major adverse developments that might occur. Good contingency planning greatly improves the speed and often the quality of response to problems.

Unlocking the value of reputation

A successful reputation improvement plan and program will only occur when the following combined forces are effective: dissatisfaction with the status quo (a sense of urgency), a vision of something better (a clear target embedded in a plan), and a few practical first steps to achieve (i.e., launching the process). Reputation is not a gift, but really hard work.

It invariably pays to recognize the nature of the barriers the executive faces. These barriers represent, first and foremost, both a lack of skills and a lack of will to take the requirements of a reputation improvement program. Three barriers are particularly hazardous:

- *defence of historic power bases*. Sometimes, managers charged with implementing a reputation improvement plan simply lack the will to drive the job through.
- *management inertia*. Reputation improvement plan efforts require managers to make substantial changes in their role (a time-consuming process). They – very often – need to manage activities differently from the way they have worked in the past.
- *widespread cynicism*. The broad body of a global company may remain unmoved by a bold new program, saying they have 'seen it all before'. Their cynicism may be reinforced if they are receiving ambivalent messages from managers and executives.

However, the most important asset of global companies is their corporate reputation. It is a priceless commodity. Successful global companies such as Apple, Google, HP, Nike, BMW, McKinsey& Company, Bang & Olufsen, Porsche and L'Oréal invest a great deal of money in developing, improving and supporting their excellent reputation. Their organization is often structured around their reputation, capitalizing their reputation with the intention of reducing their vulnerability.

Ultimately, character is all about retaining a strong identity and reputation.

A corporate reputation is a key intangible asset that helps to create economic value. It has a strong impact on profits. The 'reputation-profits' effect may operate in both directions: a global company's financial performance affects its reputation and its reputation affects its financial performance.

Global companies will become increasingly focused on managing their reputations over the next decade. 'Competitive reputation management' refers to activities undertaken by individual companies to enhance its own reputation and competitive position versus other members of the industry. At the end of the day, reputation is the most important global currency. Ergo: great reputation management beats great technology most days of the week.

References

[1] Studies' suggest that a ten percent improvement in reputation is worth between one and five percent of a company's market value. See, for instance, E.L. Black, T.A. Carnes, and V.J. Richardson, "The Market Valuation of Corporate Reputation", in: *Corporate Reputation Review*, Vol. 3, No. 1, p. 31-41, 2000.

Part V. Global Strategy and China

16

Doing Business in Today's China

Still Searching for the Pot of Gold?

The China market continues to attract new foreign multinational companies, in part because such major players as Motorola, Philips and Unilever have already been successful [1]. Philips, for instance, now has more than 50 alliances with Chinese companies. Many trade and service companies have entered the Chinese market in the tracks of their industrial counterparts. Medium-sized and smaller companies are about to follow their bigger colleagues. The question is whether China is really a genuine market or rather mostly an illusory one.

The 381 managers of European and US multinational companies I surveyed have high expectations for China's growth potential [2]. With 1,3 billion consumers who have begun to demand more expensive consumer goods such as washing machines, CD players and cars, China looks more attractive than most other countries as a new market [3].

But there is even more to lure businesses. China is also a source of relatively cheap, high-quality raw materials and an excellent launching site for the export of inexpensive semi-finished and finished products (think, for instance, of sports shoes such as Nike, Reebok, Adidas, Asics Tiger and Brooks). The growth of the Chinese market has been hovering around 9 percent annually for many years. So it is not unexpected to see that a true "run" on China has occurred. At the moment, over 450,000 multinational companies are active in China, most of which operate via alliances [4].

Foreign companies tend to believe they must simply have a presence in this market and only at later stage must they concentrate on the implications. Foreign companies that worked the Chinese market early on have managed to build up a nice lead in terms of knowledge and experience over the late entrants by now. Foreign companies that underestimated the market potential of this region until a short while ago regret this in mid-2006.

Some nuances are in place however. The average margins are still wafer-thin and most foreign companies still operate unprofitably in the Chinese market. This is due to the complexity and obscure character of this market [5].

Operating cost effectively is often an extraordinary feat. Even though many companies are in danger of drowning in a sea of red figures, they rarely consider giving up their positions. Most foreign companies are convinced that it is impossible and unwise to ignore the growth potential of the Chinese market. Many of them therefore look at the Chinese market as a long term investment and accept losses sustained in the short and the medium term.

Box 1 China profile (2005)

Population   1,335 million (since 1993, average annual growth
                    1 percent)
Population density 147 pers/km2
Literacy   87 percent
GDP/capita   US$ 555
GDP growth rate   approximately 9 percent per year since 1990

- China's population, more than three times that of Europe, is concentrated in the southern and coastal areas.
- A market economy was introduced via special economic zones (SEZ's): Deng Xiaoping led the way in the economic explosion with the Socialist Market Economy reform of 1992.
- China's economic wealth is concentrated in the southern and coastal regions.
- The main export products are at the low technology end, such as textiles, garments and shoes.
- The purchasing power of the average Chinese consumer is rapidly increasing and economic policy trends are moving from regulation driven to market driven.
- Combined, stronger domestic consumption and a more open Chinese market have sparked an impressive growth of foreign direct investment.

Source: World Trade Organization, International Monetary Fund (2005)

Entry strategies

What do entry strategies deployed by foreign companies look like?

Most foreign companies began by forming a limited number of alliances (joint ventures) because of a lack of other options available. The number of alternative entry strategies has been artificially limited for a long time because the Chinese authorities did not allow any strategies other than joint ventures and other forms of cooperation closely connected to them [6]. Moreover, until recently, the Chinese authorities decided which foreign companies could ally with whom. The government also decided which products would be involved and where they would be sold or manufactured.

Most foreign companies deliberately played along with that policy. Starting up a joint venture was an ideal opportunity for them to gain knowledge about this promising market. The narrow, politically inspired profit margins the Chinese authorities allowed were used to the maximum possible [7]. The joint ventures served as marketing tools to generate valuable information.

In time, not only the number but also the scale of these joint ventures increased as foreign companies dared to take more risks. Since the late 1990s more start-up businesses were established as Chinese authorities allowed foreign companies to generate initiatives on their own [8].

Box 2 Research methodology

This chapter is based on a survey of 381 managers of foreign multinational companies active in China, executed by the Center for International Business of the Universiteit Nyenrode, the Netherlands, in 2002 and 2003. The managers interviewed were general as well as specialized and included sales and marketing managers.

The managers interviewed worked for, among others, Motorola, Unilever, Shell, Alcatel, Philips, Kodak, Nokia, Pfizer, PepsiCo, General Motors, Procter and Gamble, Ericsson, Goldman Sachs, Siemens, FedEx, Arco, Coca Cola, Otis, PriceWaterhouseCoopers, Volkswagen, Lucent, Johnson and Johnson, AT&T, Saint Gobain, Nestlé and Anheuser-Busch.

The eight hurdles

Foreign companies that have been actively working the Chinese market for years have strikingly similar opinions on the major problems newcomers may face. According to my survey (see box 2), the following eight hurdles present major challenges for both established and new foreign businesses in China. In descending order of importance, according to the managers interviewed, they are:

Management orientation differs significantly

Chinese managers care more about the quantity of products to be manufactured rather than their quality. Most have little acquaintance with areas such as marketing and entrepreneurship, both essential management tools in a business environment where global competition rules.

The difference in management orientation is reflected clearly at the operational business management level. Foreign and Chinese companies interpret the notion "agreement" very differently. In the USA and Europe, an agreement or a contract has a binding meaning. Breaking a contract is therefore difficult to do. This is not the case in China, where agreements or contracts are not necessarily binding.

A Chinese business partner pays close attention to the status of the person signing an agreement/contract. The tentacles of Chinese hierarchy reach so far that it is important for a foreign company to check whether it is the highest authority who has signed the agreement. If this is not the case, the contract may not be binding and its implementation cannot be enforced.

Differences in culture are difficult to bridge

The difference in management orientation follows naturally from the cultural differences. US and European business people tend toward individualism, seek risks, and want to get to the heart of the matter in the shortest time possible. Chinese business people are indirect (which obscures the social and company structures), display a collectivist attitude (a fruitful breeding ground for various interest groups that are hard to manipulate) and seek to avoid risks (the hierarchy determines people's behavior). For Western business people, the welfare of the business goes before the group's best interests. For the Chinese respect for the group goes without exception before business [9].

Separating a person from a deal may seem natural in US and European business societies and also in Japanese business circles. In China, the one is inextricably interwoven with the other. In this respect foreign managers say they sometimes feel as if they are going about their business in China like bulls in a china shop.

The most striking differences in culture are explained by the far-reaching influence of Confucianism, which requires the individual to obey the superior so that a streamlined social order can be established. The group is primary in this respect. Within the group, network and hierarchy play an important role. In a Chinese network, the person who makes a decision at the top of a hierarchy is never held responsible in that capacity. Other people bear the responsibility for his decision and its implementation. Nevertheless, he will seldom fire a subordinate who does not perform optimally. A prominent Chinese politician once aptly stated:

> "In the West, people are born with individual rights, in China people are born with social obligations".

A fragmented market

Foreign companies may experience the extreme diversity in Chinese markets as a difficult hurdle [10]. The low degree of homogeneity is closely connected with the regional differences in income. The differences in disposable income - apart from the different types of consumers - largely determine which products can be marketed and in which regions.

The British/Dutch company Unilever, for instance,uses a segmented market approach for different regional markets. By entering into alliances with local companies, they first work to improve consumer goods already marketed by a Chinese partner. Unilever only introduces global brands - with which the company is normally associated - in a later stage, deploying this strategy for the Omo brand.

Implementing a step-by-step segmentation strategy is a way for Unilever to keep local talent. In the Unilever philosophy, its growth in China is determined by the quantity and the quality of local Chinese management and marketing potential. The thought behind this philosophy is that China has to be opened up by Chinese instead of Dutch or UK expatriates.

China's regional markets are so diverse that, in many aspects, the German and Greek markets have more in common than the North and the South of China. This calls for inventive and therefore risk-seeking entrepreneurship (see box 3).

Box 3 Regulation of foreign direct investment in China

Foreign direct investment is *encouraged* when it:

- engages in new agricultural technologies or comprehensive agricultural development;
- involves construction of energy, transportation or important industrial projects;
- helps bring in new and advanced technologies for the utilization of resources;
- helps boost exports of upmarket products;
- helps develop the Central and Western parts of China, and
- conforms to state law and administrative legislation.

Foreign direct investment is *restricted* when:

- domestic technologies can ensure sufficient supply to domestic demand;
- the targeted industries are monopolized by the state or attract foreign direct investments on trial basis;
- investors intend to explore domestic resources, and
- the targeted industries come within unified state planning.

Foreign direct investment is *prohibited* when:

- it threatens national security or 'social public benefit';
- it pollutes the environment or damages people's health;
- it produces negative effects on land resource development;
- it takes advantage of technologies unique to China for the purpose of production, and
- there is a ban set by state law.

The need for multiple ventures in China is unavoidable for most companies seeking to build a substantial presence. Setting up a string of alliances is the way to manage the fragmented nature of the Chinese market effectively. The far-reaching degree of decentralization and the rapid changes that presently take place at the regional and national levels serve in this respect as the last move in the direction of starting up alliance strategies.

Bureaucracy on the increase

The Communist Party wields the greatest influence, followed by the government and then the National People's Congress. Roles and responsibilities of each ministry may overlap with one another and are often poorly defined. Local interests (mainly provincial/municipal level) normally outrank national interests (when the project size is not too big), so any decision making process which involves government tends to be lengthy and complicated. Therefore, good relations at all levels of the Chinese governmental structure are crucial for foreign investors (see box 4).

The foreign managers interviewed affirm that bureaucracy is increasing, primarily due to the lack of control from Beijing. The decentralization on all levels of the decision-making process I have witnessed in past years has eroded Beijing's power considerably [11]. This means that foreign companies are increasingly forced to look for local partners and customers, as they are no longer forced to make a detour via Beijing.

At first glance, this appears to be an advantage. It saves foreign companies time and they can get to know the consumer's wishes faster. Nevertheless, decentralization of the decision-making process does have its disadvantages. One central party, although inactive, is traded in for several local parties that tend to implement their own laws. Local magistrates have wishes and preferences of their own which may deviate from the policy advanced by Beijing.

The political dimension of entrepreneurship appears to have increased rather than decrease after the large-scale administrative decentralization. The result is that working the Chinese market often becomes more expensive than initially anticipated [12].

Box 4 Volkswagen Group: a study in multi-level government relations

Step 1: goodwill gestures

- Ran training courses for large numbers of Chinese in Germany each year.
- Created business links between German suppliers and local suppliers.
- Hired famous German soccer star to coach the Chinese national soccer team.

Step 2: government attitude management

- Ongoing communication with Shanghai mayor and the media.
- Effort to expand sourcing from local Chinese suppliers created favorable attitudes on the part of government officials.
- Continued support by Volkswagen Group president despite financial difficulties.

Step 3: high-level involvement

- Principal ally in the central and municipal government was Shanghai mayor.
- Selected the best combination of partners, including CNAIC, the auto industry policy maker.
- Secured preferential treatment from Beijing and Shanghai authorities.

Step 4: leverage political support

- Negotiation started with Minister of Machinery's visit to Germany.
- Equity joint venture structure, as opposed to licensing, demonstrated Volkswagen's long-term commitment.
- The joint venture contract signed in the presence of the German Chancellor (Dr. Helmut Kohl).
- German government maintained investment commitment through the political crisis in 1989.

Lack of judicial code to do business

China lacks formal company law, so the possibility of tackling potential collisions between foreign and Chinese companies and solving them by legal means is not available. The judicial system in China is quite open and hardly concrete. As a result, foreign companies are vulnerable to the political views of local authorities.

Actions that are illegal in the West are often legal in China. That is one of the reasons why Philips, for instance, lost considerable income in recent years. Chinese companies copied CDs and software on a large scale with impunity, to the dismay of Philips executives in Amsterdam. Further, copying behavior has a lucrative global dimension. Chinese copycats do not only work the Chinese market, but also enter attractive import markets such as the USA, Japan and the EU. Philips had to compete on a worldwide scale with illegally produced CDs and software.

For the time being, there seems to be no solution because it is difficult to regulate such behavior. Intellectual property legislation has only just started in China, and it has not yet gained any experience with sanctioning.

Insufficient logistic infrastructure

The transport situation in China is inadequate in terms of quantity as well as quality [13].

Transporting energy, raw materials and semi-finished products over large distances is difficult and many foreign companies are unsure of energy supplies in certain regions. Today, various foreign companies still have to import necessary raw materials and components of semi-finished and finished products.

From a market point of view, the lack of efficient infrastructure is a disaster because the fastest growing - and therefore the most interesting - regions in China (the hinterland) are often the least accessible. Consequently, foreign companies have to keep far too big a stock, driving up the costs of doing business in China.

Poor quality of labor

The quality of people behind products is an important, if not the most critical, success factor in the competitive struggle for margins and market share. The challenge in China is that most workers are not sufficiently qualified to meet the needs of foreign companies. Only a minority has had an academic or business education.

Management techniques used by Chinese companies are often obsolete. Basic concepts such as accounting, marketing, strategy, and management information systems are unknown to them. Consequently, foreign/China joint venture duties that require specific skills are often performed by foreign managers for the time being.

Large-scale investments in the training/education of the Chinese employee has its downside. Well-trained Chinese employees actively engage in job hopping, according to the managers interviewed. Indeed, they are a scarce economic resource whose market value only increases due to the training and education they have had. The majority of the foreign companies believe that this problem will only grow in the future.

Vulnerable financial system

The Chinese financial system is a mix of Confucian and communist principles. According to the interviewees, it is insufficiently tailored to the current demand for financial services.

Banks, insurance companies and subsidy providers are highly bureaucratic and ill-equipped to meet the current demand. The first stock exchanges, an automated corporate bond market and some commodity futures markets were started only a few years ago.

The financial policy of the Chinese authorities incorporates too many financial restrictions and too few financial possibilities. Further, standard booking methods do not exist, making it difficult for foreign companies to assess the financial soundness of their Chinese business partners. Joint ventures are first and foremost "joint adventures" for foreign companies (see box 5).

Box 5 The six habits of highly-effective foreign investors in China

The advice given by the managers interviewed in the survey, listed in descendant order of importance, is general in character, but it indicates how difficult it is for a foreign company to succeed in business in China:

- *Establish a high organizational ability to adapt.* The needs of the Chinese market are evolving, so companies have to adapt constantly to the changing wishes and needs of Chinese customers. This calls for a flexible mindset.

- *Cultivate a long-term prospect.* "Contacting for contracting" usually takes a long time in Asian cultures. Executives and entrepreneurs who set their sights on the Chinese market have to leave the "big steps, quickly home" strategies they often deploy on their desks.

- *Carefully select a partner to establish an alliance.* In most cases, it is necessary to cooperate with a local Chinese company, but there are broad choices when a foreign company selects its partner nowadays. A local partner always has to fit in with a foreign company's

337

ambitions. Therefore, a partner should be carefully selected and not too rapidly (see also chapter 13).

- *Build up a critical mass of knowledge about the Chinese market.* The Chinese market is highly fragmented, which calls for a thorough analysis of different geographic and market sectors. Based on a thorough market analysis, an alliance strategy can be formulated. It is important to continue to understand that the Chinese market differs considerably from other markets. Make sure to put an exaggerated market orientation in place, instead of a production or product orientation.

- *Actively use the resources of the national, regional and local Chinese authorities.* 'Guan-Xi': build strong personal relationships with central and local authorities as well as with partners and customers. Practically all business transactions are relation-dependent.

- *Emphasize simplicity.* The executives and managers I interviewed understand that one key to excelling in China is to keep their business model as simple and manageable as possible. They typically undertake only those business activities that are critical to building a competitive advantage, focusing on core products that they know how to manufacture and sell well. Contrary to conventional wisdom, they do a minimum of product tailoring and a minimum of local design, all geared toward keeping the complexity of their China operations at the bare minimum needed to succeed.

Patience

Negotiating the eight hurdles described above does not guarantee a successful entry into the Chinese market. Being active on the Chinese market requires sound entrepreneurship and a fair share of common sense, luck, long financial breath and patience [14]. Indeed, there is a reason why one of the best-known Chinese proverbs reads: "He who treads softly will go a long way."

References

[1] See: J.E. Garten, "Opening the Doors for Business in China", Harvard Business Review, p. 167-175, May-June 1998; J. Meier, J. Perez, and J.R. Woetzel, "MNCs in China", The McKinsey Quarterly, p. 20-33, No. 2 1995; Wall Street Journal, "U.S. Tops China as No. 1 Target of Multinational Firms' Investments", March 14 1995.

[2] See also: D.F. Simon, "What is the Future for Foreign Business in China?", California Management Review, p. 106-123, Winter 1990; E. Bouteiller, "The Emergence of Greater China as an Economic Force", Long Range Planning, p. 54-60, Vol. 28, February 1995.

[3] E. Tse, "The Chinese Consumer Market", Strategy & Business, p. 10-21, Second Quarter 1998.

[4] Based on UN/EC data and Eurostat (2000).

[5] See, for example: L. Zhuang, R. Ritchie, and Q. Zhang, "Managing Business Risks in China", Long Range Planning, p. 606-613, Vol. 31, August 1998; Business Week, "The Obstacles are Huge, but Surmountable", p. 40-44, May 26, 1997.

[6] W.H. Davidson, "Creating and Managing Joint Ventures in China", California Management Review, p. 77-94, Vol. 24, No. 4, Summer 1987.

[7] I. Bjorkman and G.E. Osland, "Multinational Corporations in China: Responding to Government Pressures", Long Range Planning, p. 436-445, Vol. 31, No. 3, June 1998.

[8] See also: W.R. Vanhonacker, "A Better Way to Crack China", Harvard Business Review, p. 20-22, July-August 2000; E. Tse, "Competing in China: An Integrated Approach", Strategy & Business, p. 13-23, Fourth Quarter 1998.

[9] See also: K. Lieberthal, "Governing China", Norton, 1995.

[10] See also: Financial Times, "In Search of Fresh Pastures", December 8 1995; R. Yan, "To Reach China's Consumers, Adapt to Guo Qing", Harvard Business Review, p. 66-74, September-October 1994.

[11] For a detailed analysis: J. Frankenstein, "The Beijing Rules: Contradictions, Ambiguities and Controls", Long Range Planning, p. 70-81, Vol. 28, February 1995.

[12] For an elaboration, see: W. Vanhonacker, "Entering China: An Unconventional Approach", Harvard Business Review, p. 130-140, March-April 1997; R. Yan, "Short-term Results: The Litmus Test for Success in China", Harvard Business Review, p. 61-75, September-October 1998.

[13] See also: C. Tseng, P. Kwan, and F. Cheung, "Distribution in China: A Guide Through the Maze", Long Range Planning, p. 81-91, Vol. 28, No. 1 1995.

[14] P. Kenna and S. Lacy, "Business China", Passport Books, Lincolnwood, 1994.

17

Building Successful China Alliances

The importance of China as a key strategic market has increased rapidly and continues to do so. China is now the second or third largest market in the world for virtually every consumer and commercial product sold. Chinese companies have rapidly become some of the world's most formidable competitors and continue to gain position in a variety of world markets. Active participation in the Chinese market is the first step to meeting this global challenge.

Participation in the Chinese market is also a requirement for being a viable global competitor. And while an independent effort may at first appear to be the most attractive option, few companies have the necessary resources, skills and capabilities to become viable go-it-alone competitors in China.

An alliance with a Chinese company encompasses a broad range of potential collaboration from supply or marketing agreements to joint ventures. Although China alliances are risky and certainly face significant challenges, if properly designed and managed they are the most effective method for building and profiting from a competitive position in one of the world's toughest and most important markets.

Managing China alliances has to be learned by trial and error. It requires mutual adaptation to each other's national and business cultures and the need to live with reduced autonomy. Managers involved in China alliances must know how to deal with their foreign counterparts who may come from an entirely different type of decision-making culture.

Foreign companies such as Philips and Unilever have used various forms of China alliances for many years. But many companies have avoided them, viewing such alliances as almost a last resort because of the inherent difficulties in successfully negotiating, managing and exploiting them.

However, the past few years have seen a significant increase in their use by foreign companies to fulfil their strategic objectives and during the last 12 months hardly a day has gone by without an announcement of some significant China alliance.

Entering China

Establishing relationships with Chinese companies can be very rewarding, provided your objectives are clear and you take the time to get to know the company with which you intend to work. But although the China alliances of foreign companies share many of the characteristics of international alliances generally, there are some important differences.

First, the obstacles to becoming an "insider" in China, both real and perceived, are higher than most other countries, making alliances the primary mode of entry to the market. Differences in goals and objectives, corporate strategy, culture and competitive style appear to be far greater between Chinese and foreign companies than between, for example, North American and European companies. These differences are the key source of the problems and cause many China alliances to fall short of expectations (see box 1).

Box 1 Problem solving approaches

	Western	**Chinese**
Problem	Focused	Multifaceted
Decision making	Architectural Economic basis Rational driven	Eclectic Holistic basis Consensus driven
Approach	Linear	Fuzzy
Proof	Accepted model Integrated tools	Agreement
Solution	Specific steps	Broad visions

The lure of China

There are a number of benefits in several areas to building and maintaining a strong position in the Chinese market:

- *Financial benefits.* China is one of the world's largest and fastest growing consumer and commercial markets. The Chinese market can provide incremental income on fixed investments in R&D and manufacturing. The size of the market makes global production scale achievable.

- *Strategic learning.* Strategic learning is about learning new skills, capabilities, technology or information in one market and then transferring them within a corporation worldwide to strengthen its global competitive position. Even if the Chinese market is not so attractive on a financial basis to a particular company, the strategic lessons and skills learned from participating in the market are often valuable and can be transferred to other markets.

- *Strategic position.* A strong presence in the Chinese market can also weaken Chinese competitors' global attack by diverting resources - management time and cash - and squeezing profits in their home market. A number of foreign companies weakened their global competitive position by ceding their position in China.

Learning to successfully compete against Chinese firms requires a full understanding of the "soft" elements of Chinese competitive style and values - an understanding that can be gained only through active participation in the Chinese market. (A complex bureaucracy, old boys' network and many vague or unwritten rules and regulations in China often make access and understanding of the business and regulatory environment extremely difficult.)

Box 2 Partner selection in China: five key questions

1. Can the Chinese partner perform as required to make the alliance a success?
2. Is the Chinese partner consistent with your view of how the China alliance might evolve?
3. Are individual chemistries and corporate cultures compatible?
4. Would other partners offer greater value-creation potential?
5. Can you ensure that the alliance fits your short-term and long-term strategy?

Under certain conditions a go-it-alone strategy may be the most appropriate approach to the Chinese market. However, building and sustaining an independent position in China is extremely difficult. The nature and structure of Chinese industry creates a highly integrated network of relationships, making it difficult for a foreign firm to gain access to the essential elements of operating a business.

Developing the relationships and the soft integration skills needed to operate effectively in China requires five to ten years of dedicated effort. The choice between a go-it-alone or alliance entry is a function of the soft integration barriers, product competition and commitment to the Chinese market.

Going it alone in China may be appropriate if a foreign company has an extremely strong commitment (which requires significant investment of time, capital and management talent), a significant technological lead (which provides the time to learn soft integration skills and adapt to competing in the Chinese market) or soft integration skills are not critical to success.

In spite of the inherent difficulty in realizing the full potential value, alliances with Chinese companies are often the most effective method of establishing and building a strategic position or accessing critical resources in China:

- The Chinese partner acts as a teacher in overcoming soft integration issues by providing instant contacts, experience, intuition and credibility.
- It reduces the investment required, provides returns quickly and offers opportunities for rapid strategic learning.

The alliance approach to the Chinese market seems most appropriate when soft integration skills are critical for success (see box 3).

Box 3 Alliance negotiation approach

Western approach	Chinese approach
Do a deal	Build a relationship
Maximize shareholder value or profitability	Maximize learning and turnover
Analysis/synthesis driven	Relationship driven
"Go-no-go" decision process	Step-by-step process

Important soft integration benefits of an alliance with a Chinese firm are:

- *Immediate access to Chinese personnel at all levels of the organization.* It is difficult for foreign companies to hire people. Top-quality personnel often prefer to join a Chinese company (and stay there).
- *Access to an established supplier base.* Many of the supplier systems are relationship-based and have evolved over many years of doing business together.
- *Access to an established distribution system that is inflexible and complex.* Aggressive channel management by Chinese competitors prevents entry. Distribution scales also work against the small volumes of foreign firms.
- *Access to an established customer base.* Customers are often reluctant to experiment or switch to an unknown foreign firm. A Chinese partner provides instant credibility.

As a result, the traditional basis for a China alliance has been the foreign company providing new technology or products in exchange for the Chinese company providing market access and soft integration capabilities.

Common pitfalls of China alliances

However, fundamental differences in the strategic objectives and competitive style of foreign and Chinese firms create the potential for significant problems and even the premature failure of many alliances. Very few China alliances are regarded as successful; many fail or do not live up to the expectations of either partner. In general, the problems experienced by most China alliances fall into two areas: "frictional losses" and "shifting contributions".

Frustrations expressed by executives on both sides indicate that many China alliances that remain intact are not effective. The frictional losses in three key areas - strategy (positioning); resources (time required to reach decisions and act, and deployment of people); and finances (level and timing of investment, and profit/dividends expectations) - can affect virtually every decision and activity of the alliance.

The root cause of these losses is the wide differences in the goals, decision-making processes and competitive styles of foreign and Chinese firms.

Shifting contributions and the resulting instability is often the cause of China alliance failures. Technology and knowledge leakage by the foreign company and the aggressive learning by the Chinese partner frequently cause contributions to shift. Changes in the market, external environment and parent firm strategies can also result in contributions being out of balance. Different approaches to learning in an alliance often results in a one-way flow of information and create dramatic differences in what each partner gains.

Establishing and managing China alliances

Establishing and managing a China alliance for the benefit of both partners requires that the alliance be designed to meet specific strategic objectives and to structurally incorporate key elements that encourage flexibility, participation and continued commitment by both partners.

There are six key guidelines to designing and managing China alliances to maximize the value to both partners. Furthermore, each China alliance will need a mix of alliance-specific formal/informal organizational and managerial devices.

Setting and sharing strategic objectives from the beginning

One of the keys to minimizing frictional losses is to select an alliance form and partner that matches your strategic objectives. Setting clear strategic objectives at the beginning will help guide your efforts when evaluating potential business opportunities in China.

There are a wide variety of relationship options to use when designing the alliance to match strategic objectives. A company's specific situation and goals should be paramount in determining the appropriate business relationship. Furthermore, the appropriate form of alliance is a function of soft integration barriers and commitment to building a position in the Chinese market.

For example, the "teacher alliance" provides for a fixed-life relationship where the foreign firm learns from the Chinese company how to build the skills and capabilities necessary for an independent business in China.

In contrast to acquisitions, where much of the integration planning is often done after the deal, in alliances it is absolutely imperative to assess the mutual synergies and create detailed plans for working together before a deal is signed, since neither partner will have full control thereafter.

Clarity and mutual commitment

Defining what success means for both partners and for the China alliance and ensuring 100 per cent clarity on, and mutual understanding of, the strategic objectives at the start constitute the first hurdle on the way towards a successful China alliance. Furthermore, the alliance should be designed so that the partners are dependent on it for a key element of their overall strategy.

Partners should stay in close touch, especially during the initial stages of co-operation, and ensure that whatever deal is ultimately struck represents a win/win situation for both. Unless you plan to establish a large-scale manufacturing base in China, it is usually a good idea to begin with small, standalone projects to build a good working relationship.

Bounded autonomy of alliance

Successful China alliances seem to go through an initial phase of establishment and dependence on the parents before developing into an autonomous self-sustaining unit. As a China alliance develops capabilities independent of the parents, it becomes a self-sustaining business and the issues that plague many China alliances tend to diminish.

Creating the initial critical mass required for an alliance to reach independence and then managing the alliance to avoid conflicts with the parents are the key challenges in designing China alliances.

Strategic and operational flexibility

One key to sustained benefits for both partners in a China alliance is building in both the expectation and capability to evolve the structure and strategy of the alliance in response to change. The competitive environment, parent strategies and alliance resource requirements will change over time, necessitating changes in the scope, structure and strategy of the alliance. Potential partners should go into the alliance expecting to restructure at some point in the future.

It is important to make appropriate conflict-resolution mechanisms part of the alliance agreement. Regardless of the type of alliance, managing a China alliance successfully means being able to resolve conflicts between the partners. Therefore, anticipating potential conflicts beforehand and making conflict-resolution policies part of the final agreement is critical.

Barriers to exit

Designing barriers to exit for both partners provides incentive for foreign and Chinese companies to resolve minor differences and reduces the chances that one partner will walk away.

Examples of effective barriers to exit are "total participation" – for example, the alliance encompasses the entire business or related business segments of the Chinese partner, which neutralizes or pre-empts the competitive threat – and "exit penalties" for withdrawal such as forfeiture or buyout at book value of assets contributed.

Shared vision and rewards

There are a number of mechanisms that are used to ensure shared rewards and a common vision for the alliance among parents in a China alliance. These include:

- *Equity purchase in parents.* Purchase or exchange of equity in the parent firms signals a long-term commitment and provides sharing of alliance benefits.
- *Knowledge licensing to parents.* Cross-licensing of alliance knowledge (for example, technology) to parent firms ensures that any success is shared.
- *Total business alliance.* Incorporating complete businesses into the alliance ensures that both parents companies gain only via the alliance.
- *Share rewards.* For example, dividends, royalties, knowledge and technology.
- *Board representation.* Board seats on parent firms by alliance management or partner management helps create common commitment and vision among management from both partners.

Challenging agenda

Designing the China alliance to meet the requirements of each principle simultaneously is extremely difficult and requires an iterative approach to maximize the design for stability. This is a challenging agenda and one that contains many inherent conflicts. But with the increasing consolidation and globalization of major industries around the world, some form of China alliance may become critical for many more companies.

Part VI. Cases in Global Strategy

18 Alliance Management - KLM/Alitalia

18

Alliance Management

KLM/Alitalia

On a sunny afternoon in July 1997, Gros-Pietro - CEO of IRI, Alitalia's main shareholder – mentioned to an Italian journalist that KLM would be an ideal complementary partner for Alitalia.

Alitalia, Italy's "national treasure" and, measured in size, the fourth largest airline in Europe, was focused, at that time, on finding a suitable and attractive partner. Alitalia first courted Air France, but found out its route network overlapped with theirs. In addition, Air France was less attractive than its Dutch competitor because of its size. Being considerably larger than Alitalia, Air France was not an attractive candidate as far as Alitalia's management was concerned. They knew the French would swallow them up in the long term, and this was something they could never accept.

The Dutch airline, KLM, was considered much more attractive by the management of Alitalia. 'Quality' was the guiding adage of KLM. The Dutch airline was smaller than its French counterpart and had a complementary route network.

In addition, KLM was profitable and a market driven company: Words rarely encountered in the French company's vocabulary. The Italians embraced the cosmopolitan attitude of the Dutch, and the Italian media seemed to have taken a liking to the Dutch Swan. The politicians' view, however, was quite different. I will return to this later.

KLM, too, had been looking for a partner. This appeared to be a difficult mission. None of its dates had become serious candidates for engagement. In 1996, British Airways had looked promising, as had Swiss Air-SAS-Austrian Airlines (referred to as the "Alcazar project") a couple of years earlier, but the negotiations for an eventual engagement had not been successful.

KLM's management welcomed the interest of Alitalia. Leo van Wijk, at that time CEO of KLM, needed a serious partner after the many fruitless attempts to attract one. Alitalia was not just another date. It was seen as a very attractive candidate. It was almost equal in size, had enough growth potential for the future, flew to destinations that were not served by KLM, had two important airports and a strong position on the continent of Europe. All in all, Alitalia seemed an attractive candidate.

KLM management even confirmed, at an early stage, that it was discussing the possibilities of an alliance with Alitalia. Such an alliance should be more than just code sharing, i.e. operating under the same flight numbers. However, having learned from their past failures where they had been too optimistic about possible cooperation with other partners, KLM tried to downplay the ongoing negotiations. It did so by saying, for example, that Alitalia was just one of a number of potential candidates with which KLM was negotiating. KLM wanted to prevent Alitalia thinking it was the only candidate it was talking to.

White swan or black sheep?

KLM had opted for a careful step-by-step approach. After all, Alitalia was not the most successful of the potential European carrier candidates.

Alitalia was in fact an example of a bad-case scenario in the airline industry. It had been losing money for nine years. A state holding company, IRI, owned 90 percent of the airline shares. The remaining 10 percent was in public hands. Alitalia had been subjected to several reorganizations over the past few years; which had led to thousands of employees being fired.

Alitalia was fighting the battle for continued government support. In the second half of the 1990s, the Italian government alone had reserved 1,7 billion Euros to support its airline. However, the EU authorities did not approve of the public support of the Italian government. Brussels doubted whether the aid was compatible with common market principles [1].

Unlike competing airlines, Alitalia was always struggling to keep up with maintenance arrears. Service was bad, flights were expensive in comparison with competitors, delays and strikes due to mass dismissals occurred far too often, while "overbooking" was a popular word in the corporate jargon of Alitalia. The passengers were, of course, the victims of this deplorable service policy. In their eyes Alitalia stood for "Always Late In Take-off, Always Late In Arrival."

Despite all this, Pieter Bouw, former CEO of KLM, still considered Alitalia a suitable partner. When leaving the company, he stated in the national and international media that Alitalia was a very attractive candidate for KLM, even though the airline did not have a spotless reputation. The arguments in favor of Alitalia outweighed those against.

For insiders this statement did not come as a surprise: KLM had already been talking to the Italians since 1996, although this had never led to concrete negotiations. In the airline industry everybody is talking to everybody else, so this case was not an exception.

At some point the negotiations became more concrete. Alitalia was blessed with a South-European back yard, which KLM found interesting. This was an important strategic asset of Alitalia, one that demanded special attention by KLM. Alitalia had two airports: Rome and Milan. Its flights to Africa and the Middle and Far East also went via those two airports. For KLM, mainly operating on the North Atlantic route, this was complementary to its existing route network, i.e. it could lead to synergy advantages.

Chief executive Leo van Wijk was positive about a second hub. In the independent Dutch airline magazine, *Zakenreis*, he stated, in 1997, with regard to an extra airport (besides Schiphol), that a second hub could only be realized with a partner, i.e. a well-equipped airport not as close to Amsterdam as London, Frankfurt or Paris. The closer a second main European airport was to Amsterdam, the less interesting it would be for KLM.

Alitalia operated from an attractive, densely populated home market and flew to 57 countries. Alitalia's home market had increased by 12 percent between 1995 and 1997. This meant a growth potential that was appealing to KLM. Another advantage of the proposed cooperation was that KLM did not necessarily have to give up its identity. Cooperation with British Airways (BA), for example, would present a different picture. BA, being much larger than KLM, would completely swallow up the Dutch airline.

Moreover, through cooperation with Alitalia, KLM could increase its European market share from 7 percent to 15 percent. Increasing its market share in Europe was an important item on KLM's growth agenda; something it could not do on its own. A further advantage was that the occupancy rates for its flights in Europe would also increase. This could result in profitable European routes that were otherwise losing money.

In addition, KLM's increased presence in Europe pleased its strategic US partner, NorthWest Airlines (NWA). NWA saw Alitalia as an attractive European partner for KLM. NWA was especially interested in Milan's newly expanded airport Malpensa. KLM, in turn, was pleased with the European Union - i.e. European Investment Bank - support to the modernized Malpensa airport. It invested 1,4 billion Euros jointly with the Italian government.

Malpensa was forecast to become the second modern European hub of KLM [2]. This would be an important asset in the competition with other airlines. From an international perspective, Malpensa served an interesting group of travelers in the region. This became even more important given the problems in KLM's relationship with Schiphol.

Finally, Alitalia and KLM each had different, often not competitive, partners: KLM's partners were NWA, Braathens, Martinair, Transavia, KLM Cityhopper, Air UK, KLM Exel, Regional Airlines and Kenya Airways. Alitalia had partners such as Malèv, British Midland, Canadian Airlines, Azurra, Minerva, Eurofly, Czech Airlines, Maersk Air, Gulf Air, Cyprus Airways, Continental Airlines, Finnair, Lot and Korean Air. Partnering from different perspectives was possible.

However, the alliance with Alitalia had a negative side as well. The Italian airline carried a burden of substantial debt that had to be re-engineered. It had mostly old aircraft (the average KLM fleet was eight years old, Alitalia's was more than two times that). Furthermore, the two airlines had different corporate cultures. In the case of Alitalia, this was mirrored in organizational bureaucracy. The other downside was the close ties Alitalia had with the political world, a qualitatively weak route network, and the strong position of the unions (they were represented on the board of directors). Last but not least, the accessibility of Malpensa, in terms of roads and railways, was not sufficient, or, worse yet, non-existent.

Memorandum of understanding

Domenico Cempella, CEO of Alitalia, had already served the company for 35 years. He succeeded Mr. Schisano who had joined Alitalia in spring 1996. Schisano's task had been to make Alitalia more market oriented, a mission he failed to achieve. According to some sources, this task had been a mission impossible from the very start.

Mr. Cempella first attacked the senior management. His management style had some success. The first half-year of 1997, for example, showed profitable figures on the balance sheet. This was quite an achievement for Alitalia - the first time this had happened in ten years. There was a decrease in labor costs of 12 percent and an increase of the number of passengers of 7 percent. The occupancy rate of the airplanes increased as well; from 67,7 to 70,4 percent.

From the start, KLM held a strong position in the negotiations. The reason for this was that KLM – unlike Alitalia – had performed well over the past years. In the first half-year of 1997, KLM had, for example, a net profit in its core activities, of 296 million Euros. This was due to a structural improvement in its performance.

KLM had developed a rationalization program under the name, "Focus 2000", which was aimed at extending margins and had only been implemented a year before. The margins, in the first year, had already substantially increased. Furthermore, the price setting (tariff mix) was much better. This was also the case for its growth capacity when translated into loading rate. In short, KLM could enter the negotiations in a strong position. The airlines matched each other in terms of numbers (box 2).

Box 2 Partners in the air

	KLM	Alitalia
World ranking list in terms of income and production	13	19
Passengers in kilometers	49.1 billion	34.6 billion
Number of passengers transported	13 million	20 million
Airfreight	3.8 billion ton	2.8 billion
Airplanes	112	144
- Large	52	24
- Small	60	120
Destinations	137	102
- Europe	63	59
- Outside Europe	74	43
Flying capacity (ton kilometers)	11.835	7.122
Costs per ton kilometer	$ 0,45	$ 0,62
Turnover	$5.4 billion	$4.6 billion
Average wage costs	$ 53.909	$ 45.332

Note: KLM transports most passengers to international destinations, Alitalia mostly to domestic destinations.

Source: Annual reports

In December 1997, both carriers stated publicly that the strategic alliance between the two was almost realized. They were working on a Memorandum of Understanding for a strategic alliance.

Air France, in the background, remained KLM's competitor for Alitalia's hand. The Italian side failed to reach unanimity on partners. In the political arena in particular, there were some influential politicians with a preference for Air France. These politicians aimed at Paris' support for an important issue on their agenda: Italy entering the Economic and Monetary Union (EMU). They disliked the critical Dutch attitude, especially that of the Dutch Minister of Finance, Gerrit Zalm.

The influential Italian communist party was also in favor of Air France. Former Italian Premier, Romano Prodi, had his own political strategic agenda: According to the Italian media, he supported an alliance with Air France. Since the Italian communist party was a partner of Prodi's center-left cabinet, this was a logic conclusion. Although not a member of the cabinet, the communists were influential.

However, the senior management of Alitalia was of the opinion that the strategic alliance should be judged on its strategic and operational merits rather than on its political merits. The top management of Alitalia feared that an alliance with Air France would be a barrier to its privatization process. Air France was, after all, a state-owned company. For Alitalia, this meant "back to the dark ages". KLM was, therefore, its first choice.

The competition between Air France and KLM had some rather dramatic aspects. Air France's international position was rapidly deteriorating. Once Europe's largest airline, it had dropped to third position and lacked an American partner. Most other European airlines were engaged to partners in the US. Air France performed poorly without such a partner. In other words, Air France was in a weak position from a strategic and a financial perspective.

The once flourishing French airline was on its way to being ranked as a poorly performing company. French president Chirac tried to persuade Prodi to cancel the negotiations between Alitalia and KLM. Air France should join up with Alitalia instead. Not for the first time, it became clear that the political arena, with rules and regulations of its own, dominated the airline industry [3]. Decisions in the airline industry are rarely taken based on solid economic grounds.

Alitalia, however, chose KLM. They had resisted the pressure from the French politicians and the explicit choice to intensify relations with Air France. The managerial motives of the Alitalia management were decisive. After several battles in the Italian political arena, the politicians surrendered and managed to enter the EMU without relinquishing the partnership with KLM. Alitalia was no longer subjected to political games on either the Italian or the European playing field.

On December 16th, 1997, the Memorandum of Understanding became reality. KLM and Alitalia were to participate in each other's share capital, which meant that they did not opt for a cross-equity alliance. Their cooperation was initially to be in the commercial and technological fields. But future share and cross-equity participation was not excluded. The European and North Atlantic route network would be integrated and it was agreed that customer service (especially that of Alitalia) would be upgraded.

Harmonization of branding policy and fleet management was also part of the Memorandum, as was alignment of the incentive programs for loyal customers. With respect to the role of the partners of both airlines, the barrier of the role played by NWA was difficult to overcome. Intensifying relations between Alitalia and NWA was a difficult issue because of the fact that Italy did not have an open skies agreement with the US. Italy and the US did not as yet have free access to each other's airspace. This barrier had to be removed by politicians and Alitalia had no major influence on the matter.

In a way, the Memorandum of Understanding failed to meet expectations, because the actual alliance would only be effective as from November 1st, 1998. Until that time both airlines were to determine the best mode of cooperation. This time-scheme was not exactly on a fast track, so the risk of losing the momentum was always present.

The parties that were directly involved had to work hard to find a proper way of implementing the Memorandum. Questions such as "who is getting what and why" had to be answered. The issue was even more complicated now that NWA, as a partner of KLM, also had the right to a share. Another issue was the necessary approval of the European Commission (EC). Finally, the framework of the business plan had to be filled in. In fact the implementation of the actual alliance, a year earlier, could be seen as a trial period.

The Italians welcomed the cooperation with KLM. Apart from the advantages of the cooperation already mentioned, Alitalia was hoping to avoid the rulings from Brussels. The EC had only agreed to Alitalia being given substantial state aid on very strict conditions and those were themselves a barrier to the expansion of Alitalia. Therefore, the playing field was restricted for the Italians. Alitalia was, for example, not allowed to buy new aircraft. It was only allowed to do so after improving its health such that it would no longer need to structurally rely on state funding. The alliance with KLM could improve Alitalia's state of health and this, in turn, would allow the Italians to refrain from bringing up further (previously approved) state aid measures and re-entering the free capital market.

The Alitalia management was extremely enthusiastic about cooperation with KLM. CEO Cempella often mentioned in the media the advantages of the two carriers working together. The Dutch side was positive as well: Schiphol was in favor of expansion of the route network and an increase in flight movements. A stronger position for KLM would strengthen the position of Schiphol as mainport. The Dutch political arena welcomed the progress made by KLM in becoming a global airline.

The savings due to the alliance were substantial; although this was mainly on paper. The Italian newspaper, *Il Sole 24 Ore*, published a scoop on the subject. The newspaper assumed that a document belonging to the supervisory board of Alitalia stated that both airlines had gross revenues of between 205 and 365 million Euros as a result of the alliance; which was reason enough to be optimistic about the ongoing negotiations. However, the real work, i.e. the operational integration, had not even started. The atmosphere, as is often the case in cross-border deals, was (too) euphoric.

KLM did not pay much attention to the agreement. Even when the Memorandum was being ceremoniously signed, KLM was already focusing on the next item on its agenda for becoming a global carrier: finding a partner in Asia. KLM took a short cut from a strategic, as well as from an operational point of view, and by doing so did not pay enough attention to issues that required careful consideration.

How the ice started to crack

A moment of silence descended: Both parties wanted to get to know each other without external pressure. They were hiding their relationship from the outside world. Normally, such a period does not last long.

However, the relationship between KLM and Alitalia moved into turbulent waters. In the spring of 1998, the local Italian political scene started to make noises. Rome discovered that the alliance would result in a weaker position for its Fiumicino airport. Moreover, Alitalia was planning to shift 10 percent of its flights from Fiumicino to Malpensa in Milan. This meant a substantial economic and logistical loss for Rome.

The local politicians blamed this negative development entirely on KLM. They reasoned that Malpensa would be more in alignment with the intercontinental route network of KLM than Fiumicino. The shift of flights from Rome to Milan was thus mainly in KLM's interest. Within a couple of weeks the KLM/Alitalia partnership found itself under heavy attack.

Cempella came under such pressure that he felt obliged to defend himself in an open letter to *Il Sole 24 Ore*. He stated in that letter that the reason for the shift was purely commercial. He stressed that Alitalia was missing opportunities in the North of Italy where 75 percent of all airline tickets were sold. According to estimates, this amounted to between two and four million customers annually. These potential customers currently flew with Swissair (via Zurich or Geneva) or Air France.

The local political scene in Rome feared that Fiumicino would lose its position if the plans of the Alitalia management were to be carried out. Above all, it would harm the reputation of Rome as an international airport. Fiumicino would drop down the international ranking list. Mr. Cempella tried to nuance this line of thinking by maintaining that Rome would remain an important final and transit destination for tourists, diplomats and so on.

This did not help. Some politicians at national level supported their Roman colleagues. The Minister of Foreign Affairs, Mr. Lamberto Dini, for example, mentioned publicly that despite the strategic importance of the agreement with KLM, excluding Rome from many flights was difficult to understand in the light of the holy year 2000. Alitalia's top management was furious about Mr. Dini's public support for Rome's line of thinking. It was by no means willing to change its mind. The Italian government had to intervene. Prodi approached Dini, and in the end all national political forces proclaimed their support for Alitalia to move 10 percent of its flights from Rome to Milan.

Another major problem occurred, when it became clear that the new Malpensa airport could only become fully operational if some of the flights were moved from the old Milan airport (Linate) to the new one (Malpensa). Many foreign airlines disliked the idea. They were used to flying into Linate and had made a number of investments in the airport. Many of their clients depended on them arriving at Linate airport, which was closer to the city of Milan than Malpensa. The initiative that the Italian government took, to move flights to Malpensa, was perceived negatively by other international players. The reason behind this plan was to assure the presence of major foreign airlines, without which the expensive new Malpensa airport would hardly be able to survive.

In June 1998, the European Commissioner responsible for Transport, Neil Kinnock, stated that he did not support the Italian government's plan to force foreign carriers to fly to Malpensa. The Italian government realized the political consequences of its decision too late.

Apart from the complaints already mentioned, foreign airlines were unhappy about the inferior infrastructure around Malpensa, particularly since the airport is located 55 kilometers from Milan, the final destination of many passengers. To get to Milan, passengers were obliged to use buses or (expensive) taxis. No alternative public transport was available. The railway connection between Malpensa and Milan was not scheduled to be completed before 2000. This was a difficult message to convey to demanding passengers. The foreign carriers' criticism was understandable.

Despite the positive announcement concerning alliance projects between KLM and Alitalia, it became clear just how fragile the strategic alliance actually was. The high-profile character of the deal was hiding the reality: the alliance existed mainly on paper and had not even been formulated in detail. A smoothly operating Malpensa was a critical success factor for the alliance.

Words ... and more words ...

On November 27th 1998, the Memorandum of Understanding became a Master Cooperation Agreement: a 50-50-alliance. KLM and Alitalia each kept their own identity. A separate company comparable to a joint venture was established. It would get its own board of directors - a new phenomenon in the airline industry. The board of the joint venture would be structured under the board of KLM and Alitalia. The new organization would use human resources, materials and services from the existing companies. Financial participation in each other's companies was not foreseen, but nor was it excluded.

KLM and Alitalia wanted to put their cooperation into effect in two phases. In the first phase, the companies would cooperate in specific market segments. In the second phase, an extensive part of the passenger and freight transportation business would be carried out on the basis of joint venture contracts. A separate joint venture would be established for both activities. The respective joint ventures would rent aircraft, services and human resources from the parent companies at market prices. Ultimately, the aim was to integrate the majority of all joint commercial activities. The policy, with regard to investments, fleet management and partner airlines, would be aligned. For the moment, the labor conditions would not be harmonized. When the agreement was signed the Italian state holding, IRI, owned 51 percent of Alitalia, whereas the Dutch state owned 14 percent of KLM.

One remarkable development was that Alitalia started to perform more and more strongly. The problems of the past seemed to have disappeared. Alitalia was no longer in intensive care but, within a relatively short period of time, it had modernized itself and reconstructed its debts. The financial results of the Italian airline had significantly improved and an open skies agreement with the US was on its way. The proverb "every cloud has a silver lining" seemed appropriate in Alitalia's case. The negotiating position of Alitalia had improved, while that of KLM was slowly deteriorating.

The outside world still regarded the alliance as a masterstroke, resulting in yearly returns of $380 million for passenger and $65 million for freight transportation. The alliance was part of a ten-year agreement, which either side could call off within the first three years.

The consequences for competitors were substantial. It was estimated that Air France, Swissair and Lufthansa would lose millions of dollars in turnover, because passengers from Italy were no longer forced to use hubs in France, Switzerland and Germany for their intercontinental flights.

The European Commission still had to approve the deal, but the parties involved believed this would not be a problem. A greater threat was posed by the possibility of one of the parties exercising the cancellation clause in the agreement. The clause could be put into effect if the Alitalia privatization process were not finalized by the 30th of June 2000, or if a competitor took control of more than 25 percent in one of the alliance partners. There were other issues on the table as well: Was the privatization process proceeding too fast? Were the Alitalia employees ready for such a transformation? How stable was the political situation?

In short, there were many issues on the agenda to be resolved before the alliance could become a success. The outside world continued to perceive the deal as a success story, an image carefully polished in the media by KLM. The alliance was in many ways one of a kind. The "multi-hub system" was innovative and the alliance implied an extensive cooperation.

On paper it was a perfect marriage. But in practice it failed. The partners were unable to practice what they were preaching. The realization of the joint venture was delayed time after time. For example, it proved difficult to fill the management positions of the new joint venture since there were not sufficient candidates available internally. They had to look outside the companies for the right people. This was a bad sign.

Slowly, the basis of the strategic alliance started to crack. KLM's profitability decreased. Cost-saving measures had to be taken; which influenced its negotiating position. This also resulted in the company paying less attention to the alliance's playing field, i.e. not keeping its eye on the ball.

As if this was not enough, the European Commission blocked KLM's acquisition of Martinair. KLM already owned 50 percent of Martinair, but wanted to acquire the other half from Nedlloyd. At the same time, severe price competition was emerging on the North Atlantic network, KLM's financial backbone. In addition, the Asian economy was suffering as well. This caused KLM's turnover in Asia to drop, despite the fact that the region was becoming increasingly important for KLM and its partners. Moreover, the quality of service could not be maintained and this received negative media attention.

In 1999, it was decided that KLM would contribute 100 million Euro to the investments of Alitalia in Malpensa. The Milanese airport was important to KLM, so it was worth the investment.

On August 11th, 1999, the EC approved the alliance. Some specific conditions were, however, attached. The partners had to give up their monopoly position on the routes between Amsterdam, Rome and Milan. This meant a maximum of 40 percent of their flights. Competitors should be able to take over activities on these routes.

Turbulent waters

From January 2000 onwards both airlines moved into turbulent waters. Alitalia urgently had to adjust its corporate strategy due to its weak financial performance. Alitalia's shareholders were not pleased. This was reason enough to cancel the alliance, which was neither in the interest of the shareholders nor of the Italian politicians. The difficulties related to Malpensa started to have a negative influence on the alliance as well as on Alitalia itself. The climate deteriorated rapidly.

Alitalia's board of directors stated publicly that the financial situation would not improve in 2000. They referred to an unstable scenario regarding Malpensa, which would ultimately influence the alliance with KLM. Alitalia's share had dropped in value by 40 percent. The continuous delay in negotiations put cooperation with KLM under enormous pressure. However, both parties thought they had passed the point of no return and felt obliged to fight for their relationship. They made every attempt to escape the danger zone and move into less turbulent waters.

Malpensa remained a critical factor with respect to failure of the alliance. The transfer of flights from Linate to Malpensa was delayed due to the absence of adequate infrastructure between the new airport and Milan. The EC added to the problem by referring to related environmental issues, including inadmissible noise pollution. It examined the Malpensa case in great detail and insisted that the Italians resolve the issues.

Early in 2000, KLM's CEO, Leo van Wijk, stated publicly that the alliance would be called off if the political problems related to Malpensa continued. This statement left little room for manoeuver. KLM's own performance was declining and it needed all its energy to change the situation. In order to do so, KLM had to take some serious measures, it:
- cut the number of employees (of a total of 28,000 employees 1,500 to 3,000 flex employees would have to leave);
- cancelled destinations that were not profitable, and
- postponed ICT investments and reduced the number of aircraft.

Another setback was the fact that some foreign airlines such as Lufthansa, Air France, SAS and British Airways would not agree to transfer their flights from Linate to Malpensa. They collectively refused to change airports even though the Italian government had imposed the change. These airlines even lodged a complaint with the European Commission, citing an infringement of EU competition law.

Solution?

KLM had difficulties with the final solution proposed by the Italians. It was decided that Linate would continue to exist and serve six to seven million passengers; over three times the number originally agreed upon. This decision meant that intercontinental flights could not be provided at Malpensa airport as intended. KLM had no choice but to give in.

The deadline, April 20th, 2000, was approaching. Until then, the alliance agreement could still be called of. Negotiations were delayed again because the foreign airlines still refused to change airports. KLM had only one priority: political clarity. The problems related to Malpensa were a heavy burden on KLM, since they delayed expansion of its international network through, for example, a partner in Asia.

The Italian government had its own problems. It resigned on April 19th, 2000, and declared, just before doing so, that flights had to be transferred from Linate to Malpensa even if that meant going against the will of the foreign airlines. This was a debatable decision since it had been taken by a government that was ready to resign. The case had become even more complicated than before. This decision also clearly ran counter to the standpoint of the EC. The Commission warned the Italian government that there was a danger that it would have to revise its decision, and that this could result in damage claims. The voice of the EC was especially important since Malpensa was one of many projects that was heavily subsidized by Brussels. It was easy to imagine what the EC could do if the Italian government acted against the Commission's will.

On April 29th, 2000, KLM took the decision to call off its alliance agreement with Alitalia. Three years of negotiations had resulted in nothing short of disaster. Valuable time had been lost and competitors had emerged from left and right. KLM quickly needed to get its act together. This meant, in the first place, that it had to entirely dismantle its alliance with

Alitalia. The joint ventures for transport of passengers and freight and commercial ties had to be dissolved.

It also meant that KLM had to look for a new partner. KLM's aim was to find one before the end of the year 2000. This would prove to be a difficult exercise since most of the candidates were already courting or had engaged to other partners.

Lessons learnt

Although the problems related to Malpensa dominated the media, there were other factors that contributed to the failure of the alliance. Some seemed minor, others major, but the combination was deadly.

In this section, I will elaborate on some of those problems by painting an abstract picture in order to present some generic lessons learnt that could serve as guidelines in other alliance negotiations.

Cultural differences should be dealt with in a strategic manner

Cultural differences played an important role in the failure of the alliance negotiations. I refer to three different levels of culture: national, corporate and personal (related to employee or manager). According to Hofstede's research on cultural differences, common denominators at this first cultural level influence the second level, namely corporate culture. The third level is linked to specific individuals and cannot be generalized. People either feel compelled to work together, or they do not [4].

The KLM/Alitalia alliance faced problems on all three of the cultural levels. This does not come as a surprise, since Hofstede's research points out that the differences between the Dutch and the Italians are substantial. The friction experienced at all three cultural levels negatively impacted on the alliance negotiations in different ways.

Cultural differences played a particularly critical role in the lower hierarchies of the organizations. This could be seen during meetings between relatively small groups of employees from both airlines. The Italians, unlike the Dutch, were not acquainted with issues such as empowerment and decentralized decision-making processes. The Italians were used to working within a hierarchy, and were not allowed to make even the most minor decisions by themselves. In the eyes of their Dutch colleagues, whose decision-making powers were within a certain bandwidth, this led to bureaucracy. At the beginning it was accepted because "we are all in this together." However, after some time it resulted in irritation.

It is remarkable how easily the senior management jumped over certain cultural barriers. KLM's chief executive Leo van Wijk mentioned publicly that cultural differences did not really matter, as long as companies were speaking the same "business language."

What would be the best advice to offer in the light of this naive belief? The first piece of advice may seem obvious, however in my view it is very important: use foreign local (in this case Italian) advisors. Following this advice is a strategic starting point, which should be part of "corporate law" even though multinational corporations do not always see it that way. They are usually advised by in-house advisors who are nationals of the country where the company is based.

Secondly, the right people should be on the frontline of the negotiations. It happens far too often that people are chosen on the basis of hierarchy, i.e. based on their position in the organization. They do not necessarily have the necessary qualities to successfully finalize negotiations, such as empathy and diplomatic capabilities.

Finally, cultural differences also show up in the willingness and ability to speak other languages. The Dutch were prepared and able to speak English or sometimes even Italian. The Italians found it difficult to speak English and were not prepared to speak anything other than their mother tongue. These factors were important for the success of alliance negotiations. In the end it is all about communication, especially when companies from different countries are involved.

Strategic alliances are often a bridge too far

In the 1980s, the trend, "strategic alliance", was introduced [5]. It was only in the 1990s that it became extremely popular. The KLM/Alitalia deal itself was qualified as a "strategic alliance". However, many strategic alliances lack a strategy and embody no more than an attractive brand [6].

The positioning of the KLM/Alitalia alliance seemed to be more important on paper than as a reality. Strategic cooperation with Alitalia demanded considerable time and energy. Most companies underestimate the downside of limited resources, and so did KLM [7]. This became obvious after the failure of the alliance, when KLM had to work long and hard hours to get the company back on track.

Strategic alliances require focus. Consequently, other strategic activities (those demanding substantial investments) need to be put lower down on the priority list. Many companies are completely overwhelmed by the complexity of a strategic alliance, i.e. an alliance that is at the core of the company's corporate strategy.

KLM and Alitalia were at the forefront of developments. There was no proven best practice with respect to a successful strategic alliance in the airline industry and this had considerable influence on the negotiations. It proved impossible to bring a successful end to their negotiations. Why did they choose a "first mover strategy"? Why did they not decide on a "(fast) follower strategy"?

This last option would have been a tactical decision that could have saved time and energy. It would have been an alternative, and perhaps more successful way of implementing their European strategy of increasing market share in Europe.

Attractive advantages of a strategic alliance formulated on paper are rarely realized

It is easy to adopt a "sky is the limit" approach and produce documents claiming all kinds of attractive advantages for strategic alliances. But in practice it proves difficult to implement the agreement or to gain any strategic value whatsoever. A decision has to be based on its practical value and not on documents that hide reality behind beautiful words. The KLM/Alitalia case is a good example of this. Too many promises in the end led to skeptical reactions, both internally and externally.

My advice, therefore, is to adopt a low profile approach. This may be against the culture of many CEOs who prefer more high-profile approaches that show quick (short-term) results in the media. This mode of operation, however, often results in a lot of publicity, but unsuccessful negotiations.

'Politics' as a key factor to success should never be underestimated, especially when a politically sensitive industry is involved

Alitalia, unlike KLM, was a state-owned company. This influenced the pace at which the negotiations took place and strategic decisions could be made. Mostly political arguments played a role in Alitalia's commercial decision-making process. Alitalia's shares were, for the most part, still in the hands of the Italian state holding company, IRI.

In the airline industry political arguments always seem to dominate economic issues. This was also the case in, for example, the Fokker-Dasa deal [8]. Even KLM, a privately owned company, depends on political decisions (for example environmental regulations) for its domestic growth strategy.
By making decisions about Schiphol airport, KLM's home base, the Dutch government can indirectly determine KLM's implemention of its fast-growth scenario. The ties between the Italian airports, national and regional politics and Alitalia are even tighter. Alitalia was subjected to political decisions, over which KLM had no influence.

The Italian political infrastructure is fragile. Decisions are made late or not at all. The North-South discussion exploded during an early stage of the negotiations and continued to influence the negotiations negatively throughout the process. The Roman lobby was strong and harmful to the ongoing negotiations. The Italian government acted too slowly at critical moments during the process. The change of airports was forced upon foreign airlines at the very last minute. This resulted, understandably, in protests from these airlines, which were competitors of KLM and Alitalia. In addition, the European Commission protested against the decision.

The KLM/Alitalia case is no exception. Many companies actively involved in establishing alliances underestimate the political factor. The weight this factors bears will, of course, vary from industry to industry. Other politically sensitive industries include banking and (bio)technology. Regardless of the industry concerned, all parties involved should pay more attention to the political issues that could play a role in the negotiation process.

The negotiation process should be as short as possible

A careful decision-making process should be at the core of negotiations and this should be as brief as possible. In the negotiations between Alitalia and KLM this was not the case. The declaration of intent was signed mid-December 1997, whereas the actual alliance would only be operational from November 1st, 1998.

The question arises of course, as to why the parties involved allowed such a long time (one year) for the alliance to be established? One reason could be that the preparations were not properly executed. Whatever the reason, it is clear that when implementation of an alliance agreement takes too long, it leaves room for tensions and misinterpretations to build up. Unfortunately, in this respect, the Alitalia/KLM case was no exception.

Slippery slope

There are many more lessons that can be learned from the Alitalia/KLM case. I have chosen to elaborate on just a few in a broader, more general, context.

Successful alliance management (in the different phases of pre-alliance management, deal making and post-alliance management) is like crossing a slippery slope. You need to move carefully, be well prepared and only cross if there is an urge to do so.

References

[1] The European Commission assesses on the basis of 'The Market Economy Investors Principle (MEIP)' whether a measure is a normal commercial transaction or aid. Under the MEIP a capital transaction may be regarded as state aid if an investor, operating under normal market economy conditions, would not be prepared to make an equivalent investment in the airline. See also: P.K. Jagersma, "KLM - Waarheen Vliegt Gij?", Holland Business Publications, Heemstede, 2003.

[2] A hub is a centrally located destination that is used as a connecting point for passengers travelling between any other pair of destinations in the network.

[3] See for more political issues: P.K. Jagersma, "The Fokker-Dasa deal", Veen Publishers, Amsterdam, 1994.

[4] G. Hofstede, "Culture's Consequences", Sage, London, 1980.

[5] B.G. James, "Alliance: The New Strategic Focus", Long Range Planning, Vol. 18, No. 3, pp. 76 to 81, 1985; B. Kogut, "Joint Ventures: Theoretical and Empirical Perspectives", Strategic Management Journal, Vol. 9, pp. 319 to 332, 1988; K. Ohmae, "The Global Logic of Strategic Alliances", Harvard Business Review, pp. 143 to 154, March-April 1989.

[6] F. Berardino and C. Frankel, "Alliances: The Next Step", Airline Business, pp. 68 to 72, October, 1998.

[7] P.K. Jagersma, "KLM - Waarheen Vliegt Gij?", Holland Business Publications, Heemstede, 2003.

[8] P.K. Jagersma, "The Fokker-Dasa deal", Veen Publishers, Amsterdam, 1994.

Epilogue

Many Roads Lead Abroad

International entrepreneurship is not a sinecure. Research shows that Dutch companies are quite unanimous when it comes to the factors determining success and/or failure in international business.

Many entrepreneurs still experience difficulties with the internationalization process and many more will suffer from the same in the near future. Many a boardroom has been known to get completely bogged down by the internationalization issue in a very short space of time.

A short time ago, I started a challenging research project into the success and failure factors of internationalized companies in different parts of the world recognizing that, in a global economy, the future prosperity of a country increasingly depends on the international competitiveness of firms and industries. I examined domestic firms that are new on the path of internationalization and multinational corporations that have existing global presence, as well as manufacturing and service firms. This epilogue will address large, medium and small sized companies and their policies with regard to the internationalization process.

Many Dutch companies have started to develop cross-border business activities and many are already active on foreign markets, putting up their flags in the remaining unclaimed territories. Deals are regularly concluded in foreign countries, varying from parent companies setting up their subsidiaries, to companies acquiring other large foreign companies.

This development results in an increasing number of Dutch companies earning larger profits from their foreign subsidiaries. This does not always go smoothly, as good results are often short lived and every company that wants to expand abroad eventually ends up paying its dues. The phenomenon of cross-border activities raises many tough questions. The road to operating on a global scale has many obstacles and several interesting, though often difficult, byways. More generally, what I aim for in this epilogue is to offer clear signposts.

Approach

In this research study, I conducted individual in-depth interviews to gain insight into the factors that determine success or failure for Dutch companies with cross-border activities. In total, 375 officials from 288 Dutch companies were interviewed. These can be grouped as follows:

(1) 252 (staff) managers and members of managing boards, and
(2) 123 other executives – in particular general managers of foreign subsidiaries and export managers who were primarily or partially responsible for formulating and/or executing international business strategies.

The first group of executives is based at the headquarters in the Netherlands. The second group is based either at the headquarters in the Netherlands or at foreign subsidiaries. In practice, different companies use different terminology for their executives, both at their headquarters and at their foreign subsidiaries. For the purposes of this epilogue, I will refer to the following categories of managers: managing director, general manager and export manager.

In the end, my research portfolio included Dutch companies with a small number of cross-border activities in a limited number of foreign countries, as well as companies that owe most of their profits to the activities of many foreign subsidiaries. Of these companies, 65 percent were small and medium-sized companies (less than 250 employees) and 35 percent were large companies (more than 250 employees). The research population consisted of industrial companies (78 percent) and service companies (22 percent). The scope of this study is reflected in the nature and composition of the Dutch economy.

The personal in-depth interviews lasted on average about 80 minutes. Twenty questions were designed to be used as a connecting thread for the research process. The questions of the questionnaire were formulated around the central theme: the factors determining success or failure in international business. The interviews were taped wherever possible, provided I had permission to do so. The analysis of the conducted interviews was done at a later stage. This provided me more leeway to discuss the different issues related to international business during the interviews.

As specific management issues were central to this study, the inductive method was given preference. This allowed the possibility of making solid statements based on empirical research. In fact, replication testing was used continuously: earlier conclusions were tested against new cases and either confirmed or rejected. The study has created a great deal of material and some findings, conclusions, the lessons learnt are presented as different success and failure themes.

Process of internationalization

During the research process, success and failure factors in international business were qualified. Jagersma's (1997, 1998 and 2001) description of internationalization was used as a point of departure for this study. Internationalization can be described briefly in four phases:

- International companies are influenced by the external environment in which they operate. This environment consists of a number of sub-environments, such as a macro-economic, legal, social, political, cultural and industry environment in foreign countries where companies are active. *Accurately mapping out, analyzing and interpreting the external environment is phase I of the internationalization process.*

- Once international business policy has been formulated, it must be anchored in a business plan. International business policy is made up of strategic and operational choices. In this phase, companies involved in cross-border activities are required to make explicit choices. The main features of those choices have to be laid down explicitly, and substantiated. *International business policy formulation is phase II of the internationalization process.*

- The choices ("strategies") explained in phase two have to be implemented, resulting in local or global competitive advantages. Implementing international business strategies is not a sinecure and requires a fair amount of flexibility of companies involved in cross-border activities. *Implementing international business policy is phase III of the internationalization process.*

- International ambitions, goals and activities have to be evaluated over time. This evaluation process implies that ambitions, goals and activities are followed over a period of time. Only in this way can an international company take corrective measures and learn from its international activities. *International business policy evaluation is phase IV of the internationalization process.*

The contents of this epilogue will examine and follow these four phases of the internationalization process.

External environment

It can be concluded from the interviews that internationalization is still perceived to be difficult. This is apparent from the experiences of the 375 Dutch managing directors, general managers and export managers. Their companies operate in environments that are heavily influenced by local and global forces.

The discussion of the issue of "external environment" is dominated by the following four themes:
- socially responsible entrepreneurship;
- the political environment in a country;
- legal issues in the international business arena, and
- opportunities and threats of the Internet.

Socially responsible entrepreneurship

The importance of the company's social environment is clearly present during the conducted interviews, as is the question as to "How to adequately react to these developments in this specific environment?" The local foreign social environment of Dutch companies has become increasingly important over time. Dutch companies would be less effective in many parts of the world if they fail to gain thorough understanding of how they are perceived.

In some countries Dutch and other foreign companies are viewed with suspicion while in other countries they are welcomed with open arms. This has a great deal of influence on the performance of those Dutch companies. According to the interviewees, the world seems to be increasingly concerned with socially responsible or "sustainable" entrepreneurship.

The Dutch companies that perform the best are those that acknowledge and implement the knowledge that "good" business practices are always "best" business practices. For that reason, many Dutch companies commission independent – and sometimes scholarly – institutes to draw up international *Codes of Conduct*. Companies that have many international subsidiaries particularly benefit from these formal rules regarding how they should interact with each other and other stakeholders, such as foreign interest groups.

Dutch companies take socially responsible entrepreneurship seriously. Of the 288 companies taking part in this research, 34 percent have an international code of conduct while, of the larger companies, more than half mention that they report on sustainability. One third of the Dutch companies with an international code of conduct have them verified by an external party. International socially responsible entrepreneurship has been given a permanent place on the management agenda.

Managing directors and managers from larger Dutch companies even consider one of their main duties to be personally involved. About 75 percent of the interviewees working for larger companies feel that an international code of conduct contributes positively to better economic performance. Socially responsible entrepreneurship is, in their view, beneficial to the bottom line of a global company.

A few years ago, IHC Caland (a big shipping company) experienced how important it is to have a well-prepared socially responsible international entrepreneurship policy. IHC Caland went through a difficult period due to criticism from non-governmental organizations expressing their social concern for the situation in Burma. The company, at that time, had underestimated the complexity of socially responsible entrepreneurship.

There against, today, together with Royal Dutch Shell, it is lonely at the top with regard to socially responsible international entrepreneurship. In this respect, Royal Dutch Shell serves as an example for other companies. Royal Dutch Shell terminated 106 contracts with international partners and ended two important joint ventures in 2000 because the activities of these partners did not fit in with Royal Dutch Shell's opinion of international socially responsible entrepreneurship.

The trick to interacting successfully with customers is partially determined by the level of awareness of managing directors and export managers of social and ethical issues. What is complicated about socially responsible entrepreneurship is that the international environment presents many dilemmas; absolutely good or bad conduct does not exist. What is acceptable in one country is strictly prohibited in another. But the loosely defined thread through all of this is that ethics is an essential companion to the honorable manager.

Political environment

The position of Dutch companies in foreign markets is not only influenced by social and macro-economic climates but also by export promotion policies. In other words, it is also influenced by trade politics and the policies of the Dutch government.

Maintaining and improving the Dutch position in foreign markets is an important theme in the Netherlands. Implementing government policy that closely complements business goals was an important undertaking for the interviewees during this research. The Netherlands earns 55 percent of its gross national product beyond its borders and about one out of every three jobs is, in one way or another, related to the internationalization of Dutch companies.

This is not unique to the Netherlands; other countries, such as Belgium, Switzerland and Sweden are also dependent on international business for their prosperity and well-being. They are strongly affected by the state of affairs in their foreign companies. International business is, therefore, continuously at the forefront of political views. In virtually all countries, ministries are assisting their own companies, often in the form of export stimulating measures to promote international business. Government sponsored export instruments and programs form an important contribution to individual companies when it comes to competing for foreign clients.

Besides national schemes and subsidy devices, there are also different European and multilateral schemes, programs and devices to support Dutch companies in executing their cross-border activities.

Since the 1980s there has been a development where small and medium-sized companies in the Netherlands are encouraged to increase their export figures; which has proved to be a difficult task. Many small and medium-sized companies have "a sort of fear of the international barrier", as it was put by an interviewee. Other interviewees refer to "insufficient available management time", "insufficient knowledge about foreign product markets" and the fact that "there is a scarcity of reliable business partners that can also act as distributors", or that "there are too few of them". Small and medium-sized companies often lack the experience to make international entrepreneurship a success.

Furthermore, they are often "frustrated" - as an interviewee words it - by the "difficulty of determining the financial risks of doing cross-border business" and the "high costs involved in the internationalization process". That does not change the fact that foreign markets are an attractive opportunity for small and medium-sized companies. During the past few years there has been a structural attempt to gain insight into the opportunities for this type of company in the Dutch export sector.

Many interviewees refer to the necessity of "better co-ordination on the part of the Dutch government" with regard to its policies concerning export incentive. Implementing a high-quality and harmonious foreign/export policy seems to be an enormous task for the government. Other countries also suffer from the above-mentioned co-ordination problem. "For this reason, we must join forces", said a top manager of one of the Netherlands' largest exporters.

In the Netherlands, the network of public and private organizations for foreign/export policy is influenced by political, strategic and financial interests. According to the interviewees, these organizations play "an important stimulating and advisory role" and make a considerable contribution towards preparing Dutch companies for conducting business in foreign countries.

Legal environment

The legal dimensions of conducting business on an international scale are becoming increasingly important. Dutch companies are becoming more aware of the far-reaching effects of foreign legal developments in the countries in which they operate.

A Dutch general manager, with a South American subsidiary, illustrated this point as follows:

> "In various countries this is perhaps the most important factor for success. At first sight it doesn't seem to be a business related factor. This partially due to the fact that Dutch companies lack expertise in this field, but before they know it, they are in deep trouble".

The legal environment consists of widely varying dimensions and there are different national and transnational organizations that exert legal influence. Some examples are local (foreign) legislation and transnational legislation imposed by the UN, the WTO and the European Commission. Local and transnational legislation often have different effects on the performance of international companies.

"9/11" also appears to have far-reaching effects. Since September 11, 2001, the American government, for example, has enforced stronger measures regarding the import and export of goods. Exporters, importers and shipping agents are confronted with these measures in a variety of ways. In practice this means more intensive consultations with, rigorous checks by, and, the transfer of detailed information to, American customs officials.

Finally, transnational legislation has an important effect, especially on international companies. For example, the eCommerce Directive of the European Commission influences the behaviour of many international companies.

Another important issue concerns the contractual business documents referred to as 'letters of intent', i.e. the intention to comply with an agreement.

According to an export manager and lawyer with a Dutch trading company:

> "it involves an enormous risk, especially if negotiations about implementing a 'concluded agreement' break off prematurely. Many Dutch companies think that a letter of intent is a non-binding document abroad, without any legal consequences. In many countries, however, a letter of intent is legally valid and therefore binding for the parties involved in business negotiations. The 'intention' is an inherent part of the deal in many (especially) non-European countries. This can lead to misunderstandings and serious problems, especially in culturally unfamiliar regions like South America, Eurasia and the Far East".

Another important legal issue is (product) liability. This subject is often emphasized by the interviewees. For example, a Dutch company that introduces a product in the United States is liable, even if in fact it is not to blame for the safety risks associated with the product involved. This is a risk that Dutch entrepreneurs are increasingly confronted with in Europe, in general, and, more specifically, in Western Europe.

In this study, the liability issue is often discussed in relation to the first theme: socially responsible business practice. Product liability, in this context, is not primarily about risk liability, but first and foremost about the social responsibility that foreign companies have towards their local environments. Themes one and three substantially reinforce one another rendering the social criterion even more important.

The Internet

The emergence of the Internet has had a dramatic influence on international business. The idea that the world has shrunk because of technological developments is obvious. While the physical distance between the Netherlands and any other country remains the same, the psychological distance has decreased due to new technologies such as the Internet.

According to the interviewees, the Internet touches upon both the primary and secondary (support) value chain elements. It affects cost patterns, as well as revenue margins and offers unlimited growth possibilities for international companies. Nevertheless, the Internet also poses threats, because the greatest risk of failure is implicit in its promise of success:

- *More products can be offered via the Internet.* Since it clears away many of the geographic and information barriers, prices for those products will decrease accordingly. Competition between Dutch and locally active foreign companies for local customers will become fiercer and increasingly will be determined by price - profit margins will shrink. The emergence of price comparing robots on the Internet will fan the fire of competition even more by offering comparisons of goods and services.

- *Suppliers are forced to react immediately to actual demands for a specific product* (especially in business-to-business industries). Reacting too late or delivering a week too late is no longer an option. Local customers abroad want to (and can) obtain (online) information about products and services.

According to this study, many Dutch companies, especially small and medium-sized companies, still have a lot of homework to do on this important subject.

International business policy formulation

The most important international ambitions must be made explicitly. Moreover, a company should indicate how it intends to realize those ambitions, i.e. goals should be prioritized and listed.

During the research, I was confronted with the following dominant themes regarding the formulation of an international business policy:
- (lack of) an explicit international vision;
- an effective competitive strategy, and
- global (out)sourcing.

Developing an international vision

The word "vision" is the central guiding concept for almost all Dutch companies with cross-border activities. According to the majority of the interviewees, vision is an extremely important subject. The vision of an international company determines the course it will take. "This is important considering the level of uncertainty that Dutch companies abroad are confronted with", according to a general manager of a large Dutch service provider.

According to the interviewees, the company's international vision should be "inspiring" (since managers and employees must be prompted to do a great deal of work), "directive" (because it should sketch an appealing picture of the future) and "shared" (collective efforts should lead to the international vision becoming more tangible and clearly defined).

International visions are plentiful and come in all shapes and sizes. The interviewed companies use two different types of visions, namely organic and economic. The main attribute of 'organic visions' is that they are often holistic in nature. This type of vision refers to a symbiosis of the opinions, skills and aspirations of the founder of an international company or of a dominant leader or dominant coalition in the managing board of a company.

Comparable organic visions are often embedded in strongly shared values as far as the interviewed companies are concerned. They are often bound to long periods of time. Most Dutch companies with an international vision (see below in this paragraph) have an organic vision (about two-thirds of the visions examined were organic by nature).

An 'economic vision' has a much more tangible nature than an organic one. These kinds of visions are characterized by the words "profitability" and "turnover", often explicitly named as the most important driving force of the international company. An economic vision is more quantitative in nature than an organic vision and is favoured by larger (often public) companies over shorter periods of time, i.e. only a few years.

Dutch companies using economic visions often hire general and export managers from outside the organization. Moreover, these companies have the tendency to grow through mergers, acquisitions and alliances, i.e. anorganic instead of organic growth. Dutch companies with an organic vision usually grow autonomously and develop their own managers in as much as possible.

In contrast, many of the interviewed Dutch companies lack a driving force in the form of an explicit international vision. Only about one in five of the interviewees is able to state spontaneously during the interview, what the company's international vision is. After consultation, when the company's international vision was mailed to me later, the total score is about 35 percent. About one-third of the interviewed Dutch companies do have an explicit international vision - a formalized international ambition. In strong contrast with these results is the fact that one-fifth of all interviewees referred to "having an international vision" as the "most important driving force for international success".

Nevertheless, it is encouraging to learn that some companies have an international vision. An international vision provides a solid footing when choosing a country, region or continent when a company wants to expand. Without it, even the largest Dutch global player would collapse.

An effective competitive strategy

International companies will need to gain competitive advantages vis-à-vis their competitors. There are many different types of competitive strategies available to companies. My research has shown that Dutch companies frequently implement the following strategies:

- *Competing on the basis of low cost.* Integrated low-cost management is essential to this strategy. This means that all company activities (from R&D to production and sales) have to be carried out as cheaply as possible. Large global players (for example, DSM, Philips and Akzo Nobel) regularly reallocate their activities in such a way as to be able to profit from the accompanying cost advantages. This phenomenon is referred to as global sourcing.

- *Competing on added value.* Dutch companies can also compete globally on the basis of added value. This way they compete on issues such as service level, reputation and quality, instead of lowest prices, and so on. In some industries selling products at the lowest cost is not the only priority.

- *Competing on innovation.* Some interviewees mentioned the importance of innovation; for example, in the form of product and process innovations. Dutch chemical companies have been active in formulating and executing innovative strategies for the past few decades.

The interviewed Dutch companies expressed a preference for the low-cost strategy (65 percent), followed by the added-value strategy (25 percent). Only 10 percent of the companies make use of the innovation strategy to gain an advantage in local and global competitive rivalries. It is interesting to note that Dutch companies in highly developed markets (EU countries, Japan and North America) more often tend to compete on the basis of low-cost strategies.

Although it will become increasingly necessary to combine these three different strategies on an international scale, in practice they are seldom used harmoniously.

Global sourcing

In April 2002, Deloitte & Touche released a research report concluding that 20 percent of the larger Dutch companies were considering the option of moving a substantial part of their production activities abroad, with a subsequent loss of up to 200,000 jobs in the Netherlands. Strikingly, of the 234 researched companies with more than 50 employees, 62 percent felt that knowledge intensive R&D activities would be taken over by low-income countries in Eastern Europe and Asia.

This phenomenon is known as global sourcing. It defines developments where a company moves business activities and processes that are not bound to the local environment to parts of the world where costs and added value are most favorable.

During my research, I was also confronted with global sourcing - almost two thirds of the interviewed industrial companies are in the process of implementing global sourcing. They mention Eastern Europe as the most attractive region in the world for their global sourcing activities. Almost 70 percent of the interviewees mention this region as best-equipped for local R&D and production activities both in terms of favorable labor and facility costs, and added value (highly trained employees and managers are available).

Asia is also mentioned frequently (25 percent). In this context, China is mentioned by as many as 19 percent of all interviewed industrial companies. China is perceived as very attractive due to the promise of future business opportunities. North and South America are less popular destinations in this context.

"Go East" seems to be a favorite motto for global sourcing activities on the part of most interviewed Dutch companies. Global sourcing is not limited to Dutch industrial companies. Of all interviewed service companies, almost 25 percent express interest in moving their administrative (i.e., back-office) activities abroad to cheaper regions, seven percent of those are already in the process of moving. The companies in this category also refer to Eastern Europe (60 percent) as preferred destination, followed by Asia (22 percent).

International business policy implementation

The interviewees unanimously agreed that the following factors are the most important with respect to determining the success and failure with regard to the implementation of their international business policy:
• possessing an adequate international business model, and
• practicing solid cultural management.

An adequate international business model

All companies form part of an industry. Some industries are global while others are local. Some industries migrate from being local to global (i.e. 'emerging global industries'). Executives of international companies should continuously analyze whether or not they are operating in a global industry, an emerging global industry or a local industry. Competing in global industries demands completely different business models from competing in local industries.

Companies operating in global industries gain competitive advantage by operating beyond national borders to profit from comparative advantages, economies of scale, economies of scope and/or economies of skills. This means that subsidiaries in different countries are interdependent, i.e. the performance of a subsidiary will influence that of another subsidiary. In these types of companies, subsidiaries have specific roles.

In local industries it is worthwhile having strongly decentralized value chains at specific country level. All value chain activities (for instance, R&D, Operations, Logistics, Marketing, Sales, et cetera) should as much as possible be locally implemented. Such companies operate in such a way that subsidiaries can formulate and implement their own local (often national) strategy. International subsidiaries operate relatively independently of one another.

Industries can therefore be classified on a spectrum ranging from purely local to purely global (see box 1).

Box 1 Global, emerging global and local industries

Local	Emerging global	Global
Breweries	Medical instruments	Automobile manufacturing
Insurance	Entertainment	Electronics
Construction	Optical products	Computers
Real estate	(most) Capital goods	Software
HR consultants		Strategy consultants
Retail banking	Wholesale banking	Investment banking

My research shows that a majority of the interviewed companies operate in local (45 percent) and emerging global (32 percent) industries. About 23 percent of the interviewees operate in global industries.

Business models determine the way companies compete and how they are organized based on the characteristics of the specific international environment they are operating in. I can conclude from this study that each of the interviewed Dutch companies implement one of the four following different types of business models (corresponding to the percentage of interviewed firms):
• Country business model: 60 percent;
• Global niche business model: 16 percent;
• Regional business model: 21 percent;
• Transnational business model: 3 percent.

With respect to the country business model, most Dutch companies believe that adapting as much as possible to the local environment of the foreign country is a prerequisite for success. For example, companies such as Ahold and Unilever have a country business model. These companies have many "disciples" – more than half of the total research population used this business model and three quarters of the interviewed service companies also use this model.

Companies that made use of the regional business model adapt their activities to the specific region (such as Europe or Asia) in which they operate. For example, those companies have a European Division (a division that only offers products in Europe) or Asian Division (a division specialized in operations on the Asian market). Some examples of types of companies that use this business model are publishers (such as Wolters Kluwer), banks (such as ABN AMRO, ING and Fortis) and international construction and dredging companies (such as HBG and Boskalis).

Companies with a global niche or transnational business model have, to a great extent, standardized their products, sales and marketing practices and, unlike the companies mentioned earlier, do not adjust their practices to local conditions. Only a few Dutch companies implement the type of business model that is strongly integrated and carefully attuned to environments across national borders. Dutch companies with a global niche business model are often involved in the biotechnology (for example, Crucell) or specialized capital goods industries (for example, ASML).

Large companies, such as Royal Dutch Shell, Philips, DSM and Akzo Nobel, are clear-cut examples of companies with a transnational business model. These companies aim to obtain a competitive advantage by operating in many countries, whereby their integrated and well-orchestrated business systems providing the best (i.e. cheapest or best quality) products.

Dutch companies operating in 'emerging global' industries increasingly have to adjust their business models to the changing characteristics of those sectors. This appears to be an important success factor in international business, requiring that the companies always need a "business model fit", i.e. an international business model should match the specific characteristics of the industry.

This stands in contrast with interviewees, who mentioned that few Dutch companies have such a "business model fit". Therefore, it is important for international executives to have a good overview of the characteristics of their own industry and to subsequently review their business models in terms of the (un)changed conditions for success in the industry involved.

Cultural management

International business is often a matter of cultural management. This subject can be viewed on two levels: national and organizational culture. Attuning these two cultural levels is of the utmost importance.

According to an export manager, working in South America:

> "If it doesn't 'click' between a foreign culture and our own business culture, then conducting business will cease".

The interviewed Dutch companies are increasingly confronted by different national cultural environments, which demand sensitive cultural management. Different aspects and dimensions of a cultural environment have to be taken into consideration, as they differ from culture to culture; for example, how risk is dealt with, the impact of the hierarchy factor in an organization, and the importance attached to work and labour.

Cultural compatibility does not only play a role in national cultures; it is as important as the companies' cultures. Every international company has a corporate culture anchored in the mindset of its employees. Corporate culture is difficult to change in daily practice. This is a major challenge to Dutch companies operating in increasingly turbulent foreign markets with specific national and regional cultures which sometimes demand changes in their companies' corporate cultures.

The degree of cultural compatibility often determines the success or failure of the interviewed Dutch companies, i.e. corporate and national cultures must be in alignment. Many of these companies have failed to align their corporate culture with the national culture in regions, such as South America and Southeast Asia. Even in countries close to their home markets, Dutch companies experience problems in adapting to different national cultures.

The former CEO of Akzo Nobel, Aernout Loudon, said, years ago, during one of his lectures:

> "the capacity to associate with one's own and with foreign cultures is one of the most important, if not *the* most important, qualities for an international company. An international manager is first and foremost a 'cultural manager'".

International business policy evaluation

Too few companies evaluate their international efforts. Only one third of the interviewed companies (mainly the larger companies) evaluate their international operations structurally and systematically.

There are a number of reasons for this low score. In general, Dutch companies with cross-border activities appear to lack interest in evaluations made by executives. Formulating and implementing are preferred over evaluating. Furthermore, relatively few Dutch companies are equipped with effective international evaluation tools and the methods used are applied on an ad-hoc basis instead of in a structural way.

An international business plan

International efforts should preferably be anchored in an international business plan. This plan will eventually serve as the point of departure for an internationalization process and as the benchmark for evaluating (and adjusting) international efforts. An international business plan is, therefore, both the point of departure and the final destination of international entrepreneurship.

All interviewed Dutch companies unanimously conclude that a strong, detailed international business plan is indispensable for achieving international success. This contrasts strongly with how easily companies generally disregard the need for compiling an international business plan. About one third of the interviewed small and medium-sized companies fail to qualify and quantify their international business ambitions in an international business plan. Many of the interviewed companies are only partially aware of the preparatory steps needed to penetrate foreign markets.

That not withstanding, the interviewees state that, qualitatively better decisions can be made based on the information gathered for the international business plan. In addition, this information also makes it easier to involve other employees and managers in the companies' future challenges. An international business plan, for example, facilitates communication with employees with respect to the company's international ambitions. The process of developing a business plan is an opportunity for individual employees to become involved in the internationalization process.

In the words of a managing director of an export company, in this way:

> "managers and employees know better what they can expect in international business".

Business plans can serve as an important compass.

General management mindset

For entrepreneurs and managers, international business always starts with the right mindset and with internationalization at the top of their agenda. They should be prepared and able to invest substantial efforts towards making the international company a success.

Additionally, the celebrated sales mindset should be avoided as much as possible, because internationalization is more than just selling products in any given foreign market. The often dominant sales mindset is a supply driven instead of a demand driven attitude. Companies exist by the grace of (foreign) customer (demand) and not by wonderful products (supply) alone, i.e. a sales mindset is insufficient for achieving international success. International success is first and foremost embedded in a general management mindset.

This research study clearly shows that internationalization demands a wide range of skills, which are not always, or only partially, present in companies.

In this epilogue, I provided ten ingredients for success. Most success factors rely on personal skills and are therefore the responsibility of individual entrepreneurs/managers.

References

Jagersma, P.K., 1997, "Internationalization – From Economies of Scale to Economies of Skills", Inaugural lecture, Universiteit Nyenrode.

Jagersma, P.K., 1998, 2nd edition, "International Management", Stenfert Kroese, Leiden.

Jagersma, P.K., 2001, "Global Strategy", Inspiration Press, Brussels.

About the author

Pieter Klaas Jagersma is Professor of International Business at Nyenrode Business Universiteit, and Professor of Strategy at the Vrije Universiteit Amsterdam (PGO-MC) where he teaches (global) corporate and competitive strategy.

Professor Jagersma is "A leading global authority on competitive strategy" (Journal of Business Strategy, Spring 2005). As an executive, he serves on the boards of directors of various companies.

Professor Jagersma is the author of 24 books and over 250 articles in his field. Professor Jagersma's books include, for instance, De Fokker/DASA-deal (Veen, 1994), 400 Managementwijsheden met een Knipoog (Contact, 1996), Leasing and Marketing (Tilburg University Press, 1996), Internationaal Management (Stenfert Kroese, 1997), Management Trends (Stenfert Kroese, 1999), Global Strategy (Inspiration Press, 2001), KLM – Waarheen Vliegt Gij? (Holland Business Publications, 2003), Multibusiness Corporations (Inspiration Press, 2003), Er Leiden Vele Wegen Naar het Buitenland (AA Publishing, 2003), and (with Professor H. Ebbers) Internationale Bedrijfskunde – Van Exporteren naar Globaliseren (Pearson, 2004).

After receiving his MSc (summa cum laude) from Groningen University and Ph.D in Economics from Tilburg University, he worked with McKinsey & Company and KPN Finance (managing director). In the 1990s, Professor Jagersma became the youngest business administration professor in Dutch history.